Vṛttamālāstuti of Jñānaśrīmitra
with
Śākyarakṣita's *Vṛttamālā(stuti)vivṛti*

Studia Indo-Buddhica 1

Series initiated by
Prof. Dr. Michael Hahn

Vṛttamālāstuti of Jñānaśrīmitra
with
Śākyarakṣita's *Vṛttamālā(stuti)vivṛti*
Critical Edition

Edited by
Michael Hahn
S.S. Bahulkar
Lata Mahesh Deokar
M.A. Deokar

Deshana, Pune
&
Aditya Prakashan, New Delhi

First published: 2016

ISBN 978-81-7742-161-3

Published by Deshana, Pune
and Aditya Prakashan, 2/18 Ansari Road, New Delhi 110 002.

email: contact@adityaprakashan.com
website: www.adityaprakashan.com

Printed at Replika Press, New Delhi (INDIA).

त्वदीयं वस्तु हे विद्वन् तुभ्यमेव समर्पये ।

Preface

We are extremely delighted to offer a critical edition of Jñānaśrīmitra's Vṛttamālāstuti with Śākyarakṣita's Vivṛti to the scholarly world. During our visits to Marburg from 2012 to 2014, we got the rare opportunity to read these texts along with the Tibetan translation of the root-text with Prof. Michael Hahn. In these intensive reading sessions, we learned from him a number of things regarding text editing and the methodology of Tibetan translation. His great insight into classical Sanskrit and Tibetan was amazing and educating at the same time. It was indeed a thrilling experience to read the manuscript with him, to go through his diplomatic edition, to fill up the lacunae in the text, and to discuss various issues related to Sanskrit grammar and prosody. While going through this material, Prof. Hahn realized that there was still some scope to revise the text he had established earlier. This resulted into the first semi-critical edition of the text and its commentary in the Roman script. It was published in the form of two articles in a journal from Japan, South Asian Classical Studies (SACS), no. 8, and 9, in 2013 and 2014 respectively. Before the publication of the second part, Prof. Hahn felt that we should write a separate article discussing the grammatical explanations in the commentary, for the benefit of those readers who are not much familiar with the grammatical technicalities. The same was also published in the SACS, no. 9. Despite his deteriorating health, Prof. Hahn took pains to meticulously work with us on the text, giving a patient hearing to our comments, appreciating good suggestions on our part, and flatly rejecting the unacceptable ones. It was the first ever experience for us to have the guidance of that Guru who was always ready to help his students and his colleagues to the extent possible.

During our reading sessions with Prof. Hahn, we expressed our wish to continue our academic work in India by establishing an Institute for Buddhist and Allied Studies and to bring out some important publications as one of the activities of the Institute. Prof. Hahn welcomed the idea with great enthusiasm and suggested the name 'Studia Indo-Buddhica' for the proposed publication series. He also offered to start the new series by publishing Indian editions of three of his works, namely, the Vṛttamālāstuti together with its Vivṛti, Ravigupta's Āryākośa, and the Mahajjātakamālā, and immediately handed over to us all the relevant materials.

After the establishment of 'Deshana: An Institute of Buddhist and Allied Studies' in Pune on 24th February 2014, we started working on the critical edition of the Vṛttamālāstuti and its commentary in Devanāgarī.

In spite of the publication of the Roman edition, the task of preparing the Devanāgarī edition was not easy. Although Prof. Hahn could revise the second part of the edited text in the light of our discussions held in 2014, he could not do so for the first part that had already been released in 2013. Hence, it was our first duty to incorporate these earlier suggestions in the proposed edition. Moreover, we also noticed some new problems in the earlier edition. This made it necessary to go through the manuscript of the commentary once again, and to present the new edition in a revised form.

The present Indian edition that constitutes the text in the Devanāgarī script can be claimed as a critical edition. We have been able to read the manuscript more accurately and could rectify some of the obvious mistakes in the earlier edition. Although we have revised the main text and the commentary to a certain extent, we have taken care not to deviate, as far as possible, from the methodology Prof. Hahn had adopted and taught us. In the present edition, we have adopted the following method:

1. Here, the text of the Vṛttamālāstuti and the Vivṛti is presented in the Devanāgarī script. However, the footnotes have been retained in the Roman script, for the sake of convenience of reporting the text accurately.
2. We have reproduced Prof. Hahn's Introduction to Part I, and his Preface to Part II with some minor adaptations, which became necessary due to the revised edition of the text.
3. Indexes to the names of metres and citations have been newly incorporated.
4. Our article on the grammatical discussions in Śākyarakṣita's Vṛttamālā-(stuti)vivṛti has also been included in its slightly revised form for the benefit of the general reader.
5. We have provided positive critical apparata in this edition.
6. Apparent mistakes found in Prof. Hahn's edition either in reading the Ms. or in presenting the text are not reported.
7. Since Prof. Hahn's edition was printed in Roman, it was possible for him to indicate indistinct characters, conjectures in the place of lost characters, marginal additions, and his own additions in the main body

of the text with the help of some typographical tools. However, due to the limitations of the Nāgarī script, it was not possible to maintain the same in the present edition. Hence, following the suggestion of our colleagues in Marburg, we have presented a clean Nāgarī text for the pleasure of a Nāgarī reader, and have presented the aforesaid manuscript peculiarities in the critical apparata.

8. We have standardised the application of the sandhi. However, at places, where a sandhi might cause confusion or make the text difficult to read, we have not made it.

9. The use of the daṇḍas, and irregularities regarding the writing of *halanta akṣaras*, *visarga*, and *anusvāra* have been regularised. Similarly, the duplication of a consonant after *r* has been standardised to a single consonant. For example, *mūrttiṣu* has been standardized to *mūrtiṣu*. However, such modifications are not reported in the critical apparata.

10. Verses are printed in a different font size.

11. The pratīkas are printed in the bold face.

12. The name of the metre, its category, and caesura are marked with a dotted underline.

13. Citations and references to grammatical aphorisms are placed within quotation marks.

14. References to authors and texts are indicated with an underline.

We express our sincere thanks to Dr. Mitsuyo Demoto and Prof. Okano for giving us the permission to reprint Prof. Hahn's original Roman edition of the Sanskrit text of the Vṛttamālāstuti in Devanāgarī, and our article "Grammatical Discussions in Śākyarakṣita's Vṛttamālā(stuti)vivṛtti". These were earlier published in the *Bauddhasāhityastabakāvalī* (Indica et Tibetica, vol. 36) and SACS 2013, and 2014. We are grateful to Prof. Pradeep Gokhale and Prof. Johannes Schneider for the careful reading of the press copy and valuable suggestions. We should thankfully mention the great help received from our Marburg colleagues Prof. Jürgen Hanneder, Dr. habil. Dragomir Dimitrov, Dr. Mitsuyo Demoto, and Stanislav Jager in deciding the layout and the presentation of the text. We also appreciate the assistance we received from Ms. Sayuri Deokar in cross-checking the press copy against Prof. Hahn's edition. Thanks are also due to Mr. Aditya Goel of the Aditya Prakashan, New Delhi for showing keen interest in our work, and for bringing out this publication beautifully within a short time.

We are happy that we are able to bring out this revised edition of the Vṛttamālāstuti, on which Prof. Hahn had been working for the past forty years. We express our sense of gratitude towards him and return his own treasure to him with our modest contributions.

S. S. Bahulkar

Lata Mahesh Deokar

M. A. Deokar

Introduction I

Śākyarakṣita's *Vṛttamālā(stuti)vivṛti* on Jñānaśrīmitra's *Vṛttamālāstuti*[*]

The two professors Ratnākaraśānti and Jñānaśrīmitra, who taught Buddhist philosophy and other subjects at the university of Vikramaśīla in the first half of the 11th century, contributed two short, yet very ingenious works to the metrical literature of India. Ratnākaraśānti composed his *Chandoratnākara* or "Ocean of Metres," a concise manual, in which he gives metrical definitions of a well-chosen selection of the most frequently used metres. A brief auto-commentary explains the intention and structure of the work. The *Chandoratnākara* is available in four editions, none of which is free of mistakes. The Sanskrit text of the auto-commentary is yet to be published.[1]

Jñānaśrīmitra's *Vṛttamālāstuti* or "Praise in the Form of a Garland of Metres Counted by Syllables" illustrates 150 metres in the form of a hymn, as indicated by its title. The addressee is the Bodhisattva Mañjuśrī. After four introductory stanzas (1–4), which explain the purpose and structure of the work, 120 different metres of the *samavṛtta* category in which all the four lines have the same structure are exemplified (stanzas 5-120). The metres are arranged according to the number of syllables per line, beginning with one syllable (stanza 5) and ending with 26 syllables (stanza 118). Thereafter follow the so-called hypermetres or *daṇḍakas* (stanzas 119–124) with more than 26 syllables per line. The longest metre illustrated in the *Vṛttamālāstuti* is Pratāpodaya; it has 36 syllables per line. The *ardhasamavṛtta* category is illustrated by 16 metres (stanzas 125–140). In it, lines 1 and 3 represent one metrical pattern, lines 2 and 4 another pattern, different from the first one. The *viṣamavṛtta* section consists of 14 stanzas (stanzas 141–154) of four different categories. While 13 of its stanzas (141–152) have a different structure in all its four lines, the metre of stanza 153,

---

* Originally published in SACS 8 (2013), pp. 265-328.

1 For brief descriptions of the *Chandoratnākara* and its autocommentary, see Michael Hahn, "Sanskrit Metrics As Studied at Buddhist Universities in the Eleventh and Twelfth Century," *Journal of the Nepal Research Society*, IX (1993), pp. 57-76, and "Notes on Buddhist Sanskrit Literature. Chronology and related topics," *Studies in Original Buddhism and Mahāyāna Buddhism in Commemoration of late Prof. Dr. Fumimaro Watanabe [= Watanabe Fumimaro hakushi tsuitō ronshū. Genshi bukkyō to daijō bukkyō]*, ed. Egaku MAYEDA, Kyoto 1993, pp. 31-58.

Anaṅgakrīḍā, is in fact another *ardhasamavṛtta*, while the last stanza, whose name is not known, shows an irregular mixture of the two *samavṛtta*s Upendravajrā and Vaṃśastha.

With great ingenuity, Jñānaśrīmitra manages to include the name of each metre in the respective stanza in such a manner that it becomes a natural part of the praise of Mañjuśrī. The name can be given directly, as in following stanza:

> tīvrakleśaploṣadhvaṃsa-
> prauḍhe vaṃśe saṃbuddhānām |
> dhatte bhūṣāṃ bhātīyaṃ te
> 'mbhode yadvad vidyunmālā || 19 ||

> This (body of yours), shining in the lineage
> of the Fully Enlightened Buddhas,
> which has the power to destroy the fire
> of the fiercest defilements, adorns it
> just as *a row of lightning* adorns a cloud,
> which has the power to destroy the fire of heavy pain.

Here the name of the metre, Vidyunmālā "a garland of lightning," is used in its literal meaning in the praise of Mañjuśrī. In the next example, the name of the metre, Jaloddhatagati "[the fish] who jumps out of the water, i.e., a dolphin" has to be interpreted in an unusual manner:

> vṛṇe varam imaṃ tvad ekam atula-
> prabhāva bhavatān na mādṛśajanaḥ |
> bhavantam api yaḥ śrayañ chamasudhā-
> raseṣu viratir jaḍoddhatagatiḥ || 66 ||

> Oh you, whose majesty is incomparable,
> there is only thing I wish from you:
> May there be no one like me,
> whose mind is both dull and distraught (or: arrogant),
> who, although relying on you, shows no inclination
> for the taste of the nectar of tranquillity!

As can be seen from the commentary

> he **atulaprabhāva** | **tvat** tvattaḥ sakāśād **ekaṃ varaṃ vṛṇe** yāce | kaṃ varaṃ yācasīty āha | **mādṛśo jano na** kaś cid **bhavatān** notpadyatām | kīdṛśaḥ | **yo bhavantam api** vāgīśvaraṃ **śrayañ jaḍā** mandā **uddhatā** vikṣiptā **gatir** matir yasya sa tathābhūtaḥ san | **vigatā ratir** abhilāṣo yasya

tathā bhavati | kasmin viṣaye | **śamāḥ** śāntayas tā eva **sudhā-rasās** teṣu |

vṛttapakṣe jagatyāṃ **jaloddhatagatir** nāma | tatra ca rasesu ṣaṭsu viratiḥ ||

Jala is used as an allophone of *jaḍa* "dull," *uddhata* in the sense of *vikṣipta* "distraught" ("puffed-up, arrogant" would also be meaningful in the context of the stanza), and *gati* in the sense of "mind, understanding;" cf. pw "das Verstandenwerden, Gemeintsein."

The third device is the artificial segmentation of the name of the metre that can be done in a simple or sophisticated manner:

dadhaty api nikāmaṃ
kumāralalitāni |
tanus tava jinānāṃ
kumāra lalitaiva || 14 ||

Although your body predominantly bears a youthful attire, it is only *lovely*, Oh youth among the Victorious Ones!

kumāralalitāni śiśuceṣṭitāni **tava tanur dadhaty api nikāmam** atyarthaṃ **lalitaiva** manoharaiva | he **jinānāṃ kumāra** | loke khalu prekṣaṇe.. .. prekṣāpūrvāṇi bālavilasitāni na paritoṣam āvahanti | tava tu tanus tāni bibhraty api paritoṣakarīti virodhābhāsaḥ | vineyānurodhena tadāśrayāt parihāraḥ |

vṛttapakṣe uṣṇihi **kumāralalitā** nāma ||

Here Kumāralalitā, the name of the metre, is contained in the vocative *kumāra* and the following *lalitaiva*, in which *lalitā* is an attribute of *tanu*. The occurrence of *kumāralalitā* as part of *kumāralalitāni* in the second line is coincidental, because the name of the metre is almost always given in the last line.[1] Other examples are: Rathoddhatā as final member of the compound *bhavatparyupāsanamanorathôddhatā* (45d; *manoratha* + *uddhatā*); Śālinī in *prajñāśālinī* (46d); Indravaṃśā in *maunīndravaṃśâbharaṇôdaya-śriyam* (52d); Candravartman in *candravartma* (67d; vocative + accusative); Kalā in *sakalāyām* (68d); Mahita in *nikhilamalapaṭalavigamadīpraprathima-*

---

1 There are only three exceptions in the *viṣamavṛtta* category: Ārṣabha Śuddha-virāḍviśeṣaṇa (150bc), Vardhamāna (152b), and Anaṅgakrīḍā (153b).

guṇamahitamati jagatyām (69d); Maṇiguṇanikara in *viyad upahatanijamaṇiguṇanikaraḥ* (87d); Guṇamaṇinikara in *suyatibhir agaṇitaguṇamaṇinikaraḥ* (88d; vocative + nominative); Kuvalaya in *jinakulakuvalayam* (90d); Ramā in *kumāra mārair jitam* (96d); Vaṃśapattrapatita in *°digyativaṃśapattrapatitaṃ* (97d); Kusumitalatāvellitā in *kusumitalatā vellitevānilena* (102d); Suvadanā in *anarghasmitavasuvadanâśeṣakṛtau* (107d); Mattākrīḍam in *saṃbhogaśrīmattâkrīḍaṃ* (113d); Lavalī in *nayanavalanalavalīlā* (144d).

The following are the most sophisticated cases of embedding or forming the name of the metre:

1) The name Dodhaka:

rūparasāyanabhāvanayā te
vāsava eva paraṃ bahumānyaḥ |
yena cirāya nirastanimeṣaṃ
labdham adodhakam ambakajātam || 41 ||

Indra alone is to be praised in the highest degree
for (permanently) visualizing the elixir of your beautiful form,
because he (or: who) had attained a multitude of eyes
with which he could *drink it* (*ado-dhaka*) without blinking.

tava rūpam eva **rasāyanam** iva rasāyanaṃ nayanapuṣṭihetutvāt | tasya **bhāvanayā** abhyāsena | hetau karaṇe vā tṛtīyā | **indra eva bahu** yathā bhavati tathā **mānyaḥ** ślāghyaḥ | bahuṣu vā mānyaḥ | kathaṃ sa evety āha | **yena** vāsavena yena vā karaṇena tadā tena vāsaveneti gamyam | **nirastanimeṣam** animiṣam | **ambakajātaṃ** locanakadambakaṃ **prāptam** | kiṃbhūtam | **cirāya** cirakālam | **ada** idaṃ rūparasāyanaṃ **dhayati** pibatīty āto 'nupasargāt kaḥ | adodham | svārthe kani **adodhakam** | yasmād animiṣeṇākṣṇāṃ tu sahasreṇa ciraṃ tvadrūparasāyanaṃ pibati tato vāsava eva bahumānyo nānya ity arthaḥ |

vṛttapakṣe triṣṭubhi **dodhakam** ||

Since Dodhaka has no independent meaning, an artificial formation was necessary.

2) The name Toṭaka

tava nātha paraṃ yadi kāntisudhā-
jaladhau śramam ujjhati jhātkṛtini |

śubharūpanirūpaṇalampaṭakaṃ
parito 'ṭakam aṅga jagannayanam || 64 ||

Oh protector, would not the eye of the world,
wandering everywhere (*parito 'ṭakam*)
in its desire to behold a pure form,
completely abandon its efforts
when it reaches the nectar ocean of your beauty?

aṅgaśabdaḥ saṃbuddhau | he **nātha** | **jagannayanaṃ tava kāntir** eva **sudhājaladhis** tasmiñ **jhātkṛtini śramam** āyāsaṃ **param ujjhati** | nānyatra | samudro 'pi hi velāparaṃ-parayā jhātkāravān | bhagavān apy anavaratanityalāvaṇya-laharībhiḥ | kiṃbhūtaṃ jagannayanam | **śubhaṃ** manoharaṃ **rūpaṃ** tasya **nirūpaṇe lampaṭakam** sat **paritaḥ** samantād aṭatīty arthaḥ | tad ev**āṭakam** | ata evāsya śramaḥ | anyo 'pi hi cirabhramaṇapariśrāntaḥ samudrādimahājalāśaye śramam apanayati |

vṛttapakṣe jagatyāṃ **toṭakaṃ** ||

Toṭaka, too, has no independent meaning, therefore an artificial formation was necessary.

3) The name Narkkuṭaka

tava guṇavistarapraṇayapūtavacovibhavaṃ
varada sa eka eva sumukho mukham āvahati |
madhumayasāmadhāma yajuṣā sajuṣānugataṃ
śravaṇasudhābhimānabhavanarkkuṭakaṃ ca vidhiḥ || 98 ||

Benefactor, destiny (*vidhi*) [or: Brahma] alone,
endowed with a good mouth [or: beautiful faces],
provides one with a mouth,
whose wealth of words is purified
by the acquaintance with the abundance of your virtues,
which is the dwelling-place of songs (*sāman*) as sweet as
honey,
accompanied by pleasant sacrificial formulas (*yajus*)
and which has become a vessel of sacrificial hymns (*ṛc*),
the place of worship by nectar for the ears.

he **varada** | **tava guṇānāṃ praṇayena** paricayena **pūto vacovibhavo** yasya tādṛṅ **mukhaṃ sa evaiko vidhir ā-vahati** nānyaḥ | ata eva **sumukhaḥ** | nanu trayīparicayād eva tasya sumukhatvam astīty āha | **madhumayasya** gānamādhuryāt | **sāmno** vedaviśeṣasya **dhāma** sthānam api | apyarthasya **ca**sya pratyekābhisaṃbandhāt | tath**ānugatam** api | kena | **yajuṣā** | kiṃbhūtena | **sajuṣā** prītikareṇa | tathā **śravaṇasudhā**rūpeṇābhimananam **abhimānas** tasya **bhavanam** | kva cit śravaṇasudhābhidhāneti pāṭhaḥ | tatrāpi **śravaṇasudhe**ty abhidhānasya **bhavanam** abhidheyatvenāśrayaḥ | tādṛśām **ṛcāṃ kuṭam** iva kuṭam | svārthe kaḥ | kuṭanipāv astrīty Amaraḥ | ghaṭa ivādhāra ity arthaḥ | evaṃbhūtam api mukhaṃ sumukhatayā tadā āvahati yadā tvadguṇavistarapraṇayena pūtaṃ vacovibhavaṃ bhavati |

vṛttapakṣe 'tyaṣṭiś cchandas tathā pariṇatim avāpad yathā narkuṭakaṃ samudbhūtam ||

Again, Narkkuṭaka has no independent meaning. Therefore, an artificial formation was necessary.

4) The name Meghavisphūrjitā

parārthe sthāsnūnām atidhṛtimatām īśa viśvānukampā-
mukhonmīlannānārasarasapadākarṇayāvedayāmi |
daśāṃ tām ādhehi kṣaṇam api guro pāvanīṃ pāvanānāṃ
samantadhvāntāni praharasi yayā me 'ghavisphūrjitāni || 105 ||

O lord of those extremely firm beings
who for the welfare of others
continue to stay (in the circle of existences),
you abode of the desire for those manifold sentiments
which arise because of the compassion with everybody—
listen to what I am going to tell you:
Grant, oh teacher, only for a moment
that purest of all pure states,
by which you take away
the visible manifestations of my bad deeds (*me 'ghavisphūrjitāni*) !

he **parārthe sthāsnūnām atidhṛtimatāṃ** bodhisattvānām **īśa** | **nānā**prakāra**raso** 'bhilāṣo yeṣu **raseṣu** te | tathā **viśvānukampaiva mukhaṃ** dvāraṃ te **unmīlanto** ye **nānārasās** teṣāṃ **pada** | idam apy āmantraṇam | **ākarṇaya** śṛṇu | **āvedayāmi** | kim āvedayasīty āha | he **guro pāvanānāṃ** madhye **pāvanīṃ daśāṃ tām** api **kṣaṇam apy**

ādhehi | **yayāghānāṃ** pāpānāṃ **visphūrjitāni me harasi** | kiṃbhūtāni | **samantaṃ** sarvaṃ **dhvāntaṃ** yebhyas tāni |

vṛttapakṣe **'tidhṛtau** ūnaviṃśatyakṣare cchandasi satāṃ saṃmatā **meghavisphūrjitā** | **raseṣu raseṣu padaṃ** yatir yasyāḥ ||

Here the meaning of the name of the metre is quite clear: "the roaring of thunder." Obviously Jñānaśrīmitra could not resist to make use of the possible resolution (or separation) of *megha* "cloud" as *me 'gha* "my bad deeds."

5) The name Drutamadhyā

tattvasudhārasatṛptiviśeṣāt
sakalasamīhitasiddhivaśād vā |
tvaccaraṇānubhuvā bhavitavyaṃ
bhavamathanaśruta na drutam adhyā || 126 ||

Oh you, who are known as the destroyer of being,
he who experiences your feet
will necessarily become wise quickly,
either because he has completely become satiated
by the taste of the nectar of truth,
or because all his desires have become fulfilled.

bhavasya saṃsārasya **mathanaṃ śrutaṃ** yasya **bhava-mathane** vā **śruto** viditaḥ | tasyāmantraṇam | **tvac-caraṇam** ārādhā .. .. no **'nubhavati** yas tena puṃsā | **nāsti dhīr** yasya tathā **na bhavitavyam** | **asudhiya** iti niṣedhād iha yaṇādeśa eva | katham **adhyā na bhavitavyaṃ drutaṃ** śīghram | **tattvasudhārasatṛptiviśeṣāt sakala-samīhitasiddhivaśād ve**ty ubhayasaṃpad uktā | **tvac-caraṇānu**careṇa na bhāvyaṃ **bhavamathanaśruta na drutam adhyeti** Padyālaṃkārasūtram | tatra **adhyā tvac-caraṇānu**careṇa na na bhāvyam ity arthaḥ |

vṛttapakṣe yathoktam idam ardham ādadhatī **drutamadhyā** ||

As in the case of Meghavisphūrjitā, the artificial formation was not necessary. Again, Jñānaśrīmitra could not resist to present an unusual resolution of the compound.

6) The name Yavamatī

Since the name Yavamatī does not fit in the metrical structure that consists of a series of trochees in the first and third line and a series of Iambs in the second and fourth line, it had to be expressed indirectly. Metricians like Jayadeva have demonstrated devices how to circumscribe such 'unmetrical' names of metres. In the case of Yavamatī, he gave the following definition:

> dvī rajau tathāparau jarau guruś ca
> yavadhvaner matupstriyā samābhidheyā | 5.37

> [The odd lines consist of] twice the gaṇas *ra* and *ja*,
> the other [two] of [twice] the gaṇas *ja* and *ra* plus a long syllable;
> [this *vṛtta* metre] has the same designation as the feminine
> of the suffix *mat* after the word *yava*, i.e. *yava-mat-ī*.

This was only slightly modified by Ratnākaraśānti:

> rephajau rajau tathā jarau jragaś ca
> yavadhvaner matupstriyā samābhidhānā | 3.11

The second line of this definition was taken over literally by Jñānaśrīmitra in his illustration of the metre Yavamatī. However, he ingeniously expands the word *yava* "barley" to *avayava* "part, fraction."

> caittamātrabhāvabhāji bhāvyate kva
> parā parārthasaṃpad īdṛśī dayāyām |
> seyam etadākṛticchalād ato 'va-
> yavadhvaner matupstriyā samābhidhānā || 135 ||

> How can such an extreme perfection be accomplished
> with regard to compassion, whose true nature is merely
> spiritual?
> It is based on the deceit about his [true] form.
> Therefore its designation is identical with the feminine
> of the suffix *mat* after the word *avayava*, i.e., *avayavamatī*
> "partial."

cittasya viśeṣāvasthā **caittam** | tad eva tan**mātram** | tad**bhāvas** tattvam | tad**bhāji** caittasvabhāvāyāṃ **dayāyāṃ** dayāviṣaye **īdṛśī** sarvākārapravṛttā **parā parārthasaṃpat kva** saṃ**bhāvyate** | tasyā amūrtatvena tādṛk parārthasaṃpādanāsāmarthyāt | **ataḥ seyaṃ** dayaiṣoktalakṣaṇā yā bhagavad**ākṛtis** tad eva **cchalaṃ** tataḥ | **avayavadhvaner** avayavaśabdān **matup** | sa eva **strī** | strīpratyayāntāvasthā-parigrahāt | **tayā** anukaraṇamātrarūpayā **samam abhidhānaṃ** yasyā anukāryarūpāyāḥ | avayavavatīty arthaḥ |

vṛttapakṣe yavadhvaner matupstriyā samābhidhānā **yavamatī** | mād upadhāyāś ca mator vo 'yavādibhya iti yavādi-pratiṣedhāt vatvābhāvaḥ | ṛjunā krameṇa saṃjñāpraveśo na nirvahatīti pūrveṣām evaiṣa vākyavinyāsaḥ | ata ihaivoddhā-ryaśabdarūpavaiṣamye 'pi śleṣo 'bhimataḥ | tatra priyaṃvadā-vegavatībhadravirāṭketumatīnāṃ pratyekam ayukpādau daśā-kṣarau | yukpādāv ekādaśākṣarau | drutamadhyāhariṇaplutā-paravaktraśiśulīlānām ayukpādāv ekādaśākṣarau yukpādau dvādaśākṣarau | puṣpitāgrāyavamatyor ayukpādau dvādaśā-kṣarau yukpādau trayodaśākṣarāv iti draṣṭavyam ||

7) The name Āpīḍa

The name Āpīḍa offers the same problem as does Yavamatī, because only the last two syllables of its four pādas are long. Jayadeva solves the problem in the following manner:

iti nigaditajātau
kṛtaviṣamacaraṇaracanāyām |
dvigurunidhanaśakala iha hi yuta āṅā
samupahitasalalitayatiyutir atha bhavati pīḍaḥ | 5.17

When in the said category [of metres]
the odd pādas are arranged [in this manner],
and when all the [four pādas] are ending with two long syllables,
then this is the metre Pīḍa, preceded by the prefix ā (i.e. Āpīḍa],
adorned with beautiful caesuras.

Ratnākaraśānti's version slightly differs:

iha padacaturūrdhve
gaganidhananikhilalaghupādaḥ |
yadi mudam upanayati jagati yuta āṅā
samupahitasalalitayatigatir atha bhavati pīḍaḥ | 4.15

Jñānaśrīmitra uses the first two lines of Jayadeva in his exemplification:

iti nigaditajātau
kṛtaviṣamacaraṇaracanāyām |

laghuguruniyatibhṛti bhayam ayati ko na
bhavasi na yadi niyatam abhividhivacanam anu pīḍaḥ || 142 ||

Who would not be frightened by this form of yours,
in which your feet are placed in such a dangerous manner,
and which displays both lightness and heaviness,
if you were not a person for whom the word *pīḍa*
exists only after the designation of comprehensiveness (*ā*).[1]

ity anantaroktaprakāreṇa **nigaditāyāṃ jātau** svabhāvaviṣame tava **ko na bhayam ayati** gacchati | kīdṛśyām | **kṛtaviṣamacaraṇaracanāyām** | vihitordhvādhaḥpādavinyāsāyām | punaḥ kīdṛśi | **laghuguruniyatibhṛti** | vineyānurodhāt kva cil lāghavaṃ ca kva cid gauravaṃ ca bibhratyām | iha tu gauravam evābhipretam | sarva eva bhayam āsādayati **yadi** tvaṃ **niyatam abhividhivacanam anu pīḍo na bhavasi** | abhividhivacanam āṅ | tam anu tena saha pīḍa **āpīḍaḥ** | samantād dayāvān yadi na bhavasīty arthaḥ |

vṛttapakṣe nigaditāyāṃ padacaturūrdhvajātau kṛtaviṣamacaraṇaracanāyām etac chlokaprastārakrameṇa laghuguruniyamaṃ dadhatyāṃ satyām | abhividhivacanam anu pīḍo vyākhyātārthaḥ | atrāntimadvayadvayaṃ guru śeṣaṃ laghu | Padyālaṃkāre tu padacaturūrdhvam aniyat (?) pāṭhasaubhāgyābhāvād asmāt pṛthak darśitam | iha tu pūrvāmnāyānusāreṇoktam ||

In addition to the names of the metres, Jñānaśrīmitra also gives the names of the categories. They are given either at the beginning or at the end of a category. Furthermore, he indicates the caesuras by refined double entendres. One example may suffice:

rūpaṃ te guṇagaṇam atha kīrtiṃ
saṃvīkṣyākhilam idam atiśāyi |
bibhrāṇaṃ nijaviṣayavirāmaṃ
mandaṃ triṣṭubhi jagad upajātam || 36 ||

When the people had perceived your beautiful body,
your many virtues and your glory—all of them outstanding—

---

[1] I.e., as *āpīḍa* "compassion." Cf. German "Leid" (sorrow, pain) and "Mitleid "compassion."

they became disgusted with their own qualities
and refrained from praising them.[1]

idaṃ tavākhilaṃ rūpam atiśāyi saṃvīkṣya | **atha**śabda idam akhilam atiśāyīti pratyekatrisaṃbandhanārthaḥ | tenemam akhilam atiśāyinaṃ **guṇagaṇam** tathemām akhilām atiśāyinīṃ **kīrtiṃ** saṃvīkṣya | **jagan nija**rūpaguṇa-kīrtiv**iṣaye virāmaṃ** dhiṅ no rūpādikam ity anabhiratiṃ **bibhrat** sat | **tisṛṇāṃ** rūpaguṇakīrtīnām ātmīyānāṃ **stubh** stutiḥ | suṣāmāditvāt ṣatvam | tasyāṃ **mandam upajātam** |

vṛttapakṣe ekādaśākṣare cchandasi **triṣṭubhi** viṣayavirāmaṃ bibhrad **upajātaṃ** nāma | viṣayāś ca pañca | taiś ca pañcamaṃ sthānam upalakṣyate | evam uttaratrāpi draṣṭavyam | pañcame yatir ity arthaḥ | itaḥpūrvavṛttānāṃ pādānta evotsargasiddhā yatir nānyatra viśeṣavidhānābhāvāt | etad ārabhya pādānte tāvat sarvatra | viśeṣavidhau tu vyākhyāsyāmaḥ | **triṣṭubhī**ty adhikāra upajātiparyantam ||

The stanza contains three-fold metrical information if we single out the three terms *viṣayavirāmaṃ ... triṣṭubhi ... upajātam*. This can be translated as: "[This is,] in the category Triṣṭubh [which has eleven syllables per line, the metre] Upajāta, with a caesura after *viṣaya*, [i.e., after the fifth syllable]."

The names of the categories of the Samavṛttas are:

Name	Mentioned in stanza	Illustrated in stanza(s)
Gāyatrī	10a	vaiśva (10), tanumadhyā (11), śaraṇa (12)
Uṣṇih	13d	sātireka (13), kumāralalitā (14), ūrdhvagāmi (15)
Anuṣṭubh	16b	uttama (16), samānī (17), pramāṇikā (18), vidyunmālā (19), māṇavaka (20), kisalaya (21), citrapadā (22)
Bṛhatī	23a	kaṭākṣa (23), halamukhī (24), rūpa (25),

1 Literally: became slow in the praise of the[se] three [virtues].

		bhujagaśiśusṛtā (26), mudrā (27)
Paṅkti	28c	aravinda (28), nalinī (29), rukmavatī (30), paṇava (31), mattā (32), mayūrasāriṇī (33), śuddhavirāṭ (34), valaya (35)
Triṣṭubh	36d	upajāta (36), bhadrikā (37), vṛttā (38), svāgatā (39), bhramaravilasitā (40), dodhaka (41), upasthitā (42), upasthita (43), vātormī (44), rathoddhatā (45), śālinī (46), śyenī (47), indravajrā (48), upendravajrā (49), upajātayaḥ (50)
Jagatī	68d	vaṃśastha (51), indravaṃśā (52), pramitākṣarā (53), sragviṇī (54), vaiśvadevī (55), jaladharamālā (56), drutavilambita (57), mandākinī (58), kundalatā (59), vāgīśvaralīla (60), yamunā (61), bhujaṅgaprayāta (62), mālinī (63), toṭaka (64), puṭa (65), jaloddhatagati (66), candravartma (67), kalā (68)
Atijagatī	69a	mahita (69), kalahaṃsa (70), praharṣiṇī (71), rucirā (72), mattamayūra (73), mañjubhāṣiṇī (74)
Śakvarī	80d	vasantatilaka (75), daivata (76), aparājitā (77), praharaṇakalikā (78), asaṃbādhā (79), vasudhā (80)
Atiśakvarī	81c	anaṅgavijṛmbhita (81), mālinī (82), kāminī (83), sugatapriya (84), śaśikalā (85), sraj (86), maṇiguṇanikara (87), guṇamaṇinikara (88)
Aṣṭi	93a	acaladhṛti (89), kuvalaya (90), ṛṣabhagajavilasita (91), pattrabhaṅgaracanā (92), kumāralīlā (93)
Atyaṣṭi	94a	śikhariṇī (94), pṛthvī (95), ramā (96), vaṃśapattrapatita (97), narkkuṭaka (98), kokilaka (99), hariṇī (100), mandākrāntā (101)

Dhṛti	104d	kusumitalatāvellitā (102), karṇapūra (103), tamālapattra (104)
Atidhṛti	105a	meghavisphūrjitā (105), śārdūlavikrīḍita (106)
Kṛti	107d	suvadanā (107), siṃhavikrīḍita (108), vṛtta (109)
Prakṛti	110b	sundarī (110), sragdharā (111)
Ākṛti	112a	madraka (112)
Vikṛti	113b	mattākrīḍa (113), aśvalalita (114)
Saṃkṛti	115a	tanvī (115)
Abhikṛti	116b	krauñcapadā (116)
Utkṛti	117a	bhujaṃgavijṛmbhita (117), apavāha (118)
Daṇḍaka	119d	caṇḍavṛṣṭiprayāta (119), arṇa (120), pracita (121), pravṛtta (122), pratāpodaya (123), lalita-vṛtta (124)

In the case of the paired names Jagatī-Atijagatī, Śakvarī-Atiśakvarī, Aṣṭi-Atyaṣṭi, and Dhṛti-Atidhṛti, the names occur in neighbouring stanzas: Jagatī in the last metre of that category, Atijagatī in the first metre of that category, and so on. In all the other cases, the names occur in the first metre of the respective category.

The caesuras are indicated by the use of numerals as well as symbolic numbers. We find *catur* (28), *viṣaya* (for 5; 36, 79, 113), *cātuḥ* (40), *ambhorāśi* (for 4; 56), *dala* (for half; 60), *aṅga* (for 8; 65, 82), *rasa* (for 6; 66, 86, 94, 100, 101, 105, 118), *aṣṭa* (67), *tri* (71), *payonidhi* (for 4; 72), *muni* (for 7; 77, 107), *indriya* (for 5; 80), *ayas* (for 8; 87), *udadhi* (for 4; 88), *jaladhi* (for 4; 90), *rava* (for 7; 91), *mada* (for 8; 95), *diś* (for 10; 97, 112), *arṇava* (for 4; 100), *śruta* (for 4; 101), *bhava* (for 11; 104, 117), *bhāsvant* (for 12; 106), *māra* (for 13; 108), *vasu* (for 8; 113), *hara* (for 11; 114), *pañcamaka* (115), *svara* (for 7; 115), *karaṇa* (for 5; 116), *giri* (for 8; 117), *nava* (118).

The word used for "caesura" is either the technical term *yati* (56, 60, 73, 77, 87, 88, 91, 97, 99, 104, 106, 115), or it is circumscribed by a great variety of words meaning "pause, stop, break, breaking, crushing" *līlā* (28)[1], *virāma* (36), *cūrṇa* (40), *cheda* (46), *bhaṅga* (55, 111), *virati* (65, 66, 72, 79, 113), *bheda* (67, 94), *viccheda* (71), *saṃyata* (80, 100), *bhaṅgi* (82), *laya* (86), *yama* (90), *mardana* (95), *bhid(ā)* (101, 117), *pada* (105, 116, 118), *bhagna* (107), *khaṇḍita* (108), *anta* (112).

The commentary presented here for the first time is based on an incomplete palm leaf manuscript kept in the National Archives. Its last folio, commenting on stanzas 149 until 154, is lost. Moreover, most of the folios are damaged on their right sides as a consequence of which up to six akṣaras are lost. The manuscript consists of 43 folios. Its size is given as 30 by 5.5 centimetres. Its shelf mark is 4-711, its subject number is *Bauddha-stotra* 25. It was microfilmed by the Nepal-German Manuscript Preservation Project on September 23, 1970, and is found on reel number B 29/31. The manuscript is beautifully written and comparatively well preserved. I am grateful to Mr. Balaram Dangol (National Archives, Kathmandu) who already in 1978, during my stay in Kathmandu, gave his permission to publish the text.

Despite the loss of the last folio, which presumably contained the title of the work and the name of its author, both names could be restored with great certainty. Dpang Lo tsā ba Blo gros brtan pa, who completed the partial translation of his teacher Shong ston Rdo rje rgyal mtshan, states that he has used the commentary of a certain Śākyarakṣita. In the paper mentioned in footnote 1 (JNRC IX), I could show the traces of the commentary published here in the Tibetan translation. The title of the commentary is given as *Vṛttamālāvivṛti* in the two intermediate colophons after stanzas 124 (end of the *samavṛtta* section) and 140 (end of the *ardha-samavṛtta* section).

The commentary is a most welcome aid for understanding the intricacies of Jñānaśrīmitra's composition. The question arises whether Śākyarakṣita's interpretation is based on Jñānaśrīmitra's own explanation or that of his direct disciples. This does not seem to be the case. There are a few cases

---

1 The commentary takes *līlā* as synonym of *bhaṅgi*. This might be wrong, because in the stanza we also find *prāptapāra*, which would be a more appropriate indication of the caesura.

where the Vṛttamālāstuti was not correctly understood. One example might suffice:

> nirupamaramyarūpa jinajātadṛśvano 'ṣṭau
> madayati te 'dhikaṃ vidhutaśoka lokapālān |
> sadupadhipuṇḍarīkanakharājirājiteyaṃ
> viracitapañcacīrarucirā kumāralīlā || 93 ||

> he **nirupamaramyarūpa** | **vidhutaśoka** | **te** tava **jinajāta-dṛśvanaḥ** sugatasamūhaṃ dṛṣṭavata **iyaṃ kumārī līlāṣṭau lokapālān madayati** harṣayati | **adhikam** atyartham | jinajātadṛśvano 'pi kumāralīleyaṃ atiruciretyaty arthamadahetuḥ | kīdṛśī | **viracitapañcacīratvena rucirā** | punaḥ kiṃbhūtā | **san** śobhana **upadhir** upādhir iha svarṇaṃ yasyāḥ | sā cāsau **puṇḍarīkasya** vyāghrasya **nakharājiś** ceti tābhyām rājiteti ||

> vṛttapakṣe 'ṣṭau kumāralīlā nāma | aṣṭāv itīta ūrdhvaṃ nādhikriyate ||

Śākyarakṣita obviously refers *jinajātadṛśvano* to *te*, i.e., Mañjuśrī. This makes no sense. The attribute refers to the eight guardians of the worlds, who have already seen many Bodhisattvas and are nevertheless intoxicated by Mañjuśrī's beauty. It may be mentioned that the Tibetan translation follows the interpretation of the commentary.

Another question is whether the manuscript could be Śākyarakṣita's autograph. This can also be denied. The manuscript contains several mistakes, which the author himself would not have committed. Again, one example might suffice. In the commentary on stanza 25, the word *pāthaḥsekādibhir* is written as *yāthaḥ* | *sekādibhir*. Even by inadvertency, one would never insert a daṇḍa in the middle of a word.

This is my third major publication on Jñānaśrīmitra's *Vṛttamālāstuti*. In 1971, my doctoral dissertation of 1967 was published in the series *Asiatische Forschungen.*[1] It contains an edition of the Tibetan translation, its annotated German translation and a detailed analysis of its metrical content and its place in the Indian metrical literature. The Mongolian translation of the

---

1 *Jñānaśrīmitras Vṛttamālāstuti. Ein Beispielsammlung zur altindischen Metrik.* Nach dem tibetischen Tanjur zusammen mit der mongolischen Version herausgegeben, übersetzt und erläutert. Wiesbaden 1971. (*Asiatische Forschungen.* 33.) X, 388 S.

Tibetan text and two glossaries (Tibetan-Mongolian and Mongolian-Tibetan) are appended. In 1976, I got access to Śākyarakṣita's commentary and one year later to the original Sanskrit text of the *Vṛttamālāstuti*. At that time, I prepared a first provisional edition of the commentary and a revised edition of the *Vṛttamālāstuti*. In 2008, I published the Sanskrit text of the Vṛttamālāstuti together with its German translation in the felicitation volume for my teacher Claus Vogel.[1]

1 "The Sanskrit Text of Jñānaśrīmitra's Vṛttamālāstuti," *Bauddhasāhityastabakāvalī. Essays and Studies on Buddhist Sanskrit Literature.* Marburg 2008 (*Indica et Tibetica* 36), pp. 93-170.

Śākyarakṣita's Vṛttamālāvivṛti on Jñānaśrīmitra's Vṛttamālāstuti (II)*

In 2012 and 2013, I had the precious opportunity to revise my provisional edition of the commentary by reading it with three competent Indian colleagues from Pune during their stay in Marburg: Prof. Dr. Shrikant Bahulkar, Dr. Lata Deokar, and Prof. Dr. Mahesh Deokar. My colleague and successor Prof. Dr. Jürgen Hanneder also participated in many of our sessions. The edition has greatly profited from the advice of these colleagues and also from several splendid suggestions of Dr. Mitsuyo Demoto-Hahn. Thereafter the re-edition of the Tibetan translation in the light of the two Sanskrit texts will be a worthwhile task. The long list of corrections and emendations given in Hahn 2008, pp. 135-140, can still be expanded.

Here follows the second and final part of my edition of Śākyarakṣita's *Vṛttamālāvivṛti* (or *Vṛttamālāstutivivṛti*).[1] This paper has greatly profited from the opportunity to read and discuss the portion of the text it contains a second time with my Indian colleagues Shrikant S. Bahulkar, Mahesh Deokar, and (Mrs.) Lata Mahesh Deokar from Pune in April and May 2014. Thanks to their queries and criticism it was possible to solve several so far unclear passages, thereby improving my first draft in many places. I am particularly obliged to my friend Prof. Bahulkar for taking the trouble of comparing the edited text once more with the manuscript it is based upon—a necessary task, which my current health condition did not permit me to do myself. Prof. Bahulkar's meticulous observations were the main basis of the renewed discussion of the text.

As the reader of the *Vṛttamālāvivṛti* will notice, it contains a great number of grammatical discussions. Although I had already analyzed many of them (up to stanza 64) when I first transcribed the manuscript in 1976, I had refrained from including them in the first part of my paper, because several portions had remained unclear. Therefore it was a great boon when my Indian colleagues positively responded to my suggestion to write a separate paper that focuses on only this aspect of the

---

* Originally published in SACS 9 (2014), pp. 1-64.

1 In the extant portion of the commentary, both forms occur: *Vṛttamālāvivṛti* after stanza 140 and *Vṛttamālāstutivivṛti* after stanza 124. Unfortunately, the last folio of the manuscript containing the colophon is lost. Note that in his opening stanza, Śākyarakṣita reduces the title of the work to *Vṛttamālā*.

Vṛttamālāvivṛti. Their competent analysis can be found in this volume of *South Asian Classical Studies*.

After the edition of the commentary I have given the whole text of the *Vṛttamālāstuti* in Devanāgarī, accompanied by an index of verses. This can be regarded as a token of respect to the first editor of the text, Yogi Naraharinath, without whose work the basic text would have remained inaccessible since the original manuscript has not turned up again.

It is planned to publish, in due course of time, all the materials concerning the *Vṛttamālāstuti* in one volume: the basic text, its English translation, the revised Tibetan translation (which is an excellent piece of work), the commentary, two glossaries (Sanskrit-English-Tibetan and Tibetan-English-Sanskrit), and a facsimile of the manuscript.

We know that a second manuscript of the *Vṛttamālāstuti* and its commentary has survived in Tibet and that a microfilm of it is preserved in Beijing. For some details see Hu-von Hinüber Haiyan, "Remarks on the Manuscript of Mūlasarvāstivāda-Prātimokṣasūtra," in *Jaina-Itihāsa-Ratna, Festschrift für Gustav Roth zum 90. Geburtstag*, hrsg. von Ute Hüsken, Petra Kiefer-Pülz und Anne Peters, Marburg 2006 (*Indica et Tibetica* 47), pp. 283-337; especially pp. 283-288 amd pp. 297-334, where we find *Vṛttamālāvṛtti* as No. 227 and *Vṛttamālāstuti* as No. 228 (p. 331) in the catalogue compiled by Wang Sen. At present it seems unlikely that the permission to see and use these two manuscripts will be granted to foreign scholars. However, I hope that perhaps a Chinese scholar might be able and willing to compare them with my edition, to correct errors and fill the gaps of the fragmentary Nepalese manuscript. Then the final edition of both texts could eventually be prepared.

Symbols used in the edition

(..)	Indistinct characters
..	akṣaras lost due to a damaged folio
<..>	Not available in the manuscript
{{ .. }}	Text added in the margin
[[..]]	Text deleted in the manuscript
/////	Lost text for which no restoration could be suggested
† .. (†)	Completely unclear
.. (?)	Doubtful

VMST The Tibetan translation of the *Vṛttamālāstuti* as published in Hahn 1971 and (partially) corrected in Hahn 2008

The main text of the *Vṛttamālāstuti* is not contained in the manuscript of the commentary. It is taken from Hahn 2008, with a few modifications.

॥ वृत्तमालास्तुतिः ॥

॥ वृत्तमालाविवृत्यन्विता ॥

(1b) ओं नमो मञ्जुश्रिये ॥

ज्ञानश्रीप्रभवां वृत्तमालामिव धियां निधेः ।
ज्ञानश्रीप्रभवां वृत्तमालां वयमुपास्महे ॥

इहायं प्रकर्षपारीणगुणगणज्ञान**ज्ञानश्री**मित्रो **वृत्तमा** .. .. न्त[1]मार्यमञ्जुश्रियमभितुष्टूषुर्यतिशरीरसंज्ञाभिः स्वच्छन्दसो वृत्तभेदानपि प्रतिपिपादयिषुरादौ तावत्प्रतिपाद्यवृत्तानां सामान्येन प्रभेदप्रस्तावनामाह ।

वृत्तमित्यादि[2] ॥

वृत्तं सममर्धसमं
विषमं चेत्यामनन्ति वागीशः ।
त्रिविधं परार्थविधये
समासतो व्यासतो ऽनन्तम् ॥ १ ॥

वागीशो[3] मञ्जुश्रियस्तव **वृत्तं** चरित्र**मामनन्ति** मन्यन्त उपदिशन्ति वा । मुनीन्द्रा इति शेषः । किंभूतं तदित्याह । **समं** तुल्यं शान्तरूपमित्यर्थः । **अर्धसमं** .. ..[4]तक्रोधरूपम् । **विषमं** विकटक्रोधरूपम् । **इती**त्थं संक्षेपेण त्रिप्रकारं चरितं तव कथयन्ति । विस्तरतस्त्वेकैकस्यानन्त्या**दनन्तम्** । किमर्थमित्याह । **परार्थविधये**[5] परार्थकरणार्थम् ॥

वृत्तपक्षे तु **वागीशः** । **पिङ्गला**दयो मुनयः । **वृत्तं** पद्यभेदम् । **समं** वैश्वादि । **अर्धसम**मुपचित्रादि । **विषमं** पदचतुरूर्ध्वादि । **इती**त्थं **त्रिविधं समासत आमनन्ति**[6] । अत्रापि समादीनां प्रत्येकमनन्तत्वा**दनन्तम्** । तदुक्तम् 'अनन्तः पद्यमार्गो ऽयं विशेषः पाठशोभया'

---

1 *vṛttamālā//////////* Hahn. — Hahn suggests in a footnote: Read *vṛttamālayā bhagavantaṃ*?

2 *vṛttam ityādi* conj. Hahn] *vṛ .. .. tyādi* Ms.

3 *vāgīśo* em. Hahn] *vāgīṣo* Ms.

4 Read *śamita°* ?

5 *°vidhaye* conj. Hahn] *°vi .. ..* Ms.

6 *āmananti* conj. Hahn] *.. mananti* Ms.

इति । **परार्थविधय** इति पूर्ववत् । अथवा **परः** प्रकृष्टो यो ऽ(2a)**र्थः**[1] । तस्य **विधये** प्रतिपादनार्थम् । वृत्तनिबद्धो ह्यर्थः सुप्रतिपदो भवति ॥

पुनः किंभूतं तद्वृत्तमित्याह । **प्रतिनियते**त्यादि ॥

प्रतिनियताकृतिरूढं
वरमुनिभिर्यत्र नाम संगीतम् ।
छन्दः पदं च परमं
स्फुरति यथा विविधविन्यासैः ॥ २ ॥

यत्र येषु वृत्तेषु **प्रतिनियतास्वाकृतिषु** मूर्तिषु[2] **रूढं** प्रसिद्धं[3] **नाम वरमुनिभि**र्बुद्धैः[4] **संगीतं** संभूय गीतम् । स्थिरचक्रादिसंज्ञा संग्रन्थिता[5] । यत्र **च च्छन्दो** ऽभिलाषः । **स्फुरति** पश्यतामिति शेषः । **पदं परम**मिति । प्रतिष्ठा **च**[6] व्यवस्थितिश्च[7] श्रेष्ठं स्फुरति । कथं स्फुरति । **विविधा** ये **विन्यासाः** सत्त्वानां रुचिसमारोपा[8]स्तदनतिक्रमैः । अस्तावस्य पाक्षिकत्वादिति भावः ॥

वृत्तपक्षे तु **प्रतिनियतास्वा**[9]**कृतिषु**[10] नियतगुरुलघुक्रमस्वरूपेषु । **रूढं** प्रसिद्धं **नाम** । **वरमुनिभिः** पिङ्गलादिभिः **संगीत**मिदं वैश्वमियं तनुमध्येत्यादि । यत्र च **च्छन्दो** गायत्र्यादि[11]संज्ञेति[12] । कथं **विविधा** ये **विन्यासा**स्तत्र तत्र गायत्र्यादि[13]संज्ञानिवेशास्तदनतिक्रमैः । **पदं चे**ति यतिः । तच्चोत्कृष्टं **स्फुरति** । अत्रापि **यथाविविधविन्यासै**[14]रिति

---

[1] *yo 'rthaḥ* conj. Hahn] *... thaḥ* Ms.

[2] {{*mūrttiṣu*}} Ms.

[3] *prasiddhaṁ* conj. Hahn] *prasi ...* Ms.

[4] *buddhaiḥ* Ms.] *budhaiḥ* em. Hahn

[5] *saṁgranthitā* Ms.] *saṁgrathitā* em. Hahn

[6] *ca* em. Hahn] *cā°* Ms.

[7] *°sthitiś ca* conj. Hahn] *°sthi .. ..* Ms.

[8] *°samāropās* p.c.] *°samāropas* a.c.

[9] *°niyatāsv* p.c.] *°niyatasv* a.c.

[10] *ākṛtiṣu* conj. Hahn] *.. kṛtiṣu* Ms.

[11] *gāyatryādi°* p.c.] *gāyitryādi°* a.c.

[12] *°saṁjñeti* conj. Hahn] *°sa ... ti* Ms.

[13] *gāyatryādi°* p.c.] *gāyitryādi°* a.c.

[14] *°vinyāsai~* conj. Hahn] *°vi .. sai~* Ms.

योज्यम् । 'विश्रामो ऽर्धे पदे भङ्गः पादांशे वक्ष्यतो यतिः' इति वचनात् । अथवा शुद्धविराडार्षभादावेकादिस्थानेषु भावात् । यतेर्**यथा** यादृशा ये **विविधा**[1] (2b) **विन्यासास्**तैः । तद्वृत्तमामनन्तीति पूर्वेण संबन्धः । तत्र **प्रतिनियताकृती**ति सामान्येन शरीरस्य प्रस्तावना । **नामसंगीत**मिति संज्ञायाः । **पद**मिति यतेः । **छन्दश्चे**ति च्छन्दसः ।

ननु[2] हरिहरादिभ्यो गुणाधिक्ये भगवतस्तत्परिहारेण स्तुत्यर्हता ॥ तदेवं[3] तद्गुणगौरवं[4] कथमवगतमित्याह **प्रतिरूपे**त्यादि ॥

प्रतिरूपदर्शनादपि
शक्याः सकलक्रमेण गुरुलघवः ।
विगणयितुं धीमद्भिः
किमपरमत्रानुयोगेन ॥ ३ ॥

प्रतिरूपाः प्रतिकृतयः । **तद्दर्शनादपि**[5] । इमे **गुरवो** न केवलं निरूपणाद् गुणगौरवादिमे **लघवो** गुणलाघवादिति **सकलक्रमेण** सर्वप्रकारं **विगणयितुं** परिसंख्यातुं **धीमद्भिः शक्यन्ते**[6] । तदुक्तम् 'रूपमहो यथेदमाह्लादि पटे ऽपि हि नाथ तावकम्' इति । अतः **किमपरं** प्रयोजनम**त्र** स्तुतिप्रस्तावे ऽनुयोगेन पर्य**नुयोगेन** कृतेन[7] किम् । नान्यदित्यर्थः[8] ॥

वृत्तपक्षे तु ननु पूर्वाचार्यप्रणीतभादिसंज्ञामन्तरेण कथं नियतगुरुलघुक्रमनिश्चय इत्याह । **रूपाणि** सूत्रश्लोकाः । तेषां **प्रतिरूपाणि** प्रस्ताराः[9] । **तद्दर्शनादपि** । न केवलं भादिसंज्ञाद्वारेण । अतो भादिसंज्ञां विना कथं गुरुलघुक्रमनिर्णय इत्यत्र प्रश्नेन किं फलम् । भादिसंज्ञया[10] ग्रन्थगौरवात् प्रतिपत्तिगौ(3a)रवाच्चेति[1] भावः ॥

---

1 *ye vividhā* conj. Hahn] *(y)e (.)i .. ..* Ms.

2 *nanu* conj. Hahn] *.. nu* Ms.

3 *tad evaṁ* em.] *tad eva* Ms., Hahn

4 *tadguṇa°* em.] *taguṇa°* Ms.; *guṇa°* Hahn

5 *taddarśanād api* conj. Hahn] *tadda .. .. d api* Ms.

6 *śakyante* conj. Hahn] *.. .. nte* Ms.

7 A mark of addition below *°te°*. The upper margin is broken off. No addition elsewhere on the folio.

8 *nānyad* conj. Hahn] *.. .. d* Ms.

9 *prastārāḥ* conj.] *pra(st). ...* Ms.; *pra(stu)<tāni* |> Hahn. —Hahn suggests in a footnote: Or *pratyu<tāni>* ?

10 *°saṃjñayā* em. Hahn] *°saṃjñāyā* Ms.

इदानीमस्य ग्रन्थस्य भङ्ग्या प्रवृत्तिप्रयोजनमुपदर्शयितुमाह । **प्रभवत्वित्यादि** ॥

प्रभवतु विभ्रमहतये
विचिन्त्यमानं तदादराद्भवताम् ।
सुकृतिमुखाभिजनानां
वाचां निजमेकमाभरणम् ॥ ४ ॥

॥ प्रस्तावना ॥

तद्भगवतो वृत्तम् । **आदराद्विचिन्त्यमान**मभ्यस्यमानं **भवतां विभ्रमहतये**[2] विपर्यासप्रहाणाय **प्रभवतु** । श्रुतमय्या हि प्रज्ञया प्रथममवधार्य चिन्तामय्याभ्यस्यमानमभ्यासप्रकर्षाद्भगवद्वृत्तं विभ्रमसंभ्रंशाय भवति । किंभूतं तद्वृत्तमित्याह[3] । **सुकृते**ति । **सुकृतिमुखमभिजन** उत्पत्तिस्थानं यासां तासां **वाचां निज**मनागन्तुकमसाधारणं वा । **एक**मन्याभावात् **आभरण**मलंकारः । उपवर्ण्य[4]मानेन हि वागीशस्य वृत्तेन सुकृतिनां वचांस्यलंक्रियन्ते । तदनेन भगवतो वृत्तचिन्ता विपर्यासनिरासप्रयोजनिका । तद्वर्णनं च वाचां भूषणायालमिति[5] भवतामपि सन्त[6]स्तच्चिन्तावर्णनयोः प्रवृत्तिरुचितेति दृष्टादृष्टलक्षणं प्रवृत्तिप्रयोजनं प्रकाशितम् ॥

वृत्तपक्षे तु **तत्स**मादिवृत्तं तात्पर्यतो **विचिन्त्य**[7]**मानं भवतां** श्रोतॄणां **विभ्रमहतये** वृत्तविषयाज्ञानप्रहाणाय **प्रभवतु** । कथंभूतं तदित्याह । **सुकृते**त्यादि । वृत्तं हि कविगिरामाभरणभूतम् । पादबद्ध(3b)त्वेन[8] वाल्मीकिना प्रथममवतारितत्वादिति[9] । प्रयोजनं पूर्ववदवगन्तव्यम् ॥

प्रस्तावनेति । अभिधास्यमानस्यार्थस्योपोद्घात इत्यर्थः ॥

धीगीःश्रीणामिति ॥

---

1 °*gauravāc ceti* conj. Hahn] .. *ravāc ceti* Ms.

2 °*hataye* conj. Hahn] °*hata* .. Ms.

3 *tadvṛttam* conj. Hahn] *ta* .. ..*m* Ms.

4 *upavarṇya*° conj.] *upa* .. ..° Ms.; *upa(la)<kṣya>*° Hahn

5 *alam iti* conj. Hahn] *a* ..*m iti* Ms.

6 Read *satāṃ taccintā*° ?

7 *tātparyato vicintya*° conj. Hahn] *tātpa(rya)*.. .. *cintya*° Ms.

8 °*bhūtam* | *pādabaddhatvena* conj. Hahn] °*bhūta*. .. .. *tvena* Ms.

9 °*tāri{{tā}}tvād* Ms.

धी-
गीः- ।
श्री-
णाम् ॥ ५ ॥

निजै-
कभूः ।
विभा-
तिया ॥ ६ ॥

एकाक्षरस्योक्त[1]नाम्नश्छन्दसः **श्री**संज्ञकमिदं वृत्तम् । यद्यपि षडक्षरादिभिरेव काव्यवर्त्मनि व्यवहारो दृश्यते नैकाक्षरादिभिरसुन्दरत्वात् । तदुक्तं पद्यविवेके

उक्तमत्युक्तकं[2] मध्या प्रतिष्ठा सुप्रतिष्ठया ।
प्रायः प्रयोगबाह्यत्वादभव्यत्वाच्च नाश्रिताः ॥

तथा च जयदेवः 'गायत्रं छन्दसामाद्यम्' इति । रत्नाकरे च 'च्छन्दांसि विदुः षड्कैरारभ्यै-कैक[3]वृद्धिभिः पादैः' इति । इहापि वक्ष्यति **गायत्रीव च्छन्दःस्वाद्या** इति । पद्यालंकारे ऽपि 'गायत्र्यादीन्येव[4] च्छन्दांसि दर्शितानि' । लं

इह तु श्लोकबन्धान्तरेण[5] च्छन्दोवृत्तनाम नोक्तम् । तथापि संभवमात्रेण निर्देशाददोषः । किं च प्रयोगो **ऽप्यन्यत्र** दृश्यते । यथा

धीः श्रीः । तेस्ताम् ॥
सर्वैः कार्या । बुद्धे भक्तिः ॥
सौगतं[6] मङ्गलम् ।
सूदितं युक्तिभिः ॥
शीलैराढ्याः सर्वे सत्त्वाः ।

---

1 *ekākṣarasyokta°* conj. Hahn] *e .. .. kta°* Ms.

2 *uktam atyuktakaṁ* conj. Hahn] *ukta. .. .. ktakaṁ* Ms.

3 *ṣaṭkair ārabhyaikaika°* conj. Hahn] *ṣa .. .. rabhyaikaika°* Ms.

4 *gāya°* p.c.] *gāyi°* a.c.

5 *°bandhāntareṇa* conj. Hahn] *°bandhāntare ..* Ms.

6 *saugataṁ* conj. Hahn] *sauga .. .* Ms.

सौख्योपेताः संपद्यन्ताम् ॥
सर्वविदाज्ञा यो ऽनुविधत्ते ।
तं च सदर्थाः के न भजन्ते ॥

रङ्गरचनायां च 'स्मृतिहेतवे[1] (4a) पुरुषोत्तमः । भरतादिषूद्धरते लवम्' इति ॥

तत्र **धीर**त्रानास्रवा[2] प्रज्ञा । **गीर**नवद्या वाक् । **श्रीः** लौकिकलोकोत्तरा संपत्तिः । तासां **निजा** स्वभावसिद्धा । **एका** अद्वितीया **भूर्भू**मिराश्रय[3] उत्पत्तिस्थानं वा । सा नीलोत्पल-पाणेर्मञ्जुश्रियो मूर्तिर्जयतीति वक्ष्यमाणेन संबन्धः ॥

निजैकभूर्विभाति येति द्व्यक्षरस्यात्युक्तनाम्नश्छन्दसः सुखं नाम वृत्तम्[4] ॥

पुनः किंभूता सा मूर्तिरित्याह । **तद्गुणाशंसिभिः सेव्यते चानिश**मिति ॥

तद्गुणा-
शंसिभिः ।
सेव्यते
चानिशम् ॥ ७ ॥

त्र्यक्षरस्य मध्याभिधानस्य मृगी नामेदं[5] वृत्तम् ।

न केवलं धीगीःश्रीणां निजैकभूः[6] । **तस्या**स्तनोर्ये **गुणा** लक्षणानुव्यञ्जनादयस्ता**नाशंसितु-**मभिलषितुं शीलं येषां तैः । धीगीःश्रीगुणाशंसिभिर्वा **सुरासुरादिषूद्गतै**र्वा[7] । सुरनरप्रधानैः **सेव्यते** चोपास्यते या तनुरिति योज्यम् ॥

किंभूतैस्तैरित्याह । **समाश्रयस्खलन्मलै**रिति ।

समाश्रय-
स्खलन्मलैः ।

---

1 °*hetave* conj. Hahn] °*heta* .. Ms.

2 °*sravā* em. Hahn] °*śravā* Ms.

3 *bhūmir āśraya* conj. Hahn] (*bhū*) .. .. *śraya* Ms.

4 *nāma vṛttam* conj. Hahn] *nā* .. .. *ttam* Ms.

5 *nāmedaṃ* em. Hahn] *nāṃmedaṃ* Ms.

6 °*śrīṇāṁ nijaikabhūḥ* conj. Hahn] °*śrī* .. .. .. *jaikabhūḥ* Ms.

7 °*ṣūdgatair vā* conj. Hahn] °*ṣūdgatai* .. Ms.

सुरासुरा-
दिषूद्गतैः ॥ ८ ॥

समाश्रयो भगवदाश्रयणम् । तस्माद्धेतोः[1] **स्खलन्तो मला** रागादयः क्लेशा येषां तैः । तद-यमर्थः । यत एव ते सुरासुरादिप्रवरा भगवतस्तनुगुणमाशंसन्ति । तत एव तैः सा सेव्यते ऽनिशं तद्व(4b)शाच्च[2] स्खलन्मलतया क्रमेण तद्गुणलाभिनो भवन्तीति ।

समाश्रयस्खलन्मलैः सुरासुरादिषूद्गतैरिति चतुरक्षरस्य प्रतिष्ठानाम्नो जया नाम वृत्तमेतत् ॥

पुनः किंभूतैरित्याह[3] । **नैकभवीये**त्यादि ॥

नैकभवीया-
भ्यासविवृद्धम् ।
बोधविशेषं
साधु दधानैः ॥ ९ ॥

इदं पञ्चाक्षरस्य सुप्रतिष्ठाख्यस्य पङ्क्तिनामधेयं वृत्तम् । उक्तादिसु[4]प्रतिष्ठान्तस्य च्छन्दः-पञ्चकस्यापरे ऽपि वृत्तविशेषा[5] .. .. राजेन दर्शिताः । तत्रैवावबोद्धव्याः । नैकभवो नखादित्वान्नलोपाभावः । तत्र भवो वृद्ध्यादित्वाच्छः । **नैकभवीयो ऽभ्यासः** । तेन **विवृद्धो** वृद्धिं गतो यः स **बोध**[6]**विशेषो** विपर्यासादिदोषरहितः । तं **साधु** शोभनं **दधानैः** । एतेन भगवदाश्रयस्खलन्मलत्वे ऽपि तदुपदेशा[7]भावेनानेक[8]जन्मपरंपराभ्यास[9]विवृद्धबुद्धिविशेष-स्याभावान्नानल्पकल्पोप[10]चितपुण्यज्ञानसंभूतभगवद्देहगुणविशेषलाभ इति प्रकाशयति ॥

---

1 °*āśrayaṇam* | *tasmādd hetoḥ* conj.] °*āśrayaṇa* . .. . Ms.; °*āśrayaṇa*<*m* | *tasya hetoḥ*> Hahn

2 *sevyate 'niśaṁ tadvaśāc ca* conj. Hahn] *se* .. .. *śāc ca* Ms.

3 *punaḥ kiṁbhūtair* conj. Hahn] .. .. *r* Ms.

4 °*su*° em. Hahn] °*ṣu*° Ms.

5 °*viśeṣā* conj. Hahn] °*viśe* .. Ms.

6 *gato yaḥ sa bodha*° conj. Hahn] *ga* .. .. *bodha*° Ms.

7 *tadupadeśā*° p.c.] *tadupadiśā*° a.c.

8 °*bhāvenāneka*° em. Hahn] °*bhāvenānekaṃ* Ms.

9 °*paraṁparābhyāsa*° conj. Hahn] °*paraṁ* .. ... *sa*° Ms.

10 °*analpakalpo{{pa}}*° Ms.

पुनः कीदृशी[1] सा तनुरित्याह[2] । **गीते**त्यादि ॥

> **गीता गायत्रीव**
> **च्छन्दःस्वाद्या सद्भिः ।**
> **वृत्तं भावि श्रेयो**
> **यस्यां सद्वा वैश्वम् ॥ १० ॥**

या **सद्भिर्गीता** । यथा **गायत्री**[3] **च्छन्दःसु** मध्य **आद्या** तथा सापि **च्छन्दसा**भिलाषेण **स्वाद्येव** स्वाद्या आस्वादनीया । अभिलाषवृत्तिरपि च्छ(5a)न्दः[4]शब्दो ऽस्ति । यथा च्छन्दसा हि वचसां प्रवृत्तिरिति । **यस्यां** च तनौ विश्वस्येदं **वैश्वं श्रेयः** । **वृत्तं** भूतम् । **भावि** भविष्यत्[5] । **सद्वा** विद्यमानं च ॥

वृत्तपक्षे इयमाद्या **गायत्री**[6] च्छन्दःसु यस्यामिदं **वैश्वं** वृत्तम् । गायत्री[7] च्छन्दःस्वाद्या यस्यामिति शरणं यावदधिकृतं वेदितव्यम् ॥

नीलोत्पलपाणेरित्यादि योजितम् ।

> **नीलोत्पलपाणे-**
> **र्लीलानिलयस्य ।**
> **शास्तुर्जयतीयं**
> **मूर्तिस्तनुमध्या ॥ ११ ॥**

लीलानिलयो विलासभवनम्[8] । **तनु** क्षामं **मध्यं** यस्याः सा **तनुमध्या** ॥

वृत्तपक्षे गायत्री[9] च्छन्दःस्वाद्या यस्यामियं[10] **तनुमध्या** नाम ॥

---

1 *kīdṛśī* em.] *kīdṛśā* Ms., Hahn

2 *ity āha* conj. Hahn] *i .. ..* Ms.

3 *gāyatrī* p.c.] *gāyitrī* a.c.

4 *api cchandaḥ°* conj. Hahn] *a .. .. ndaḥ°* Ms.

5 *bhaviṣyat* em. Hahn] *bhaviṣyati* Ms.

6 *gāyatrī* em. Hahn] *gāyitrī* Ms.

7 *gāyatrī* em. Hahn] *gāyitrī* Ms.

8 *°bhavanam* conj. Hahn] *°bhava ...* Ms.

9 *gāyatrī* em.] *gāyitrī* Ms., Hahn

10 *{{yasyā}}m iyaṁ* Ms.

प्रसीदेत्यादि ॥

प्रसीद भगवन्
विलोकय मनाक् ।
जडं जनमिमं
त्वदेकशरणम् ॥ १२ ॥

हे **भगवन् प्रसीद** प्रसन्नो भव । तादृशश्च मादृशि । **जडमज्ञं**[1] **जनं विलोकय** । किंभूतम् । **त्वदेकशरणम्** । त्वमेकः शरणमाश्रयो यस्येति हेतुभावेन विशेषणम् ॥

वृत्तपक्षे गायत्री[2] च्छन्दःस्वाद्या यस्यां **शरणं** नाम वृत्तम्[3] ॥

जाज्वलीतीत्यादि ॥

जाज्वलीति शासनं
त्वां समेत्य सौगतम् ।
सूर्यधाम दुःसहं
सातिरेकमुष्णि हि ॥ १३ ॥

त्वां समेत्य प्राप्य । सुगतस्येदं **सौगतं शासनं** प्रवचनं[4] तदर्थो वा । **जाज्वलीति** अत्यर्थं ज्वलति । देदीप्यत इत्यर्थः । **हि**शब्दः[5] सादृश्ये । यथा **उष्णि**[6] उष्णसमये । 'उष दाहे' । औणादिकः पूषादित्वात् कनिन् । **सूर्यधाम** । अतिरेक आधिक्यं तेन सह वर्तते **सातिरेकम**धिकं **दुःसहं** भवति[7] । (5b) तत्र सूर्यतेजःस्थानीयं शासनम् । उष्णसमयकल्पो भगवान् । जाज्वलीतीति च सातिरेकदुःसहता सूचितैव ॥

---

1 *jaḍam* conj. Hahn] .. *ḍam* Ms.

2 *gāyatrī* p.c.] *gāyitrī* a.c., Hahn

3 *nāma vṛttam* conj. Hahn] *nā* .. .. *ttam* Ms.

4 *pravacanaṃ* p.c.] *pravacanoṃ* a.c.

5 *hiśabdaḥ* conj. Hahn] *hiśa* ... Ms.

6 *uṣṇi uṣṇasamaye* em. Hahn] *uṣṇiṣṇaṣṇe* (?) Ms.

7 *bhavati* conj. Hahn] *bha* .. .. Ms.

वृत्तपक्षे **उष्णिहि** सप्ताक्षरे छन्दसि[1] **सातिरेकम्** । ऊर्ध्वगामिपर्यन्तमु[2]ष्णिहीत्यधिकारः । पद्यालंकारे 'जातौ बहुवचने उष्णिहम्' इति निर्देशो ऽन्तिमस्य गुरुत्वज्ञापनार्थः । इह तु समवृत्तप्रस्तावात् पादान्तरसाहचर्याद्गुरुत्वसंगतिः[3] ॥

दधत्यपीत्यादि ॥

दधत्यपि निकामं
कुमारललितानि ।
तनुस्तव जिनानां
कुमार ललितैव ॥ १४ ॥

कुमारललितानि शिशुचेष्टितानि **तव तनुर्दधत्यपि निकाम**मत्यर्थं **ललितै**व मनोहरैव । हे **जिनानां कुमार** । लोके खलु[4] प्रेक्षणे.. .. प्रेक्षापूर्वाणि बालविलसितानि न परितोषमावहन्ति । तव तु तनुस्तानि बिभ्रत्यपि परितोषकरीति[5] विरोधाभासः । विनेयानुरोधेन तदाश्रयात्परिहारः[6] ।

वृत्तपक्षे उष्णिहि **कुमारललिता** नाम ॥

जायत इत्यादि ॥

जायते जनराशे-
र्यामनुस्मरतो ऽपि ।
निर्धुताधरभाव-
मूर्ध्वगामि च रूपम् ॥ १५ ॥

यां तव तनु**मनुस्मरतो** ऽनुध्यायतो **जनराशेः** । **निर्धुतो** निःशेषेण धुतो ध्वस्तो **ऽधरभावो** जातिगुणादिभिरधरता येन तथाभूतं **रूपं** स्वभावो **जायते** । न केवलम् । किं **तूर्ध्वगामि** च जातिगुणादिभिरेवोर्ध्वगमनशीलमुत्कृष्टपदवर्ती(6a)ति यावत् ॥

वृत्तपक्षे उष्णिहि **ऊर्ध्वगामि** वृत्तम् । अन्येषामुद्धता नाम ॥

---

1 The Ms. consistently reads *cchandasi* despite a preceding long letter.

2 °*paryantam* conj. Hahn] °*pa .. .. m* Ms.

3 *gurutvasaṁgatiḥ* conj. Hahn] *guru(tva) .. .. tiḥ* Ms.

4 *kha{{lu}}* Ms.

5 °*karīti* em. Hahn] °*kārīti* Ms.

6 *tadāśrayāt pari°* conj. Hahn, though not reported] *tadāśrayā . ..ri°* Ms.

पुनः किंभूता सा तनुरित्याह । **यद्गुणे**त्यादि ॥

> यद्गुणस्तुतिविस्तरा-
> दस्तसङ्गमनुष्टुभि ।
> धीरमेकमुदीरय-
> न्त्युत्तमं पदमुद्गताः ॥ १६ ॥

यस्यास्तनोर्गुणस्तुतिस्तस्या अस्तसङ्गं स्वार्थासक्तिरहितं यथा भवति तथा **विस्तरणात्** प्रथनात् । **धीरं** पण्डित**मेकम**द्वितीय**मुदीरयन्ति** कथयन्ति[1] । के ते । **उत्तमम**मुत्कृष्टं **पदमुद्गताः** प्राप्ताः । बुद्धा इत्यर्थः । कस्मिन् विषये धीरमुदी[2]रयन्तीत्याह । **अनुष्टुभि** । 'ष्टुभु स्तम्भे' । अनेकार्थत्वादिह स्तुत्यर्थः । अनुरूपं स्तोभनमनुष्टुभ् । उपसर्गात् सुनोतीत्यादिना षत्वम् । य एव स्वसुखनिरपेक्षो[3] मञ्जुघोषतनुगुणस्तुतीस्तनोति तमेवानुरूपस्तुतिविधौ विज्ञो ऽयमिति व्यपदिशन्ति मुनीन्द्रा इत्यर्थः । अथवा अस्तसङ्गमिति धीरमित्यस्य **पद**[4]मित्यस्य वा समाना[5]धिकरणम् ॥

वृत्तपक्षे **ऽनुष्टुभि** अष्टाक्षरे च्छन्दसि **उत्तमं** नाम । **अनुष्टुभी**त्यधिकारश्चित्रपदां यावत् ॥

पुनः किंरूपा तनुरित्याह । **घोरे**त्यादि ॥

> घोरमोहतामसाव-
> रुद्धबुद्धिलोचनस्य ।
> रत्नयष्टिदीपिकैव
> या समान्यभूज्जनस्य ॥ १७ ॥

या तव तनुः । **रत्न**मयी[6] (6b) **यष्टिः** सैव **दीपिका** सैव **जनस्य समान्यभूत्** । साधारणीभवति स्मेति च्व्यन्तः । किंभूतस्य जनस्य । तम एव **तामसम्** । **मोह** एव **तामसं** तत्त्वदर्शनविबन्धकत्वात् । **घोरं** **यन्मोह**[7]**तामसं** तेनावरु**द्धं** **बुद्धिलोचनं** यस्य ॥

---

1 {{*kathayanti*}} Ms.

2 *dhīram udī°* conj. Hahn] *dhīra . .. dī°* Ms.

3 *nirapekṣo* conj. Hahn] *nirape ..* Ms.

4 *dhīra{{m ity asya pada}}m* Ms.

5 *samānā°* conj. Hahn] *sa .. nā°* Ms.

6 *ratnamayī* conj. Hahn] *ra .. .. ..* Ms.

7 *yanmoha°* conj. Hahn] *yanmo ..°* Ms.

वृत्तपक्षे ऽनुष्टुभि **समानी** नाम[1] ॥

जगत्त्रयेत्यादि ॥

> जगत्त्रयातिशायिनीं
> मुनीन्द्रसंपदं प्रति ।
> स्फुरन्त्यशेषनायक
> प्रमाणिकापि सैव नः ॥ १८ ॥

किं च हे **अशेषनायक** । **सैवो**क्तरूपा तव तनुः **नो** ऽस्माकं[2] प्रमाणं प्रमितिं करोतीति **प्रमाणिका** परिच्छेदिका । किं प्रति प्रमाणिका[3] । **जगत्त्रयमतिशयितु**मतिभवितुं शीलं यस्यास्तथाभूतां **मुनीन्द्राणां** लोकोत्तर**संपत्तिं**[4] **प्रति** । कीदृशी सतीत्याह । **स्फुरन्ती** दीप्यमाना । अन्य**दपि** हि प्रमाणं परिस्फुरदेव परिच्छेदकं प्रमेयस्य । तथा भगवतो ऽपि तनुर्महापुरुषलक्षणैः[5] परितः स्फुरन्ती मुनीन्द्रसंपदः परिच्छेदिका । यत्राकृतिस्तत्र गुणा वसन्तीति न्यायात् ॥

वृत्तपक्षे ऽनुष्टुभि **प्रमाणिका** ॥

तीव्रेत्यादि ॥

> तीव्रक्लेशप्लोषध्वंस-
> प्रौढे वंशे संबुद्धानाम् ।
> धत्ते भूषां भातीयं ते
> ऽम्भोदे यद्वद्विद्युन्माला ॥ १९ ॥

इयं ते तनुः **भाती** दीप्यमाना सती **भूषा**मलंकारं **धत्ते** करोति । कुत्र । **संबुद्धानां वंशे** । किंभूते । **क्लेशैः** कृतः **प्लोषो** दाहः । **तीव्रो** यः **क्लेश**[6]**प्लोषस्**तस्य **प्रध्वंसः** । तत्र **प्रौढे** प्रगल्भे । किं यत्र रो(7a)चमानं यथा भूषां धत्त इत्याह । यथा **विद्युन्माला** सौदामनीदाम ।

---

1 *nāma* em. Hahn, though not reported] *nām* Ms.

2 *no 'smākaṁ* conj. Hahn] *no '(smā)* ... Ms.

3 *pramāṇi{{kā}}* Ms.

4 °*saṁpattiṁ* conj. Hahn] °*saṁ .. ttiṁ* Ms.

5 °*lakṣaṇaiḥ* conj. Hahn] °*lakṣa ..* Ms.

6 *{{kle}}śa*° Ms.

अम्भोदो जलदो ऽपि । **तीव्रः क्लेशः**[1] क्लिष्टिः **प्लोषश्च** दाहः । तयो**र्ध्वंसे**[2] **प्रौढः** । मञ्जुनाथतनोरपि भासमानया विद्युन्मालया साम्यम् ॥

वृत्तपक्षे ऽनुष्टुभि **विद्युन्माला** ॥

केतनदण्डमित्यादि ॥

केतनदण्डं दधतो
ऽध्यापयितुं नीतिमिव ।
सद्गुरुलीला भवतो
भाति जगन्माणवकम् ॥ २० ॥

भवतो मञ्जुश्रियः । **सद्गुरुलीला** सद्गुरोश्चेष्टा **भाति** । किंभूतस्य । **केतनं** चिह्नमुत्पलं तदेव **दण्ड** इव सनालत्वाद्दण्डस्तं **दधत** इति हेतुभावेन विशेषणम् । किं कर्तुम् । **जगदेव माणवक** इव । माणवको बटुर्बालो वा । तं धर्म**नीतिमध्यापयितुं**[3] पाठयितुम् । उपाध्यायो ह्यनभियुक्तशिष्याणां भयोपदर्शनार्थं दण्डं धारयन्नध्यापयति[4] ॥

वृत्तपक्षे ऽनुष्टुभि **माणवकम्** ॥

त्रिजगत इत्यादि ॥

त्रिजगतो निजगतिं
प्रथयतः पृथुधियः ।
करतलं तव चलत्-
किसलयं तुलयति[5] ॥ २१ ॥

तव पृथुधियः[6] कर एव **करतलम्,** भूतलवत् । त**च्चलत्किसलयं**[7] **तुलयति** । तद्वदित्यर्थः । किंभूतस्य । **त्रिजगत**स्त्रैधातुकस्य । **निजां** शुभाशुभकर्मादिक्षिप्तां देवादि**गतिं**[1] निजस्वभावं

---

1 *tīvraḥ kleśaḥ* em.] *tīvrakleśaḥ* Ms., Hahn

2 *dhvaṃse* em. Hahn] *dhvaṃśe* Ms.

3 *adhyāpayituṁ* conj. Hahn] *adhyāpa .. ...* Ms.

4 Hahn suggests in a footnote: Read *cālayan* ?

5 Although Hahn treats *tulayati* as an indication of caesura, Śākyarakṣita does not make any such comment in his *Vivṛti*.

6 *pṛthudhiyaḥ* conj. Hahn] .. .. *dhiyaḥ* Ms.

7 *°kisalayaṃ* em. Hahn] *°kiśalayaṃ* Ms.

वा **प्रथयतः** कथयतः[2] । धर्मदेशनासमये भावाभिव्यक्त्यभिनयेन पाणेश्चलनाच्चलत्पल्लवेन साम्यमुक्तम् ॥

वृत्तपक्षे ऽनुष्टुभि **किसलयम्**[3] ॥

साधिगम(7b)मि[4]त्यादि ॥

साधिगमं समकालं
तत्त्वरसेषु विधत्ते ।
विश्वमधीश्वर चित्रं
चित्रपदा तव वाणी ॥ २२ ॥

हे **अधीश्वर तव वाणी** भारती । **चित्राणि** नानाप्रकाराणि **पदानि** यस्याः सा तथाभूता सती । **विश्वं** सर्वं विनेयजनं **सममेककालं तत्त्वे रसेषु** परमार्थरस[5]विषये **साधिगमं** सप्रतिवेधं **विधत्ते** यत्त**चित्र**[6]माश्चर्यम् । भगवतः खल्वभिन्नापि भारती विनेयानामाशयभेदेन भिद्यमाना नानापदव्यञ्जनैः चर[7].. .. .. धमाधत्ते ॥

वृत्तपक्षे ऽनुष्टुभि **चित्रपदा** ॥

बृहत्यामित्यादि ॥

बृहत्यां विभूत्यां त एके
पदन्यासमासादयन्ति ।
क्षणं यत्र ते लब्धलक्ष्यः
कटाक्षो ऽपि विश्रान्तिमेति ॥ २३ ॥

---

1 *devādigatiṁ* conj. Hahn] *de .. .. .. tiṁ* Ms.

2 {{*kathayataḥ*}} Ms.

3 *kisalayaṃ* em. Hahn] *kiśalayaṃ* Ms.

4 *sādhigamam* conj. Hahn] *sā .. .. .. m* Ms.

5 *paramārtharasa°* conj. Hahn] *paramārtha .. ..°* Ms.

6 *citram* em. Hahn] *cittam* Ms.

7 *°vyañjanaiḥ cara* em. Hahn] *°vyañjanaiḥ ra* Ms.

यत्र येषु । **ते** तव । **लब्धलक्ष्यः** सन् **कटाक्षो ऽपि** । न केवलं वचनादि । **क्षणं विश्रान्तिमेति** विश्राम्यति[1] । **त एवैके** त्वत्कटाक्षपातपूता **बृहत्यां** महत्यां **विभूत्यां** चक्रवर्त्यादिसंपदि **पदन्यासमासादयन्ति** प्रतिष्ठां लभन्त इति यावत् ॥

वृत्तपक्षे **बृहत्यां**[2] नवाक्षरे च्छन्दसि **कटाक्षो** नामापूर्वम् । **बृहत्या**मिति मुद्रापर्यन्तमधिक्रियते ।

त्वद्दृशैवेत्यादि ॥

त्वद्दृशैव परिमलनाद्
भव्यतामियमुपगता ।
भाति भूमिरिव जनता
संतताहितहलमुखी ॥ २४ ॥

किं च **त्वच्चक्षुषैव परिमलनात्** परिचयात् कारणात् । **इयं जनता** जनसमूहः । **भव्यतां** शान्तिफलभाजनता**मुपगता** सती **संतताहितहलमुखी भूमिरिव भाति** । **संततं** निरन्तर**माहितं हलस्य मुखं** यथा[3] तथा । य(8a)था खलु सततहलमुखप्रहता[4] भूमिर्भाविफलनिष्पत्तौ योग्या तद्वदुक्तरूपापि जनतेत्यर्थः ॥

वृत्तपक्षे बृहत्यां **हलमुखी** ॥

ननु भगवन्नयनपरिमलनमात्रेण जनताभिमतफलनिष्पादनयोग्या । न हि हलपरिकर्ममात्रादसति सलिलसेक[5]बीजवपनादौ भूमिरपि सस्यप्रभूतिहेतुः प्रतीयते । तत् कथं तस्या भव्यतावगतिरि[6]त्याह । **वरदे**त्यादि ॥

वरद सा हि संजन्यते
परिणतिस्तयास्यां यतः ।
वचनबीजमुप्तं त्वया
फलति शान्तिरूपं फलम् ॥ २५ ॥

---

1 *viśrāmyati* conj. Hahn] *vi .. .. ti* Ms.

2 *bṛhatyāṁ* conj. Hahn] *bṛ .. tyāṁ* Ms.

3 *(yathā)* Ms.

4 *sa<ṃ>tata°* Hahn

5 *salilaseka°* em. Hahn] *salilameka°* (?) Ms.

6 *°avaga(ti)r i* Ms.

हे **वरद** । **तया** त्वद्दृशा परिमलितया **सा** कापि **परिणतिः** प्रतिसर्गमुप[1]चीयमानपुण्यसंभारादिभिर्विशिष्टात्मभावावस्था पाथःसेकादिभिरिव[2] भूम्याः । **हि**र्यस्मात् । **संजन्यते** संतत्या निष्पाद्यते । **यतः** परिणतिपरंपरायाः । **अस्यां** जनतायाम् । सामर्थ्यमवधार्य **त्वया वचन**मेव **बीजमुप्तम्** । **शान्तिः संक्लेशोप**[3]शमस्तल्लक्षणं **फलं फलति** निष्पादयति । सलिलावसेकादिपरिकर्मितायां भुवि बीजमुप्तं सस्यमिव ॥

वृत्तपक्षे बृहत्यां **रूपं** नाम ॥

कलयितुमि[4]त्यादि ॥

> कलयितुमिह कः शक्त-
> स्तव खलु चरितानीश ।
> सतमसि समये तोये
> भुजगशिशुसृतानीव ॥ २६ ॥

हे **ईश** । **इह** जगति **तव चरितानि खलु** निश्चितं **को** ऽर्वाग्दर्शी **कलयितुं** ज्ञातुमीशः **शक्तः** । कुत्र किं यथेत्याह । **सतमसि** सान्धकारे **समये** । .. ..[5] **य**(8b)**था**[6] **भुजगशिशोः सृतानि** गमनानि । सलिले सर्पस्यापि विचरितानि न लक्ष्यन्ते प्रागेव तच्छिशोः । तत्रापि सावतमससमये[7] । तथा च तव चरितानीत्यर्थः[8] ॥

वृत्तपक्षे बृहत्यां[9] **भुजगशिशुसृता** ॥

भवादृशो ऽपि तर्हि भगवच्चरितापरिचयेन मौन[10]मेवोचितमित्याह । **किंत्वि**त्यादि ॥

---

1 *°sargam upa°* em. Hahn] *°surgarūpa°* Ms.

2 *pāthaḥsekādibhir iva* em. and conj. Hahn] *yāthaḥ* | *sekā(d)i .. r iva* Ms.

3 *śāntiḥ saṁkleśopa°* conj.] *śā .i . .. kleśopa°* Ms.; *śā<nt>i<rūpaṃ> kleśopa°* Hahn

4 *kalayitum* conj. Hahn] *ka .. .. tum* Ms.

5 Hahn suggests in a footnote: Read *toye jale*?

6 *yathā* conj. Hahn] .. *thā* Ms.

7 *sāvatamasasamaye* em. Hahn] *āvatamaṃ saṃsasamaye* Ms.

8 *cari{{tā}}nīty arthaḥ* Ms.

9 *bṛhatyāṁ* conj. Hahn] *bṛ .. ...* Ms.

10 *maunam* em. Hahn] *maulam* Ms.

किंतूदस्यति धैर्यध्वस्त्री
त्वत्कीर्तिश्रुतिजन्मानन्दः ।
स्वप्रौढिप्रतिपत्तिन्यस्तां
लोकस्याननमुद्रामीश ॥ २७ ॥

तथापि हे **ईश त्वत्कीर्तेः श्रुति**राकर्णनम् । त**ज्जन्मा**[1] **आनन्दो** हर्षः । **लोकस्य** मादृशो जनस्य । **आननमुद्रां** चरितविषये मौन**मुदस्यति** क्षिपति । किंभूताम् । **स्वस्या**त्मनः । **प्रौढिः** प्रागल्भ्यम् । त**त्प्रतिपत्त्या न्यस्तां** निवेशिताम्[2] । यद्यसावात्मज्ञतया स्वप्रौढिं प्रतिपन्नवान्नाहमस्मिन्विषये समर्थ इति तदा धैर्यमधिष्ठाय तिष्ठतो ऽस्यानन्दो ऽपि कथमाननमुद्रामुदसितुमीश[3] इत्याह **धैर्यध्वस्त्री**ति ॥

वृत्तपक्षे तु बृहत्यां **मुद्रा** नाम ॥

श्रीत्यादि ॥

श्रीनिकेत लीलाचतुरं ते
प्राप्तपार विद्याचरणानाम् ।
भाति वर्ष्म बुद्धात्मजपङ्क्तौ
यद्वदम्बुजन्मस्वरविन्दम् ॥ २८ ॥

हे **श्रियां निकेत** निवास । पुनः संबोध्यते । **प्राप्त**मधिगतं **पारं** पर्यन्तो येन । केषाम् । **विद्याश्चरणानि** च तेषाम् । विद्याचरणान्यार्याष्टाङ्गो मार्गः । सम्यग्दृष्टिर्विद्या शेषाण्यङ्गानि[4] चरणानि । न ह्यपश्यन्नचरणो वा गन्तुं[5] (9a) समर्थ इति । तिस्रो[6] वा शिक्षा विद्याचरणानि । अधिप्रज्ञं शिक्षा विद्या । अधिशीलमधिचित्तं च चरणानि । प्रज्ञायाः पूर्वपरिकर्मरूपत्वात्[7] पुनश्चरणं चरणमिति कृत्वा विद्यायास्तु पूर्वग्रहणम् । तत्परिशुद्ध्या शीलसमाधिपरिशुद्धितः । तया हि प्रज्ञाचक्षुषैव पश्यंस्ताभ्यां शीलसमाधिभ्यां चरणाभ्यामिव गच्छन् गन्तव्यमनुप्राप्नोतीति विद्याचरणशब्देन तिस्रः शिक्षा निर्दिश्यन्ते । **तव वर्ष्म** वपुः

---

1 *tajjanmā* conj. Hahn] *tajja ..* Ms.

2 *niveśitām* conj. Hahn] .. *veśitām* Ms.

3 *ānanamudrām* em. Hahn, though not reported] *ānanamutām* Ms.

4 *śeṣāṇy* em. Hahn, though not reported] *śeṣāny* Ms.

5 *gantuṁ samartha* em.] *gantuṁ sa* (?) *samartha* Ms.; *gantuṃ sa samartha* Hahn

6 *tisro* em. Hahn] *trisro* Ms.

7 *°rūpatvāt* em. Hahn] *°rupatvāt* Ms.

। **बुद्धात्मजानां** बोधिसत्त्वानां **पङ्क्तौ** पर्षन्मण्डले **भाति** । किंभूतम् । **लीलया** विलासेन **चतुरं**[1] मनोहरम् । कुत्र यथा किं भातीत्याह । **यथा अम्बुजन्मसु** कुमुदोत्पलादि**ष्वरविन्दं** महोत्पलम् । एतेनार्यमञ्जुश्रियः श्रीनिकेतत्वेन प्राप्तविद्याचरण[2]पारत्वेन च लीलाचतुरस्य वपुषो ऽपरबोधिसत्त्वापेक्षयोत्कर्ष उक्तः । अरविन्दस्यापि श्रीनिकेततया लीलायां च केलिविषये चतुरतया जलजन्मा[3]न्तरापेक्षमुत्कृष्टत्वं स्फुटमेव ॥

वृत्तपक्षे दशाक्षरे च्छन्दसि **पङ्क्तौ अरविन्दं** नामापूर्वम् । चतुर्णामन्त**श्चतुरन्तः** । तत्र **लीला** भङ्गिर्यतिरिति यावत् । **पङ्क्ता**वित्यधिकारो[4] (9b) वलयं यावत् ॥

त्वामित्यादि ॥

> त्वामुद्गीतकुलोदयशैलं
> प्रज्ञालोकमुपायरथस्थम् ।
> वन्दे जाड्यविखण्डनशौण्डं
> त्रैलोकीनलिनीसवितारम् ॥ २९ ॥

त्वां वन्दे इति संबन्धः । किंभूतम् । त्रयो लोका[5]**स्त्रैलोकी** । चातुर्वर्ण्यादित्वेन ष्यञि स्त्रियां षिल्लक्षणो ङीष् सामग्रीवत् । सैव **नलिनी** । तस्याः **सवितेव** सविता[6] प्रकाशकत्वात् । **उद्गीतं** ख्यातं यत् **कुलम्** । बोधिसत्त्ववंशः ब्राह्मणादिवंशो वा । तत्रैव परार्थं जन्मसंदर्शना**दुदयशैल** इव यस्य । **आलोको** रश्मिः । **प्रज्ञै**वालोको यस्य[7] । **उपायो** बोधिसत्त्वानां सर्वसत्त्वापरित्यागाशयाद्यनेकप्रकारः । स एव **रथः** संसारभ्रमणश्रम[8]विनोदहेतुत्वात् । तदुक्तम्

> बोधिसत्त्वरथं प्राप्य सर्वदुष्खश्रमापहम्[9] ।
> एवं सुखात् सुखं गच्छन् को विषीदेत् सचेतनः ॥ इति ।

---

1 *caturaṁ* conj. Hahn] *ca .. raṁ* Ms.

2 *°caraṇa°* conj. Hahn] *°cara ..°* Ms.

3 *jalajanmā°* conj. Hahn] *jalaja ..°* Ms.

4 *ity adhikāro* conj. Hahn] *ity a .. .. ..* Ms.

5 *lokās* em. Hahn] *lokas* Ms.

6 *savitā* conj.] *sa .. ..* Ms.; *sa<padi>* Hahn

7 *yasya* conj. Hahn] *.. sya* Ms.

8 *°bhra{{maṇaśra}}ma°* Ms.

9 *sarvaduṣkhaśramāpaham* conj.] *{{sarva}}duṣkhaśramāpa* ... Ms.

तदेवं रूपकालंकारेणादित्यसाधर्म्यमभिधाय भगवतः स्वार्थसंपत् प्रदर्शिता । परार्थसंपदमावेदयन्नाह[1] । **जाड्यं** जगदज्ञानम् । तस्य **विशेषेण खण्डनम्** । तत्र **शौण्डः** शक्तः । सूर्यपक्षे जाड्यं शैत्यम् ॥

वृत्तपक्षे पङ्क्तौ **नलिनी** । अदो ऽप्यपूर्वम् ॥

बुद्धेत्यादि ॥

बुद्धसुतानामभ्युदयोर्वी
भाति भृशं भूत्या तव नाथ ।
शैलविशेषस्येव शिखाभू
रुक्मवती रत्नाङ्कुरकान्त्या ॥ ३० ॥

हे **नाथ** । **बोधिसत्त्वानामभ्युदयस्य** गुणविभूते**रुर्वी** आश्रयता मुदितादिभूमिर्ज्ञानविशेषावस्थालक्षणा । **तव गुणसंपत्त्या भृश**मत्यर्थं **भाति** । कस्य यथा किं केन कीदृग् भाती(10a)त्याह । **रुक्मं** स्वर्णम् । यथा **शैलविशेषस्य** सुमेरोः **काञ्चनमयी शिखरभूमी**[2] **रत्नाङ्कुराणां कान्त्या**त्यर्थं शोभते । तद्वत् ॥

वृत्तपक्षे पङ्क्तौ[3] **रुक्मवती**[4] । केषांचिन्मते चम्पकमालेयम् ॥

निःशेष इत्यादि ॥

निःशेषस्तव विजयध्वानं
तन्वन् भ्राम्यति भुवनोद्योत ।
सानन्दः कृतिनिवहः स्वामिन्
विष्वग्घोषणपणवो यद्वत् ॥ ३१ ॥

भुवनोद्योत स्वामिन्निति संबोधनद्वयम् । यथा राजादेर्विजयशब्दं विस्तारयन् घोषणपटहः परितो **भ्राम्यति** तथा **तवापि घोषणपणव इव कृति**जन[5] इति । शेषं सुबोधम् ॥

वृत्तपक्षे पङ्क्तौ **पणवः** ॥

---

1 *āvedayann āha* conj. Hahn] *āvedaya .. ha* Ms.

2 {{*śi*}}*khara°* Ms.

3 *paṅktau* conj. Hahn

4 *rukmavatī* em. Hahn] *rukmatī* Ms.

5 *°(ja)na* Ms.

वादीत्यादि ॥

वादिव्रातप्रवरशिरोऽब्ज
श्रीधाम्नस्ते गुणमधुयोगात् ।
धीमन् धीरानपि मदयन्ती
त्रैलोकीवाग्[1] विलसति मत्ता ॥ ३२ ॥

वादिव्रातानां वादिवृन्दानां ये **प्रवराः** श्रेष्ठाः । तेषां **शिरोऽब्ज** । वादिव्रातानां वा प्रवरशिरोऽब्ज[2] । शिरःस्वब्जमिवाब्जमुत्कृष्टत्वेन मण्डन[3]भूतत्वात् ॥ शिरोमणिवदिति संबोधनीयम् । **तव श्रीधाम्नो गुणा** एव **मधूनि** । **तद्योगात्** संबन्धतश्च[4] तद्वाचकत्वेन[5] **त्रैलोकीवाक्** स्वयं **मत्ता** सती **धीरानपि** त्वद्गुणाख्याने निरुद्योगानपि **मदयन्ती** उत्सुकयन्ती **विलसति** । अब्जस्यापि श्रीधाम्नो मधुयोगान्मत्ता[6] भृङ्गादिमाला धीरानपि[7] मदयन्ती विलसति ॥

वृत्तपक्षे पङ्क्तौ **मत्ता** नाम ॥

विश्वेत्यादि ॥

विश्वचक्रवर्तिनां जिनानां
वंशभूषणे त्वयि स्फुटैव ।
म्लायतीव सा कुमारताख्या
या मयूरसारिणीष्यते तु ॥ ३३ ॥

या पुनः **स्फुटैव**[8] व्यक्तरूपैव[9] **मयूरेण सर्तुं शीलं यस्य तस्मिन्** कार्त्तिकेये **कुमारताया आख्या** (10b) प्रसिद्धि**रिष्यते सा विश्वचक्रवर्तिना**मधिपतीनां[10] **जिनानां वंशभूषणे त्वयि**

---

1. *trailokī vāg* Hahn
2. *°śiro'bja* conj. Hahn, though not reported] *°śi .. bja* Ms.
3. *maṇḍana°* em. Hahn] *maṇḍala°* Ms.
4. *saṁbandhataś ca* em. Hahn] *saṁbandhaś ca* Ms.
5. {{*ta*}}*dvācakatvena* Ms.
6. *madhuyogān* em. Hahn] *madhupayogān* Ms. — Hahn suggests in a footnote: Read *madhūpayogān* or *madhupānayogān*?
7. *dhīrān api* conj. Hahn] *dhīrā .. pi* Ms.
8. *sphuṭaiva* em. Hahn] *sphuṭeva* Ms.
9. *vyaktarūpaiva* em. Hahn] *vyaktaṃrūpaiva* Ms.
10. *°vartinām* em. Hahn] *°vattinām* Ms.

कुमारे सति **म्लायतीव** । यतस्त्वं[1] बहूनां त्रैलोक्यचक्रवर्तिनां वंशभूषणभूतः कुमारः । स चैकस्यैव[2] कामधात्वीश्वरस्य शम्भोः । अतस्त्वयि तस्य कुमारताख्या म्लायतीवेत्यर्थः ॥

वृत्तपक्षे पङ्क्तौ **मयूरसारिणी** ॥

नानेत्यादि ॥

> नानारत्नमरीचिमालिनी
> प्रोन्मीलन्निजकान्तिसंपदा ।
> प्रत्यङ्गं तव भूषणावली
> नीता शुद्धविराट्पराभवम् ॥ ३४ ॥

तव भूषणावली पराभवं नीता प्रापिता .[3] । किंभूता । **नानारत्नानां मरीचिमाला** यस्या अस्ति । व्रीह्यादित्वादिनिः । कया । **प्रत्यङ्गं प्रोन्मीलयन्ती** या नवकुमारदशाभाविनी **कान्तिसंपत् तया** । हे **शुद्धविराड्**इति संबोधनं[4] हेतुभावेन । विशेषेण राजत इति विराट् । यस्मात्त्वं शुद्धो निर्भूषणो विशेषेण[5] राजस इति ॥

वृत्तपक्षे पङ्क्तौ **शुद्धविराट्** ॥

पात्वित्यादि[6] ॥

> पातु जगत्तव तत्त्वनया-
> ख्यानविधौ करवल्गितकम् ।
> वादिपते व्यतिघट्टनतो
> वल्गुनिनादचलद्वलयम् ॥ ३५ ॥

हे **वादिपते** । **तव करयो**[1]**र्वल्गितकमी**षच्चलनं **जगत् पातु** । कुत्र तदित्याह । **तत्त्वनयस्य** परमार्थवर्त्मन **आख्यान**करणकाले । किंभूतम् । **व्यतिघट्टनतो** व्याख्यानमुद्राबन्धेनान्योन्यसंपर्का(11a)त्[2] । **वल्गुनिनादं चलद्वलयं** कङ्कणं यत्र ॥

---

[1] *tvaṁ* em.] *tu* Ms., Hahn

[2] *caikasyaiva* conj. Hahn] *caikasyai ..* Ms.

[3] Possibly, only the daṇḍa is lost.

[4] *saṁbodhanaṁ* conj. Hahn] *(saṁ) .. dhanaṁ* Ms.

[5] *viśeṣeṇa* em. Hahn] *viśeṣaṇa* Ms.

[6] *pātv* em. Hahn] *yātv* Ms.

वृत्तपक्षे पङ्क्तौ **वलयं** नामापूर्वम् ॥

रूपमित्यादि ॥

> रूपं ते गुणगणमथ कीर्तिं
> संवीक्ष्याखिलमिदमतिशायि ।
> बिभ्राणं निजविषयविरामं
> मन्दं त्रिष्टुभि जगदुपजातम् ॥ ३६ ॥

इदं तवाखिलं रूपमतिशायि संवीक्ष्य । **अथ**शब्द इदमखिलमतिशायीति प्रत्येकाभिसंबन्धनार्थः[3] । तेनेममखिलमतिशायिनं[4] **गुणगणं** तथेमामखिलामतिशायिनीं **कीर्तिं** संवीक्ष्य । **जगन्निज**रूपगुणकीर्ति**विषये विरामं** धिङ् नो रूपादिकमित्यनभिरतिं[5] **बिभ्रत्** सत् । **तिसृणां** रूपगुणकीर्तीनामात्मीयानां **स्तुभ्** स्तुतिः । सुषामादित्वात् षत्वम् । **तस्यां मन्दमुपजातम्** ॥

वृत्तपक्षे एकादशाक्षरे च्छन्दसि **त्रिष्टुभि**[6] विषयविरामं[7] बिभ्र**दुपजातं** नाम । विषयाश्च पञ्च । तैश्च पञ्चमं स्थानमुपलक्ष्यते । एवमुत्तरत्रापि द्रष्टव्यम् । पञ्चमे यतिरित्यर्थः । इतःपूर्व[8]-वृत्तानां[9] पादान्त एवोत्सर्गसिद्धा यतिर्नान्यत्र विशेषविधानाभावात् । एतदारभ्य पादान्ते तावत् सर्वत्र । विशेषविधौ तु व्याख्यास्यामः । **त्रिष्टुभी**त्यधिकार[10] उपजातिपर्यन्तम्[11] ॥

तनुरित्यादि ॥

> तनुरतनुदयाद्रवोपम-
> स्फुरदनुपमकान्तिसंततिः ।

---

[1] *karayor* conj. Hahn] .. *rayor* Ms.

[2] *°saṁparkāt* conj. Hahn] *°saṁpa .. t* Ms.

[3] *°nārthaḥ* em. Hahn] *°nārthaṃ* Ms.

[4] *akhila{{m ati}}śāyinaṁ* Ms.

[5] *rūpādikam ity* conj. Hahn] *rūpādika ..ty* Ms.

[6] *triṣṭubhi* conj. Hahn] .. *ṣṭubhi* Ms.

[7] *viṣaya°* em. Hahn] *rviṣaya°* Ms.

[8] *itaḥ pūrva°* Hahn

[9] *vṛttānāṁ* conj. Hahn] *vṛ .. ...* Ms.

[10] (*triṣṭubhīty adhikāra*) Ms.

[11] *°jātiparyantam* conj. Hahn] *°jā .. .. ryantam* Ms.

जनयति भवतो न कस्य वा
मुदमधिप समन्तभद्रिका ॥ ३७ ॥

हे **अधिप** । **भवतस्तनुः समन्तं भद्रं** कल्याणं यस्यास्तथाभूता **कस्य वा न मुदं जनयति** । सर्वस्यैव जनयतीत्यर्थः । कीदृशी पुनः । **अतनुर्घना**[1] (11b) या **दया तद्द्रवेणोपमा**[2] यस्यास्तादृशी **स्फुरन्ती** अन्येनानुपमा **कान्तिसन्ततिर्यस्याः** सा तथा । भगवतो देहस्य द्युतिप्रवाहः करुणाया अन्तर्व्याप्य बहिः स्रवन्त्या[3] द्रव इव लक्ष्यत इत्यर्थः ॥

वृत्तपक्षे त्रिष्टुभि **भद्रिका** नाम ॥

शरदित्यादि ॥

शरदमृतकरकरश्रेणी-
समहिमगतमलगौरीयम् ।
गुणसमुदितिरिव मुक्ताली
विलसति हृदि भवतो वृत्ता ॥ ३८ ॥

यथा भवतो[4] **गुणानां** प्रज्ञादयादीनां **समुदितिः**[5] संहतिर्**हृदि विलसति** तथा **मुक्तावल्यपि** । कीदृशी गुणसमुदितिः । **वृत्ता** सच्चरित्रा वर्तुलमुक्तायोगान्मुक्तावलीव । तथा **शरदमृत-करस्य** शरच्चन्द्रस्य या **करश्रेणी** । तया **समा** तुल्या **हिमा** शीतला । **गतमल**त्वादेव **गौरी** विशदा[6] च ॥

वृत्तपक्षे त्रिष्टुभि **वृत्ता** नाम ॥

गीयमानेत्यादि ॥

गीयमानसुमनःसुमनस्व-
ज्ञातिकीर्तिविजयेव तवेयम् ।

---

1 *atanur ghanā* conj. Hahn] *atanu .. ..* Ms. The restoration is only tentative.

2 *taddraveṇopamā* em. Hahn] *tadraveṇopamā* Ms.

3 *sravantyā* em. Hahn] *śravantyā* Ms.

4 *bhavato* em. Hahn] *bhagavatā* Ms.

5 *samuditiḥ* em. Hahn] *samuditaḥ* Ms.

6 *viśadā* em. Hahn] *viṣadā* Ms.

भाति दूरततसौरभलोभ-
स्वागतालिपटलक्वणितेन ॥ ३९ ॥

स्फारामोदा मधुनिधिरधिकं
चूर्णं चातुःसममिव दधती ।
नीलाब्जश्रीर्दलसुखशयना-
संपर्याप्तभ्रमरविलसिता ॥ ४० ॥

पद्यद्वयम् । **तव नीलाब्जश्रीर्भाति**[1] । किंभूता । **सुमनसां** मध्ये **सुष्ठु मनस्वती**[2] मनस्विनी । परिमलादिगुणेनोन्नता या **जातिः** पुष्पजातिर्जातिपुष्पं वा तस्याः **कीर्तिस्**तस्या **विजयः** पराजयः । स **गीयमानो** यस्याः सा तथा । साक्षात्तद्गानाभावा**दिव**शब्दः । केन गीयमान इत्याह । **दूरं ततं** विततं यत् **सौरभं** तेन स्वागताया अलिमालायाः **क्वणितेन** । सापेक्षत्वेऽपि गमकत्वात् समासः ॥

वृत्तपक्षे त्रिष्टुभि **स्वा**(12a)**गता** ॥

पुनः किंरूपा नीलाब्जश्रीरित्याह । **स्फारामोदे**त्यादिना पदद्वयं व्यक्तम् ॥

अधिकं चूर्णं परागं **दधती** । कीदृशम् । चतुःसमं कुङ्कुमादि । तस्येदं **चातुःसमम्**[3] । चूर्णमित्यत्रापि योज्यम् । त**दिवा**धिकं भातीति पूर्वेणैव वा संबन्धः । शय्यतेऽस्मिन्निति शयनम् । **दलं**[4] पत्त्रम् । तदेव **सुखं शयनम्** । तत्र दले वा सुखेन शयनम् । तेन **असंपर्याप्त**मपरिपूर्णम् । अभिलाषाविच्छेदात् । **भ्रमराणां विलसितं** यस्यां सा तथा ॥

वृत्तपक्षे त्रिष्टुभि **भ्रमरविलसिता** । चत्वारश्च ते समाश्च वर्णास्तेषु भवम् । चतुर्षु वा समं तदेव **चातुःसमं चूर्णनं** भङ्गं बिभ्रती भ्रमरविलसिता । तथा च पद्यालंकारे 'वेदच्छेदे भ्रमरविलसिता' इति ॥

रूपेत्यादि ॥

रूपरसायनभावनया ते
वासव एव परं बहुमान्यः ।

---

1 *nīlābjaśrīr* em. Hahn] *līlābjaśrīr* Ms.

2 *manasvatī* em. Hahn] *manasvati* Ms.

3 *cātuḥsamam* em. Hahn] *cātuḥsama* Ms.

4 {{*dalaṁ*}} Ms.

येन चिराय निरस्तनिमेषं
लब्धमदोधकमम्बकजातम् ॥ ४१ ॥

तव रूपमेव **रसायन**मिव रसायनं नयनपुष्टिहेतुत्वात् । तस्य **भावनया** अभ्यासेन । हेतौ करणे वा तृतीया । **इन्द्र एव बहु** यथा भवति तथा **मान्यः** श्लाघ्यः । बहुषु वा मान्यः । कथं स एवेत्याह । **येन** वासवेन येन[1] वा करणेन तदा तेन वासवेनेति गम्यम् । **निरस्तनिमेष**मनिमिषम् । **अम्बकजातं**[2] लोचनकदम्बकं **प्राप्तम्** । किंभूतम् । **चिराय** चिरकालम् । **अद** इदं रूपरसायनं **ध**(12b)**यति** पिबतीति आतो ऽनुपसर्गात् कः । अदोधम् । स्वार्थे कनि **अदोधकम्** । यस्मादनिमिषेणाक्ष्णां तु सहस्रेण चिरं त्वद्रूपरसायनं पिबति ततो वासव एव बहुमान्यो नान्य इत्यर्थः ॥

वृत्तपक्षे त्रिष्टुभि **दोधकम्** ॥

भक्त्येत्यादि ॥

भक्त्यानतरत्नकिरीटचक्रै-
राबद्धकराञ्जलिभिः प्रहृष्टैः ।
धन्यैः सुचिरं चरणद्वयी ते
वीतान्यविधेयमुपस्थितेयम् ॥ ४२ ॥

भक्त्या आ समन्ता**न्नतानां रत्न**मयानां **किरीटानां चक्रं** समूहो येषाम् । **तथाबद्धः करयोरञ्जलिः** संपुटो[3] यैः करिकलभवत् । **तै**र्**धन्यै**रेव **ते चरणद्वयी सुचिरमुपस्थिता** पर्युपासिता । अन्येषामभाजनत्वात् । **वीतान्यविधेयं** त्यक्तान्यकार्यम् ॥

वृत्तपक्षे त्रिष्टुभि[4] **उपस्थिता** ॥

किमित्यादि ॥

किमिन्द्रविभवैर्ब्रह्मश्रिया वा
ततो ऽप्यतिशयिन्या संपदा किम् ।

---

1 *yena* conj. Hahn] *ye ..* Ms.

2 °*(jā)taṁ* Ms.

3 *saṁpuṭo* em.] *sampucatā* Ms.; *saṃpuṭatā* Hahn, though not reported

4 {{*tri*}}*ṣṭubhi* Ms.

प्रसिध्यति धियो ऽधीश प्रकामं
त्वदङ्घ्रिकमलस्योपस्थितं चेत् ॥ ४३ ॥

हे **धियो**[1] **ऽधीश** । यदि **त्वदङ्घ्रिकमलस्योपस्थित**मुपस्थानं **सिध्यति** तदा **किं** प्रयोजन-**मिन्द्रस्य विभवैः** समृद्धिभिः । **ब्रह्मणः संपदा किम्** । **ततस्ताभ्यामतिशायिन्या**[2] आरूप्य-समापत्त्यादि**संपत्त्यापि किम्** । न किंचित् । यतस्त्वच्चरणकमलाराधनेन[3] बोधिरप्यधि-गम्यत इति भावः ॥

वृत्तपक्षे त्रिष्टुभि **उपस्थितम्** ॥

त्वदित्यादि ॥

त्वत्संसेवाविमुखं जन्मदुर्गे
कर्मक्लेशौ विवशं नाशमस्मिन् ।
संभूयालं नयतो ऽवश्यमुग्रौ
वातोर्मी पोतमिवाम्भोधिमध्ये ॥ ४४ ॥

जन्मैव दुर्गमस्मिन् । **विवशं** पराधीनम् । **तव संसेवायां विमुखं** जनम् । **कर्म** शुभाशुभम् । **क्लेशो** रागादिः । तावु**ग्रौ संभूय** । **अल**मत्य(13a)**र्थम्** । **अवश्यं**[4] नियमेन । **नाशं नयत** इति संबन्धः । कौ किं कुत्र यथा । **वातश्चोर्मिश्च** तौ यौ तं वहित्र**मम्भोधिमध्ये** यथा नाशं नयत इति ।

वृत्तपक्षे त्रिष्टुभि **वातोर्मी**[5] नाम वृत्तम् । वातोर्मिमालेत्यन्ये । यतिं चाम्भोधाविच्छन्ति । तथा च कलिकालसर्वज्ञः 'मो वा स्तौ वा यदि वातोर्मिमाला' इति । तथापि †कुरुयैव† पूर्वानुरोधात्तु दर्शितेति पद्यालंकारः ॥

दूरेत्यादि ॥

दूरदर्शिमनसामनागसां
कापि विस्फुरति चित्तसंततिः ।

---

[1] *dhiyo* em. Hahn] *adhiyo* Ms.

[2] According to the basic text, one expects *atiśayinyā*.

[3] *tvaccaraṇa°* em.] *taccaraṇa°* Ms., Hahn

[4] *sambhūyālam* em. Hahn] *sambhūpālam* Ms.

[5] *vātormī* em. Hahn] *rvātormī* Ms.

निर्विरामतममाभवं भवत्-
पर्युपासनमनोरथोद्धता ॥ ४५ ॥

अनागसो निर्दोषाः । अत एव ते **दूरदर्शिमनसस्तेषां निर्विरामतमं** मनागपि विच्छेदाभावात् । **काप्य**वाच्या **चित्तसंतति**र्विशेषेण **स्फुरति** । किंभूता । **आभवं** भवपर्यन्तं यत् **भवत्पर्युपासनं** त्वदाराधनम् । तत्र **मनोरथो** ऽभिलाषस्ते**नोद्धता** । पृथग्जनत्वे ऽपि आयतिपथ्यदर्शिनस्तदात्वे च निष्पापाः । तेषामेव यथोक्ता चित्तसंततिः स्फुरति नान्येषामित्यर्थः ॥

वृत्तपक्षे त्रिष्टुभि **रथोद्धता** ॥

च्छेद इत्यादि ॥

छेदे हृद्या विभ्रमाणां चतुर्णां
तूर्णप्राप्तावार्यसत्यामृतानाम् ।
पुण्यावस्था त्वत्कटाक्षेक्षणे ऽपि
प्रौढप्रज्ञाशालिनी काप्युदेति ॥ ४६ ॥

तव कटाक्षेक्षणे ऽपि पुण्यावस्थाभ्युदेति । जनस्येति शेषः । किंभूता । **प्रौढया प्रज्ञया**[1] **शालिनी** समन्विता । 'शाली संबन्धितो ज्ञेय' इत्यभिधानात् । पुनः किंभूता । **चतुर्णां विभ्रमाणां** विपर्यासानामनित्यानात्मदुःखाशुचिषु नित्यात्मसुखशुचि(13b)ग्रहस्वभावानां **च्छेदे** सति **हृद्या**[2] । किमर्थं तेषां च्छेद इत्याह । **आर्याणां** यानि **सत्यानि** । दुःखसमुदयनिरोधमार्गलक्षणानि[3] तेषां **तूर्णं** शीघ्रं **प्राप्ति**निमित्तम् ॥

वृत्तपक्षे त्रिष्टुभि **शालिनी** । सा चतुर्णां च्छेदे भङ्गे हृद्या[4] ॥

कीर्तिरित्यादि ॥

कीर्तिरर्तिकर्त्तंतस्तव स्तव-
स्तोमसद्मनो ऽतिसद्मनोहृतः ।

---

1 *prauḍha{{yā prajña}}yā* Ms.

2 *hṛdyā* em. Hahn, VMST (*dga' ba*)] *hṛtyā* (?) Ms.

3 *°mārgalakṣaṇāni* em. Hahn] *°mārggaḥ lakṣaṇāni* Ms.

4 *hṛ{{dyā || kīrtir ityādi || artiḥ pīḍā tatkarttatas tava kīrtiḥ | alam atyartham | daśa diśo 'laṁkaroti | kiṁbhūtasya | stavastomasya stutinicayasya sa}}dmanaḥ* Ms.

सान्द्रचन्द्रचन्द्रिकार्द्रचन्दन-
श्येन्यलंकरोत्यलं दिशो दश ॥ ४७ ॥

अर्तिः पीडा **तत्कर्त्ततस्तव**[1] **कीर्तिः** । **अलमत्यर्थम्** । **दश दिशो ऽलंकरोति** । किंभूतस्य । **स्तवस्तोमस्य** स्तुतिनिचयस्य[2] **सद्मनः** पात्रस्य । पुनः किंभूतस्य । अत्यर्थं सतां मनो हरतीत्य**तिसद्मनोहृतः** । विकल्पितत्वात् अमभावाभावः । कीदृशी कीर्तिः । **सान्द्रा**[3] या **चन्द्रस्य चन्द्रिका** ज्योत्स्ना **आर्द्रं**[4] च **चन्दनं** तद्वत् **श्येनी** श्वेता । श्येत[5]शब्दात् ङीप्रत्यये तकारस्य नत्वे रूपम् ॥

वृत्तपक्षे त्रिष्टुभि **श्येनी** ॥

त्वदित्यादि ॥

अभ्युद्गतानेकशिखाभिरुच्चै-
स्त्वत्संश्रयाद्दुस्त्यजसत्त्वदृष्टिः ।
प्रध्वस्तमन्वञ्चति शैलमूर्ति-
स्तीव्रेन्द्रवज्राहतिदारितेव ॥ ४८ ॥

तव संश्रयाद्दुस्त्यजा सत्त्वदृष्टिरात्मदृष्टिः **प्रध्वस्तमनु**क्रमेणा**ञ्चति** गच्छति । किंभूता । **अनेकशिखाभिः** विंशतिशिखरै**रुच्चैरभ्युद्गता** । **यथा शैलस्य मूर्ति**रनेकशिखरैरभ्युद्गतापि **तीव्रा** या **इन्द्रवज्रेणाहति**स्तया **दारिता** सती प्रध्वस्तं गच्छति । तथा रूपमात्मा रूपवानात्मा रूपे आत्मा रूपमात्मनि । एवं वेदनादिषु । इत्थं विंशत्या शिखरैरुन्नता[6] भगवदाशयनैरात्म्य[7]ज्ञानाशनिना नाशमन्वञ्चति ॥

वृत्तपक्षे त्रिष्टुभि **इन्द्रवज्रा** ॥

विरूढेत्यादि ॥

---

1 *kartatas* em. Hahn] *kartanas* Ms.

2 °*nicayasya* em. Hahn] °*niścayasya* Ms.

3 *sāndrā* conj. Hahn] *sā* .. Ms.

4 *ārdraṃ* em. Hahn] *ādraṃ* Ms.

5 *śyeta*° em.] *śveta*° Ms., Hahn

6 One rather expects the object, namely, *sattvadṛṣṭiḥ|ātmadṛṣṭiḥ* here.

7 *nairātmya*° em. Hahn] *nairātma*° Ms.

विरूढधर्माधिपभावभव्य-
प्रतुङ्गसिंहासनसंनिषण्णम् ।
उपासते कान्तशिवाः शिवाप-
त्युपेन्द्रवज्रायुधवेधसस्त्वाम् ॥ ४९ ॥

शिवापतिश्च उपेन्द्रश्च वज्रायुधश्च वेधाश्च ते **त्वामुपा**(14a)**सते** । किंभूताः । **कान्त**मिष्टं **शिवं** निर्वाणं येषां तथा सन्तः । किंभूतं त्वाम् । **विरूढो** वृद्धिं गतो यो **धर्माधिपभावो** धर्मैश्वर्यं तस्मिन् **भव्यं** योग्यं यत्[1] प्रो**त्तुङ्ग**मुच्चैः **सिंहासनं** तत्र **संनिषण्ण**मुपविष्टम् ॥

वृत्तपक्षे[2] त्रिष्टुभि **उपेन्द्रवज्रा** ॥

अनन्तरेत्यादि ॥

अनन्तरोद्भावितलक्षणाढ्यौ
पादौ भवेतामपि गोचरौ ते ।
यासां दृशः श्रव्ययतिप्रपञ्चौ
धन्याः सुराणामुपजातयस्ताः ॥ ५० ॥

अनन्तरमुद्भावितानि यानि **लक्षणानि** किमिन्द्रविभवैरित्यादिना । अभ्युदयनिःश्रेयसहेतुत्वादीनि स्वरूपाणि । **तैराढ्यौ** संपन्नौ । आनन्तर्यं चात्र सजातीयाव्यवधानात् । यथा 'विक्रमादित्यानन्तरं श्रीहर्षो राजा बभूव' इति । अथवा अनन्तरोद्भावितलक्षणेति भगवतः संबोधनम् । आढ्यता च पादयोर्लक्षणादिभिरेव । तथा **श्रव्यः** प्रवचनादौ **यतिप्रपञ्चो** गतिसंयमविस्तारो विक्षेपाभावाद्**ययोः** । **तावे**वंभूतौ तव **पादौ यासां** मनुष्यादिजातीनां **दृशो**[3] **ऽपि गोचरौ भवेतां ता जातयो धन्याः** । **सुराणां** च **उप** समीपे वर्तन्त इति योज्यम् । देवादिगतेरासन्नीभावात् ॥

वृत्तपक्षे **ऽनन्तरोद्भाविताभ्या**मिन्द्रवज्रोपेन्द्र[4]वज्रा**लक्षणाभ्यामाढ्यौ**[5] **पादौ**[6] । तथाभूतौ च **श्रव्ययतिप्रपञ्चौ**[1] **यासां भवेताम्** । पादान्त एवात्र यतिः प्रपञ्चश्च प्रतिपादं बहुषु भावात्

---

1 {{ya}}t Ms.

2 *vṛttapakṣe* em. Hahn] *vṛtte* Ms.

3 *dṛśo* conj. Hahn] .. *śo* Ms.

4 *°vajropendra°* conj. Hahn, though not reported] *°vajrope ..°* Ms.

5 *°lakṣaṇābhyām* em. Hahn] *°lakṣaṇābhyāṃm* Ms.

6 *pādau* em. Hahn] *pādyau* Ms.

भवेताम् । ता **उपजातय**श्चतु(14b)र्दश[2] विज्ञेयाः । बहुवचननिर्देशात् । तेन त्रिष्टुभि चतुर्दशप्रकारा **उपजातयो** वृत्तानि । प्रायेणात्र **शान्ति**सूत्रसमस्याप्रकाराणि सूत्राणीति । क्वचित्त्विष्टिरप्यदृष्टैव ॥

असंशयमित्यादि[3] ॥

असंशयं त्वामपरेषु सत्स्वपि
प्रकामसर्वात्मगुणानुहारिषु ।
अनन्यसाधारणयाधियाधिपा
उशन्ति वंशस्थमनङ्गजिष्णवः ॥ ५१ ॥

आत्मनो बोधिसत्त्वानामेव ये **सर्वे गुणाः प्रकाम**मत्यर्थं तै**रनुहर्तुं** शीलं येषाम् । आर्यमञ्जुश्रिय एव वा ये सर्वे गुणाः प्रज्ञावाह्याः[4] प्रकामंताननुहर्तुं शीलं येषाम् । तेष्वन्येषु बोधिसत्त्वेषु विद्यमानेष्वपि **असंशयं** निश्चयेन । **अनङ्गस्य जयनशीला** बुद्धा **अधिपा** बोधिसत्त्वानां नाथाः[5] । वंशे बुद्धवंशे[6] तिष्ठतीति **वंशस्थं** त्वामेव । **उशन्ति** वदन्ति । कया । **धिया**[7] प्रज्ञया । कथंभूतया**नन्यसाधारणया**[8] ॥

वृत्तपक्षे त्रिष्टुभीति निवृत्तम् । जगत्यामिति वक्ष्यमाणम् । तेन जगत्यामिति द्वादशाक्षरे **च्छन्दसि वंशस्थं** नाम ॥

बालेत्यादि ॥

बालाकृतिं कान्त विचित्रभूषणं
हेमाभमक्षोभ्यसनाथशेखरम् ।
वागीश्वरं वाङ्मतिमूर्तिभिर्नमे
मौनीन्द्रवंशाभरणोदयश्रियम् ॥ ५२ ॥

---

1 *°prapañcau* em.] *°prapañco* Ms., Hahn

2 *caturdaśa* conj. Hahn] *ca .. rdaśa* Ms.

3 *asaṁśa{{ya}}m ityādi* Ms.

4 Or *°vādyāḥ*? Or *°bāhyāḥ*?

5 *nāthāḥ* em. Hahn] *nākhāḥ* Ms.

6 *buddhavaṁśe* conj. Hahn] *buddha .. śe* Ms.

7 *dhiyā* em. Hahn] *dhipā* Ms.

8 *°sādhāraṇayā* em. Hahn, though not reported] *°sādharaṇayā* Ms.

वाङ्मतिमूर्तिभिरिति कायवाङ्मनोभिः[1] । मुनीन्द्राणामयं **मौनीन्द्रो वंशः** । तस्या**भरणभूता अभ्युदयश्री**र्यस्य । शेषं सुबोधम् ॥

वृत्तपक्षे जगत्या**मिन्द्रवंशा** नाम[2] । वंशस्थस्यैवादिगुरुत्व[3] इन्द्रवंशेत्यनयोर्भेदः ॥

(15a) **अतिविस्तरै**रित्यादि ॥

अतिविस्तरैरपि गिरां सुगिरो
गुणपारमीयुरधिनाथ न ते ।
निजमोदमात्रजननीति नुतिः
प्रमिताक्षरापि सुभगैव मम ॥ ५३ ॥

हे **अधिनाथ**[4] । **ते** तव **गुणानां पारं** पर्यन्तं **गिरां विस्तरैरपि न ईयु**र्न गताः । के । शोभना[5] गीर्येषां ते **सुगिरो**[6] मुनयः । तव तर्हि स्तुतिरनुचितेत्याह । **प्रमितान्यक्षरा**णि[7] यस्यां तादृश्यपि **मम नुतिः सुभगैव** शोभनैव । यस्य **निजः** स्तोतुरात्मनो **हर्षः** । स एव **तन्मात्रं** स्तुत्यगुणपर्यन्तागमनात् । सा **जन्यते** यया ।

वृत्तपक्षे[8] जगत्यां **प्रमिताक्षरा** वृत्तम् ॥

दीप्यमानेत्यादि ॥

दीप्यमानाखिलालंकृतिश्लाघिनी
पुण्यभाजां मुखाम्भोजलब्धोदया ।
भारती भारतीश स्वभावोज्ज्वला
त्वामुपैति स्वयं सद्गुणस्रग्विणी ॥ ५४ ॥

हे **भारतीश** । **भारती** सरस्वती **स्वयं स्वयंवरे** च **त्वामुपैत्या**श्रयति[1] । किंभूता । **स्वभावेनोज्ज्वला**[2] निस्तवचर्ण[3].. ..सात् । **सन्तो** ये **गुणा** भगवत एव तेषां **स्रग्मा**ला । सा यस्या

---

1 *kāyavāṅmanobhiḥ* em. Hahn] *kāyavāṅmatimūttibhir iti kāyavāṅmanobhiḥ* Ms.

2 °*nāma* em. Hahn, though not reported] °*nāṃ* Ms.

3 °*syaivādi*° em. Hahn] °*saivādi*° Ms.

4 *adhinātha* em. Hahn] *adhīnātha* Ms.

5 *śobhanā* em. Hahn] *śobhavanā* Ms.

6 *sugiro* em. Hahn] *sugirayo* Ms.

7 *pramitāny* conj. Hahn] (*pra*) .. *tāny* Ms.

8 °*pakṣe* conj. Hahn] °*pa* .. Ms.

अभिधेयत्वेनास्ति । मत्वर्थीयः स्रजो विनिः । तथा **दीप्यमाना अखिला** या **अलंकृतयः** काव्यालंकृतय[4]स्ताभिः **श्लाघा** यस्याः । व्रीह्यादित्वादिनिः । पुनः किंभूता । **पुण्यभाजां** बोधिसत्त्वानां **मुखाम्भोजाल्लब्ध**[5] **उदय**[6] उत्पत्तिर्यया सा तथारूपिण्यपि[7] सरस्वती **दीप्यमानाखिलालंकारश्लाघिनी**[8] । **पुण्यभाजां** ब्रह्मणां[9] **मुखाम्भोजलब्धोदया स्वभावेन चोज्ज्वला** । सर्वशुक्ला सरस्वतीति वचनात् । सन् शोभनो गुणः सूत्रं यस्यां तादृशी स्रगस्या अ(15b)स्तीति[10] **स्रग्विणी** । सापि त्वां स्वयमभ्युपैति श्रीपतिपरिहारेणेति वार्थः ।

वृत्तपक्षे जगत्यां **स्रग्विणी** ॥

भङ्गमित्यादि ॥

भङ्गं नीतास्ते पञ्चबाणस्य बाणाः
शान्तो द्वेषाग्निर्मोहजाड्यं निरस्तम् ।
नाथ त्रैलोक्यानुग्रहव्यग्रमूर्ते
संपत् संप्राप्ता वैश्वदेवी त्वयैव ॥ ५५ ॥

हे **नाथ** । विश्वे च ते देवाश्च तेषामियं **वैश्वदेवी संपत्त्वयैव संप्राप्ता**[11] नान्येन । कथमित्याह । यतस्त्वया **पञ्चबाणस्य** ते **बाणा भङ्गं नीताः** प्रापिताः । एतेन कामनिर्जयः कथितः । तथा त्वया **शान्तो द्वेषाग्निः** । कुतः । शान्त इत्यन्तर्भूतण्यर्थे[12] रूपम्[13] । **मोहजाड्यं** च **निरस्तम्** । अत्र च विनापि तेन चार्थो लभ्यते । शम्भुना पुनः काम एव जितः । ब्रह्मणा

---

1 *upaity* em.] *upety* Ms., Hahn

2 *~nojjvalā* em. Hahn] *~nojjalā* Ms.

3 *ni(stavacarṇa)* or *°stuṣacanta°* Ms.

4 *kāvyālaṁkṛtayas* conj.] *kāvyā(laṁ)* .. .. .. *s* Ms.; *kāvyālaṁ<kārā>s* Hahn

5 *mukhāmbhojāl* em. Hahn] *mukhyāmbhojāta* Ms.

6 *udaya* em. Hahn] *uda* Ms.

7 *°rūpiṇy api* conj. Hahn] *°rūṇy api* Ms. The restoration is uncertain.

8 *dīpyamānākhilā°* conj. Hahn] *dīpya* .. .. *khilā°* Ms.

9 *brahmaṇāṃ* em. Hahn] *brahmāṇāṃ* Ms.

10 *srag asyāstīti* conj. Hahn] *sra* . .. .. *stīti* Ms.

11 *saṁprāptā* conj. Hahn] *saṁ* .. *ptā* Ms.

12 *i(ty antarbhūta)ṇyarthe* Ms.

13 *rūpam* conj. Hahn] .. ... Ms.

द्वेषः । रविणा जाड्यम् । त्वया तु सर्वेषामेषां संपत्तिरधिगतेति विशेषः[1] । **त्रैलोक्यानुग्रह-व्यग्रमूर्ते**[2] इति हेतुभावेन विशेषणम् । न हि स्वयमसिद्धः परार्थं साधयितुमधीष्ट इति । अथवा यदि रागादयो भगवतः प्रहीणास्तदा .. त्वत्प्रेसत्त्वार्थ[3]हानिरित्याह । त्रैलोक्येत्यादि । अनेन करुणया भवे ऽवस्थानं सूचितम् ।

वृत्तपक्षे जगत्यां **वैश्वदेवी** । **बाणाः** पञ्च **ते** चात्र **भङ्गं नीताः** ॥

संपूर्णेत्यादि[4] ॥

> संपूर्णो ऽन्तर्गुणगणरत्नैश्चित्रै-
> रम्भोराशेर्यतिमतिधैर्याद्धत्से ।
> संक्लेशाग्निप्रशमनसद्धर्माम्भो-
> धारासारैर्जलधरमालालीलाम् ॥ ५६ ॥

अन्तर्गता[5] ये **गुणा**स्त एव[6] **रत्नानि** । तैश्चित्रैर्नानाप्रकारैराश्चर्यकरैर्वा संपूर्णः । **गुणगण-रत्नै**र्वा । **अन्तः संपूर्णः** सन् । **अतिधैर्या**च्च **अम्भोराशेः** समुद्रस्य[7] (16a) **यतिं**[8] संयम-माचारं[9] **धत्से** । तथा **जलधरमालाया लीलां** धत्से इति योज्यम् । कैः । **संक्लेश** एवाग्निस्तं **प्रशमयति** । संप्रशम्यते[10] वानयेति[11] । सा चासौ[12] **सद्धर्माम्बुधारा**[13] च तस्या

---

[1] *viśeṣaḥ* conj. Hahn] .. .. *ṣaḥ* Ms. The restoration is uncertain.

[2] *°mūrte* em. Hahn] *°mūte* Ms.

[3] *(tvatpre)sattvrtha°* Ms.

[4] *saṁpūrṇetyādi* conj. Hahn] *saṁpū .. tyādi* Ms.

[5] *antargatā* conj.] *anumatā* Ms., Hahn

[6] *guṇā(s ta e) va* Ms.

[7] *samudra(sya)* Ms.

[8] *yatiṃ* em. Hahn] *patiṃ* Ms.

[9] Read *saṃyamācāraṃ* ?

[10] *saṃpraśamyate* conj.] *saṃpraśamya* Ms., Hahn

[11] *(vā)nayeti* Ms.

[12] *cāsau* em.] *cālau* Ms., Hahn

[13] *saddharmmā°* em. Hahn] *sarddharmmā°* Ms.

[14] *āsārāḥ* conj. Hahn] .. .. Ms.

सवातास्तैः । वारिराशिरपि चित्रै रत्नैः संपूर्णो ऽतिधीरश्च । मेघमालापि धा[1]रासारैरग्निं शमयतीति साम्यम् ॥

वृत्तपक्षे **ऽम्भोराशेर्यतिमति** जगत्यां **जलधरमाला**[2] धत्त इति संबन्धनीयम्[3] ।

तवेत्यादि ॥

> तव पुरः परमोत्तमसंमताः
> प्रतिभया विकलाः प्रतिवादिनः ।
> सुलभमूकदशा बहु मन्वते
> द्रुतविलम्बितमप्युदितं वचः ॥ ५७ ॥

हे **परम** तव **पुरत उत्तमत्वेन संमता** अपि **प्रतिवादिनो** बृहस्पत्यादयः । **परमोत्तमे**ति वा संबोधनम् । उत्तमत्वेन[4] संमता ये ते । **द्रुतं** वा **विलम्बितं** वा यद**ुच्चारितं वचः** । क्रियाया विशेषणं वचसो वा । **तदपि बहु** मन्यन्ते । किंभूताः । **सुलभा मूकदशा येषाम्** । कथं ते तथेत्याह । **प्रतिभया** स्फूर्त्या **विकलाः** । प्रतिभानरहितानां हि मूकतैवोचिता । ते ऽपि यदि द्रुतं विलम्बितं वा वचनमुच्चारयन्ति । तदा तदपि बहु मन्यन्ते मृताद्वरं दुर्बलतेति न्यायात् ।

वृत्तपक्षे जगत्यां **द्रुतविलम्बितम्** ॥

त्रितयेत्यादि ॥

> त्रितयमपि पवित्रयन्ती जगत्
> तुहिनकरकरावदातद्युतिः ।
> प्रभवति भवतश्च कीर्तिश्चिरं
> सुरगिरिशिरसश्च मन्दाकिनी ॥ ५८ ॥

त्रितयमपि **जगत् पवित्रयन्ती भवतः कीर्तिः प्रभवति** । **सुरगिरेः शिरसश्च**[5] (16b) **मन्दाकिनी** स्वर्नदी प्रभवति । सा द्युतिधानान्तरमेरुश्ङ्गे प्रभवति । पठ्यते मन्दाकिनीशब्दः

---

[1] *vā* corrected to *dhā*?

[2] *jaladhara°* conj. Hahn] *ja .. .. ra°* Ms.

[3] *saṃbandhanīyam* em. Hahn] *saṃbandhīyam* Ms.

[4] *uttamatvena* conj. Hahn] .. .. *matvena* Ms.

[5] *śirasaś ca* em. Hahn] *śiraś ca* Ms.

स्वर्नद्याम् । पठितो ऽपि कविसमये त्रिपथगापि[1] .. .. या दृश्यते । तेन त्रितयमपि पवित्रयन्ती[2]त्युक्तम् । किंभूता । भवतः कीर्तिर्मन्दाकिनी च । **तुहिनकरकरवदवदाता द्युतिर्यस्याः**[3] सा तथा । भगवतश्च कनकाभत्वान्मेरुशिखरसाम्यम् ॥

वृत्तपक्षे[4] जगत्यां **मन्दाकिनी** ॥

हरतीत्यदि ॥

हरति नितान्तमियं तव कीर्तिः
कृतिहृदयानि दयानिजवास ।
प्रसवचयेन चितेव समन्ता-
द्दिशि दिशि कुन्दलता दलतालम् ॥ ५९ ॥

यथा **समन्ताद्दलता** विकसता **प्रसवचयेन** पुष्पनिवहेन **चिता** व्याप्ता **कुन्दलता** । **अलम**त्यर्थम् । **दिशि दिशि कृतिनां** सुकृतिनां[5] **हृदयानि हरति** । तथा हे **दयानिवास**[6] । **इयम**नन्तरोदिता तव कीर्तिर्दिशि दिशि समन्तात् प्रसरन्ती पण्डितहृदयानि नितान्तं हरति[7] ॥

वृत्तपक्षे[8] जगत्यां **कुन्दलता** नामापूर्वम् ॥

दलयतीत्यादि ॥

दलयत्युपात्तशोभासमवायो
जगतामघानि को ऽप्येष कृपाब्धिः ।
बहुबुद्धकोटिनिर्माणपटीयान्
धृतधर्मधातुवागीश्वरलीलः ॥ ६० ॥

---

1 *tripa(tha)gā(pi)* Ms.

2 *pavitrayantī* conj. Hahn] .. *vitrayantī* Ms.

3 *dyutir* em. Hahn] *rdyutir* Ms.

4 °*pa(kṣe)* Ms.

5 *sukṛtināṁ* conj. Hahn] .. *kṛtināṁ* Ms.

6 *dayāni<ja>vāsa* Hahn. However, the addition of the *akṣara ja* is not necessary, for the commentator frequently uses a paraphrase for the *pratīka*.

7 *harati* Ms.] *ruṇaddhi* em. Hahn, though not reported

8 *vṛttapakṣe* conj. Hahn] *vṛ(tta)* .. *kṣe* Ms.

धृता धर्मधातुवागीश्वरस्य बुद्धस्य **लीला** येन स **एष को ऽपि कृपासमुद्रः । जगतामघानि** पापानि[1] **दलयति**[2] । किंभूतः । **उपात्तः** संभृतः **शोभानां समवायो** येन तथा । **बहुबुद्ध-कोटीनां निर्माणं** स्फरणं जननं वा । तत्र **पटीयान**त्यर्थं समर्थः । आर्यम(17a)ञ्जुश्रियो[3] देहादनेकबुद्धकोटीनां स्फरणात्तवाराधनेन च प्रादुर्भावात्तथाभिधानम् ॥

वृत्तपक्षे **दलमर्धं** पादानां तत्र **यत्या प्राप्तः** सन् **शोभासमवायो** येन स तथा । जगत्यां **वागीश्वरलीलो** नामापूर्वम् ॥

प्रविकिरतीत्यादि ॥

प्रविकिरतीव वियत्तरङ्गिणी-
तरलतरङ्गरुचां[4] रुचां चयान् ।
विलसति शश्वदसिर्दशान्तरे
तव यमुनाजलवीचिमेचकः ॥ ६१ ॥

तव दशान्तरे मूर्त्यन्तरे ऽरपचनादौ **शश्वद्विलसति** सति । **असिस्तव यमुनाजलवीचि-वन्मेचकः** श्यामः । **रुचां चयान्** तवैव कायकिरणनिकराणां कान्त्या[5] **प्रकर्षेण**[6] **विकि-रतीव** च्छुरयतीव[7] । कीदृशान् । **वियत्तरङ्गिण्यास्तरलतरङ्गाणा**मिव **रुक्** कान्तिर्येषां तेषा-मपि विशदत्वात् विच्छिन्नविसारित्वाच्च[8] । एतेन गङ्गायमुनासंभेदसाम्यमुपदर्शितम् । अथवा तव दशान्तरे यथोक्तरुचां चयान्[9] प्रविकिरति सति । तत्रैवोक्तगुणो निस्त्रिंशः शश्वद्विलसतीति योजना ॥

वृत्तपक्षे जगत्यां **यमुना** नाम ॥

मन इत्यादि ॥

---

1 *pāpā(ni)* Ms.

2 *dalayati* conj. Hahn] .. *layati* Ms.

3 *āryamañjuśriyo* conj. Hahn] *ā* .. .. *ñjuśriyo* Ms.

4 °*rucāṁ* em.] °*ruco* Edition, Hahn

5 *kāntyā* em. Hahn] *ekāntyā* Ms.

6 The text here is confusing. One expects *kāyakiraṇanikarān prakarṣeṇa.*

7 *cchurayatīva* em. Hahn, though not reported] *cchurayatīya* Ms.

8 Hahn suggests in a footnote: Read *avicchinna*°?

9 *cayān* conj. Hahn] *caya* .. *yan* Ms.

*मनोहारिहारावलीरम्यमीदृक्
क्व ते नाथ रूपं सुरूपाधिराज ।
क्व तच्चातिदुर्दान्तसत्त्वप्रशान्त्यै
स्फुरद्भीमभूषाभुजङ्गप्रयातम् ॥ ६२ ॥*[1]

हे **नाथ** । **मनोहारिण्या**[2] **हारावल्या रम्यं तव क्वेदृशं रूपम्** । **सुरूपाधिराजे**त्यनेन[3] रूपाभिमानिविनयनार्थं तादृङ् महाराजलीलादिनिर्माणं दर्शितमिति दर्शयति । **क्व चाति**-श(17b)यं[4] **दुर्दान्तसत्त्वानां प्रशमार्थं स्फुरन्त**श्चलन्तो **भीमा** भयानका **भूषार्थं** ये **भुजङ्गा**-स्तैः **प्रयात**माश्रितं यमार्यादिरूपम् । अतिविस्मयकरं[5] रूपद्वयं तवेत्यर्थः ॥

वृत्तपक्षे जगत्यां **भुजङ्गप्रयातम्** ॥

अविरलेत्यादि ॥

अविरलमौक्तिकप्रकरभूषा
हरति न कस्य चित्तमियमीश ।
सुरुचिरमल्लिकासमयसेव्य-
प्रतिनवमालिनीव तव मूर्तिः ॥ ६३ ॥

हे **ईश** । **सुष्ठु रुचिरा मल्लिकायाः समये** यौवनदशायां **सेव्या प्रतिनवा** अभिनवा या **माला** यद् वा सुरुचिरा[6] मल्लिका काले सेव्या या प्रतिनवा माला मल्लिकाया एव सा **यस्या** अस्ति मूर्तेः । सैव **तवेयं मूर्तिः कस्य न चित्तं हरति** । सर्वस्यैव हरतीत्यर्थः । किंभूता । **अविर-लेन मौक्तिकप्रकरेण**[7] । स एव वा **भूषा यस्याः सा** ॥

वृत्तपक्षे जगत्यां **नवमालिनी** ॥

तवेत्यादि ॥

---

1 The stanza is missing in the edition and its manuscript. It is reconstructed from VMST and the commentary.

2 *°hāri(ṇyā)* Ms.

3 *surūpādhi°* em. Hahn] *surūpātyadhi°* Ms.

4 *cāti(śa)yaṁ* Ms.

5 *°vismayakaraṁ* em. Hahn] *°vismakaraṁ* Ms.

6 *(su)rucirā* Ms.

7 *°prakareṇa* em. Hahn] *°prakāreṇa* Ms.

तव नाथ परं यदि कान्तिसुधा-
जलधौ श्रममुज्झति झात्कृतिनि[1] ।
शुभरूपनिरूपणलम्पटकं
परितो ऽटकमङ्ग जगन्नयनम् ॥ ६४ ॥

अङ्गशब्दः संबुद्धौ । हे **नाथ** । **जगन्नयनं तव कान्ति**रेव **सुधाजलधि**स्तस्मिञ्**झात्कृतिनि श्रम**मायासं **परमुज्झति** । नान्यत्र । समुद्रो ऽपि हि वेलापरंपरया झात्कारवान् । भगवानप्यनवरतनित्यलावण्यलहरीभिः[2] । किंभूतं जगन्नयनम् । **शुभं** मनोहरं **रूपं** तस्य **निरूपणे लम्पटकं** सत् **परितः** समन्तादटतीत्यर्थः । तदेव**ाटकम्** । अत एवास्य श्रमः । अन्यो (18a)ऽपि[3] हि चिरभ्रमणपरिश्रान्तः समुद्रादिमहाजलाशये श्रममपनयति ॥

वृत्तपक्षे जगत्यां **तोटकम्** ॥

वरदेत्यादि ॥

वरद विरतिभाञ्जि व्यक्तमङ्गा-
न्यतिभव भविता नो ऽवश्यमेव ।
तव वचनसुधायाः पानपात्रं
श्रवणयुगपुटो ऽयं प्रीतिहेतुः ॥ ६५ ॥

हे **वरद** । **अतिभव** भवमतिक्रान्त । **नो** ऽस्माक**मङ्गानि** हस्तपादादीनि । **व्यक्तं विरतिम**नभिरतिं **भजन्ते** । सुखहेतवो न भवन्तीत्यर्थः । **श्रवणयोर्युगं** तस्य **पुटः** । स पुन**रवश्यमेव नः प्रीतिहेतुर्भविष्यति**[4] । कथम् । **तव वचनसुधायाः पानपात्रं**[5] यस्मात् ॥

वृत्तपक्षे जगत्यां **पुटो** नाम । अत्र **चाङ्गान्यष्ट विरतिभाञ्जि** ॥

वृण इत्यादि ॥

वृणे वरमिमं त्वदेकमतुल-
प्रभाव भवतान्न मादृशजनः ।

---

1 *jhātkṛtini* em. Hahn, though not reported; commentary] *jhāṅkṛtini* Edition

2 *anavaratani(6)pya(ṇylā)vaṇya°* Ms.

3 Read *pāntho 'pi* ?

4 *prīti°* em. Hahn] *prīta°* Ms.

5 *pāna°* em. Hahn] *yāna°* Ms.

भवन्तमपि यः श्रयञ्छमसुधा-
रसेषु विरतिर्जडोद्धतगतिः ॥ ६६ ॥

हे **अतुलप्रभाव** । **त्व**त्त्वत्तः सकाशा**देकं**[1] **वरं वृणे** याचे । कं वरं याचसीत्याह । **मादृशो जनो न** कश्चिद् **भवता**न्नोत्पद्यताम् । कीदृशः । **यो भवन्तमपि** वागीश्वरं **श्रयञ्जडा** मन्दा **उद्धता** विक्षिप्ता **गति**र्मतिर्यस्य स तथाभूतः सन् । **विगता रति**रभिलाषो यस्य तथा भवति । कस्मिन् विषये । **शमाः**[2] शान्तयस्ता एव **सुधारसा**स्तेषु ।

वृत्तपक्षे **जगत्यां जलोद्धतगति**र्नाम । तत्र च **रसेषु** षड्सु **विरतिः** ॥

त्वदित्यादि ॥

त्वत्प्रसादसमुदीर्णशुभवशा-
दष्टभेदि सुखमेव कृतिजनः ।
लोचनोत्सवविधासु तनुभृतां
चन्द्र वर्त्म समुपैति भवभिदाम् ॥ ६७ ॥

हे **तनुभृतां लोचनोत्सवविधासु** नयनानन्दकृतिषु **चन्द्र** । **तव प्रसादेन समु**(18b)**दीर्णं** समृद्धं **यच्छुभं तत्सामर्थ्यात्**[3] **कृतिजनः सुखमेवा**कष्टेनैव **भवभिदा**मार्याणां **वर्त्म** मार्गं **समुपैति** प्राप्नोति । कीदृशम् । **अष्टभेदि** । आर्याष्टाङ्गलक्षणम् ॥

वृत्तपक्षे **जगत्यां**[4] **चन्द्रवर्त्म** नाम । त**च्चाष्टभेदि** अष्टमयतिकमित्यर्थः ॥

सुखेत्यादि ॥

सुखदुःखातिशयादिहेतुजातै-
रविलुप्तस्मृतयो भवन्ति भव्याः ।
तव पादाश्रयलब्धबुद्धिसाराः
सकलायामपि वादिराज गत्याम् ॥ ६८ ॥

हे **वादिराज** । **सुखं** च **दुःखं** च तयो**रतिशय आदि**र्येषां †सुखमाद्यादीनां†[1] तेषां **हेतु**[2]**जातै**-रपि । **अविलुप्ता स्मृति**र्येषां ते **भव्याः** । **सकलायामपि** देवादि**गतौ** वर्तमानास्तथा **भवन्ति**

---

1 *sakāśād* em.] *śakāśād* Ms.

2 *śamāḥ* em. Hahn] *samāḥ* Ms.

3 *tatsāmarthyāt* em. Hahn] *tatsāmarthāt* Ms.

4 *jagatyāṁ* conj. Hahn] *jaga* ... Ms.

। ननु लोको निरतिशयसुखादिहेतुमासाद्य विनष्टस्मृतिर्भवति[3] । तत्कथमिदमुच्यत इत्याह । **तव पादाश्रयेण लब्धो बुद्धेः सारो** बलं यैस्ते तथाभूता यस्मात् । अथवा सकलायां वादिराजानां गतौ सर्वविवादव्यवहारे[4] । शेषं समानम् ॥

वृत्तपक्षे जगत्यां **कला** नामापूर्वम् । इत ऊर्ध्वं **जगत्या**मिति नानुवर्तते ॥

तवेत्यादि ॥

> तव चरणपरिचरणरुचीनां
> किमपि सुखमुदयति कृतिरूपम् ।
> निखिलमलपटलविगमदीप्र-
> प्रथिम[5]गुणमहितमति जगत्याम् ॥ ६९ ॥

तव चरणयोः परिचरणे परीष्टौ **रुचि**र्येषां तेषां **सुखं** यथा भवति तथा **किमप्यद्भुतं कृतिनां रूपं** स्वरूपं कृतित्व**मुदयति जगत्याम्** । कथमद्भुतमित्याह । **निखिलस्य मल-पट**(19a)**लस्य**[6] **विगमाद्दीप्रो** दीपनशीलः **प्रथिमा** पृथुत्वं येषाम् । **तद्गुणै**र्वक्तृत्वादिभि-र्महती[7] **मतिरवबोधविशेषो** यत्र तत्तथा । अथवा निखिलमलपटलविगमदीप्रं[8] च तत्प्र-थिमगुणेन महितमति चेति कर्मधारयः ॥[9]

वृत्तपक्षे **ऽतिजगत्यां**[10] त्रयोदशाक्षरे च्छन्दसि **महितं** नाम ॥

कलेत्यादि ॥

---

1 Hahn suggests in a footnote: Read *sukhaduḥkhātiśayādīnāṃ*?

2 *hetu°* conj. Hahn, though not reported] *he ..°* Ms.

3 *°smṛtir* conj. Hahn] *°.. tir* Ms.

4 *sarvavivāda°* conj.] *sarva .. vāda°* Ms.; *sarvavāda°* Hahn

5 *°dīpraprathima°* em. Hahn, commentary] *°dīpraṃ prathita°* Edition, which is also meaningful.

6 *°paṭalasya* em. Hahn] *°paṭalasyā* Ms.

7 This is either a mistake for *mahitā* or its paraphrase.

8 *°dīpraṃ* em. Hahn] *°dīghrañ* Ms.

9 Apart from the two possible interpretations suggested by Śākyarakṣita, it is also possible to understand the word *nikhilamalapaṭalavigamadīpra* as a vocative.

10 *°pakṣe 'tijagatyāṁ* em. Hahn] *°pakṣe jagatyāṁ* Ms.

कलधौतकान्तवपुरुत्तमलीलः
पटुभारतीवरटया वरिवस्यः ।
इह मञ्जुघोष इति वः प्रथितो ऽव्या-
ज्जिनमानसैकनलिनीकलहंसः ॥ ७० ॥

इह जगति **मञ्जुघोष इति प्रथितः** ख्यातो **जिनमानसम**वैका उत्कृष्टा या **नलिनी** तत्र कलहंस इव **कलहंसो वो** युष्मान् **अव्यात्**[1] । किंभूतः । **कलधौतं** स्वर्णं तद्वत् **कान्तं वपु-**र्यस्य । तथा च रभसः[2] 'कलधौतं स्वर्णे रूप्ये' इति । **पद्वी** या **भारती** सैव **वरटा** हंसीति तया सततानुगमात् । **वरिवस्यः** परिचार्यः । नलिन्यां कलप्रधानो ऽपि हंस इह जगति मञ्जुर्घोषो ऽस्येति मञ्जुघोष इति प्रथितः । पटुवाणीलक्षितया वरटया[3] सेव्यः । **उत्तमचेष्टः** कलधौतं रूप्यं तद्वत् शुद्धवपुश्च भवति ॥

वृत्तपक्षे **ऽतिजगत्यां कलहंसो** नाम । अस्य चिरन्तनं भ्रमरीत्यपि नाम ॥

विच्छेद इत्यादि ॥

विच्छेदस्त्रिषु यदि दुःसहेष्वमीषु
क्लेशेषु स्फुटमणुशो ऽपि दुष्करः स्यात् ।
प्राप्येत क्व नु खलु नाथ मूर्तिरीदृक्
त्रैलोक्ये[4] नयनमनःप्रहर्षिणीह ॥ ७१ ॥

हे **नाथ** । **अमीषु** रागद्वेषमोहेषु **त्रिषु दुःसहेषु क्लेशेषु स्फुटं** व्य(19b)क्तं[5] यो **विच्छेदो** विगमः स यदि **दुष्करः स्यात्** । **अणुशो ऽपी**ति । स्थूलप्रचाराणां तावद्विच्छेदस्य दुष्कर-त्व **ईदृग्मूर्तिर्न प्राप्यते** । अणुशो ऽपि सूक्ष्मप्रचाराणामपि[6] यदि विच्छेदो दुष्करः[7] कर्तुम-

1 *avyāt* em. Hahn] *vyāt* Ms.

2 *rabhasaḥ* conj. Hahn] *ra .. saḥ* Ms.

3 *varaṭayā* em. Hahn, though not reported] *varaṭāyā* Ms.

4 *trailokye* em. Hahn, commentary] *trailokī°* Edition. —The reading of the edition may also be retained as it also makes good sense. In that case, *trailokī°* should be taken as a compound. The word *trailokī* has also been used elsewhere by Jñānaśrīmitra. Cf. verses 29, 32, and 101.

5 *vyaktaṁ* conj. Hahn] *.. ktaṁ* Ms.

6 *°pracārāṇām* em. Hahn] *°pracārāṇāṃm* Ms.

7 *duṣkaraḥ* conj. Hahn] *.. ṣakaraḥ* Ms.

शक्यः स्यात्तदेह **त्रैलोक्ये** ईदृग्भवतो मूर्तिः **क्व नु खलु प्राप्येत**[1] नैव प्राप्येतेत्यर्थः ।[2] कीदृशी । **नयनं** च **मनश्च** ते **प्रहर्षयितुं शीलं** यस्याः सा तथा । तदुक्तम् 'मूर्तिरेव तवाचष्टे भगवन्[3] वीतरागताम्' इत्यादि ॥

वृत्तपक्षे **ऽतिजगत्यां विच्छेदस्त्रिषु** यदि स्यात्तदा **प्रहर्षिणी** ॥

पयोनिधावित्यादि ॥

पयोनिधौ विरतिमपां विधाय च
स्फुरन्महाकिरणकलापरत्नधौ ।
भवादृशां वपुषि च कान्तिसंततिः
समीक्ष्यते यदि रुचिरेयमीदृशी ॥ ७२ ॥

इयमीदृशी **रुचिरा कान्तेः संततिर्भवादृशां** महाबोधिसत्त्वानामेव[4] **वपुषि** पर**मीक्ष्यते** । **अपां विरतिं** विगमं **विधाय यदि** कदाचित्तस्मिन्[5] । कल्पितोपमेयं यथागमे[6] 'उभौ यदि व्योम्नि पृथक्प्रवाहौ' इत्यादि ॥

वृत्तपक्षे **ऽतिजगत्यां पयोनिधौ विरतिं विधाय** इयमीदृशी **रुचिरा** समीक्ष्यते ॥

मन्द्रेत्यादि ॥

मन्द्रध्वानैर्यामृतधारास्त्वयि रम्या
मुञ्चत्युच्चैर्विस्फुरति प्रीणितभव्ये ।
नाथान्वेति व्यक्ततयात्यन्तमनोज्ञं
वर्षाम्भोदं सैव यतिर्मत्तमयूरम् ॥ ७३ ॥

हे **नाथ** । **मन्द्रध्वानैः** गम्भीरनिर्घोषै**रमृतधाराः** प्रवचनप्रवाहान् **मनोहर**[7] **मुच्चैस्त्वयि**[1] **मुञ्चति** । अत एव **प्रीणितभव्ये या यति**श्चरितं **विस्फुरति सैव** यति**र्वर्षा**(20a)**म्भोदं व्यक्त-**

---

1 *nu khalu prāpyeta* em.] *na khalv aprāpyata* Ms., Hahn

2 The text is unclear.

3 *bhagavan* em. Hahn] *bhagan* Ms.

4 °*sattvānām eva* em. Hahn] °*satvānāṃ meva* Ms.

5 *kadācit tasmin* em. Hahn] *kadācitastasmina* Ms.

6 *yathāgame* conj. Hahn] *yathā .. me* Ms.

7 Should we read *manoharān* ? Or did the commentator read *ramyaṃ* in the VMS?

तया स्फुटमन्वेति[2] । **अत्यन्तमनोज्ञ**त्वात् प्रावृषेण्यस्य मन्द्रध्वानैरमृतधारामोचनं सूचितम् । **मत्ता मयूरा** यस्मात् । तत्त्वेन प्रीणितभव्यत्वम् ॥

वृत्तपक्षे रुचिराया या **यति**रनन्तरोक्ता चतुर्थे सैवातिजगत्यां **मत्तमयूरं** वृत्तमन्वेति ॥

जयतीत्यादि ॥

जयतीयमुत्पलतरोरनुत्तर-
त्रिजगत्प्रमोदजनने मधाविव ।
त्वयि नेत्रकान्तकुसुमोद्गता लता
मधुमत्तभृङ्गरवमञ्जुभाषिणी ॥ ७४ ॥

त्वयि त्रिजगतां प्रमोदस्य जनने जननिमित्तं जनके वा । **मधाविव**[3] वसन्त इव वर्तमानस्योत्**पलतरोः** केतनेन्दीवरवृक्षस्य **लता** शाखा **जयति** । कीदृशी । त्रिजगतो **नेत्राणां कान्तं** यत्**कुसुमं** तेनो**द्गता** । तथा **मधुमत्तानां भृङ्गाणां रवेण मञ्जु भाषितुं शीलं यस्याः सा** तथा । मधुसमयो ऽपि त्रिजगत्प्रमोदजननः । तत्र चोत्पलतरोः शाखा नेत्रकमनीयसुमनोभिरुल्लसिता तन्मकरन्दपानमत्तमधुकरझांकारैः मनोहरव्याहारिणीव भवति ॥

वृत्तपक्षे ऽतिजगत्यां **मञ्जुभाषिणी** । इयं तु पूर्वं[4] **कुसुमोद्गता** नाम[5] । अत एवात्र द्वयमुपात्तम् ॥

सर्वेत्यादि ॥

सर्वातिशायिगुणनिर्भरलब्धमोदै-
र्विद्वन्मधुव्रतकुलैरुपगीयमानम् ।
मन्यामहे जिननयाभरणं तवैव
वृत्तं वसन्ततिलकं नवचूतमेव ॥ ७५ ॥

यथा **नवचूतं वसन्तस्य तिलक**मलंकारभूतं तथा **तवैव वृत्तं** चरित्रं **जिननयस्याभरणं मन्यामहे**[6] । (20b) किंभूतम् । **विद्वांस** एव **मधुव्रता**स्तेषां **कुलैरुपगीयमान**मुत्कीर्त्यमानम्

---

[1] *tvayi* em. Hahn] *tv api* Ms.

[2] *anveti* em. Hahn] *artheti* Ms.

[3] *madhā(v) iva* Ms.

[4] *pūrvaṁ* conj. Hahn] *pū ..* . Ms.

[5] *nāma* em. Hahn, though not reported] *nām* Ms.

[6] *manyāmahe* conj. Hahn] *manyāma ..* Ms.

। किंभूतैः । **सर्वातिशायिनस्तवैव ये गुणास्तैर्निर्भरं लब्धो मोदो** यैः । चूतमपि सर्वातिशायिभिर्निजैः सौरभादि[1]गुणैर्निर्भरलब्धमोदानि यानि मधुव्रतकुलानि तैर्वन्दिवृन्दैरिवोपगीयमानम् । एव इवार्थे । तथा चाजयः 'एवौपम्ये[2] ऽवधारणे' इति ॥

वृत्तपक्षे[3] शक्करीभूषणेति वक्ष्यते ॥[4]

संमुखेत्यादि ॥[5]

> संमुखवलन्मुखमृगाधिपतिपृष्ठा-
> रूढमतिगाढदयमभ्युदयकन्दम् ।
> सुन्दरिमबन्धुरितहेमहिमपादं
> वादिकुलदैवतममन्दमभिवन्दे ॥ ७६ ॥

वादिकुलदैवत[6]**ममन्दं** यथा भवति तथा **अभिवन्दे** । किंभूतम् । भगवत एव **संमुखं**[7] **वलन्**[8] **मुखं** यस्य तस्य **मृगाधिपतेः पृष्ठारूढमतिगाढ**[9]**दय**मतिशयितकृपम् । **अभ्युदयस्य** विभूतेः **कन्दं** मूलम् । तथा **सुन्दरिमा**[10] सौन्दर्यम् । तेन **बन्धुरितावधरितौ हेमहिमपादौ** येन । वर्णस्य सौन्दर्येण हेम बन्धुरितं कान्तेश्च हिमपादश्चन्द्र[11] इत्यर्थः ॥

अत्रापि वृत्तपक्षे **शक्करीभूषणं दैवतं** वृत्तम् । केचिदिदं सिंहललितमाहुः । तथा च जयदेवः 'सिंहललितं च कथितं भजसनोगौ[12]' इति ॥

---

[1] *nijaiḥ saurabhādi°* conj.] *ni .. . .. rabhādi°* Ms.; *nij<asau>rabhādi°* Hahn

[2] *evaupamye* em. Hahn] *evopamye* Ms.

[3] *°pakṣe* conj. Hahn, though not reported] *°pa ..* Ms.

[4] The name of the metre Vasantatilaka is missing. One expects the following text: *vṛttapakṣe śakvarībhūṣaṇaṃ vasantatilakam* | *śakvarībhūṣaṇeti vakṣyate* |.

[5] *saṁmukhetyādi* conj. Hahn

[6] *vādikuladaivatam* conj.

[7] *sa(ṃ)mukhaṁ* Ms.

[8] *valan mukhaṁ* em.] *valayamukhaṁ* Ms.; *valaya<n> mukhaṃ* Hahn

[9] *atigāḍha* conj. Hahn] *gāḍha°* Ms.

[10] *sundarimā* p.c.] *sundarima* a.c.

[11] *himapādaś* conj.] *hi .. padaś* Ms.. Hahn conjectures *°padaś* with a suggestion to read *°pādaś*.

[12] *bhajasanogau* conj. Hahn] *bhajasa .. gau* Ms. This definition is not found in the *Jayadevacchandas* !

प्रशमितेत्यादि ॥

प्रशमितसकलप्रपञ्चनिरावृति-
प्रसरदमलधीसमाधिसुधाजुषः ।
दमयति भवतो हताहितविक्रमा
मुनियतिरपराजिता भुवनत्रयम् ॥ ७७ ॥

भवतो मुनेर्यतिर्मुनिजनोचितः[1] संयमः । **अपरै**र्बाह्यमुनिभि**रजिता भुवनत्रयं दमयति** विनयति । किंभूता । **हतो ऽहितानां** मा(21a)राणां[2] **विक्रमो यया** । किंभूतस्य भगवतः । **प्रशमितः** प्रशमं नीतः **सकलः प्रपञ्चो** ग्राह्यग्राहकादि[3]विकल्पो यः । यच्च **निरावृति** आवरणाभावः । ताभ्यां यथासंख्यं **प्रसरन्तावमलौ** यौ **धीसमाधी** तावेव **सुधा** तां **जुषमाणस्य** ॥

वृत्तपक्षे शक्करीभूषणा **अपराजिता** । सा च **मुनियतिः** । मुनयः सप्त ॥

प्रतिभयेत्यादि ॥

प्रतिभयवपुषामकरुणचरित-
प्रशमनविधये क्वचिदपि कृपया ।
तव भुजपरिघावलिरतिविषमा
विलसति विविधप्रहरणकलिका ॥ ७८ ॥

तव क्वचिद्धञ्रभैरवाद्यवस्थाविशेषे **भुजपरिघाणां** दोर्दण्डाना**मावलिः** संहति**रतिविषमा विलसति** । किंभूता । **विविधानि प्रहरणानि कलयती**ति[4] ण्वुल् तादृशी । किमर्थम् । **प्रतिभयं** भयंकरं **वपु**र्येषा**मकरुणं**[5] **यच्चरितं** तस्य **कृपया प्रशमनविधये**[6] ॥

वृत्तपक्षे शक्करीभूषणा **प्रहरणकलिका**[1] । अन्येषां प्रहरणकलिता । सप्तमे च यतिः । तथा च शान्तयः 'प्रहरणकलिता ननविननवितैः[2]' इति । जयदेवे तु यतिर्नास्ति । यत्सूत्रं 'प्रहरणकलिता[3] च ननभनलगैः' इति ॥

---

1 *rmuni°* em. Hahn] *rmunir°* Ms.

2 *mārāṇāṁ* conj. Hahn] .. *rāṇāṁ* Ms. The restoration is uncertain.

3 *°grāhakādi°* em. Hahn] *°grāhahādi°* Ms.

4 For the meaning, see *Dhātupāṭha* 1.526: *kala śabdasaṃkhyānayoḥ*; 1.527: *kalla avyakte śabde.*

5 *akaruṇaṃ* em. Hahn] *akaraṇaṃ* Ms.

6 *°vidhaye* em. Hahn] *°vidhaya* Ms.

श्रेय इत्यादि ॥

> श्रेयःसंभोगं विषयविरतिमव्यग्रां
> मारप्रध्वंसं त्रिभुवनहितसंपत्तिम् ।
> दुष्प्रापाहार्यं पदमभिलषतां तच्च
> त्वद्भक्तेरन्या वरद न दिगसंबाधा ॥ ७९ ॥

श्रेयः पुण्यं तत्प्रभवश्चक्रवर्त्यादि**संभोगः** । **तच्छब्दः** प्रत्येकमभिसंबध्यते । तेन तं **श्रेयःसंभोगमभिलषतां** प्रजानाम् । हे[4] (21b) **वरद त्वद्भक्तेर्नान्या**[5] **दिगसंबाधा** । नान्यो मार्गः प्रतिपक्षासंकटः । लौकिकीं संपत्तिमुक्त्वा लोकोत्तरामाह । तां च **विषयेभ्यो** रूपादिभ्यः पञ्चकामगुणेभ्यो **विरतिमभिलषतां**[6] श्रावकगोत्राणां न केवलम् । तं च **मारप्रध्वंसम्** । तथा बोधिसत्त्वानां **त्रिभुवनहितस्य संपत्ति**र्लाभस्ताम् । तच्च **पदं** यत[7] **दुष्प्रापमसंहार्यं**[8] चाभिलषताम् । त्वद्भक्तेर्नान्या[9] दिगसंबाधेति सर्वत्र योज्यम् ।

वृत्तपक्षे **विषयाः** पञ्च । तेषु **विरति**मभिलषतां कवीनां शक्करीभूषणा **असंबाधा** नाम ॥

भवत इत्यादि ॥

> भवतः कलां किमपि संयतैरिन्द्रियैः
> क्वचिदादरस्तिमितधीर्यदि ध्यायति ।
> अचिरात् स्वयं वरयतीयमेनं जनं
> वसुधा ध्रुवं जलधिशक्करीभूषणा ॥ ८० ॥

---

1 °*kalikā* em. Hahn] °*kalilā* Ms.

2 The two editions of the *Chandoratnākara* (Huth, Hahn) read: *praharaṇakalitā nanavananava tair* | (Hahn 2.51). The text given here is to be preferred.

3 °*kali*(*tā*) Ms.

4 *prajānām* | *he* conj.] *pra* .. .. Ms.

5 *bhakter* p.c.] *bhaktir* a.c.

6 *viratim abhilaṣatāṁ* conj. Hahn] *vira*(*ti*). .. .. .. *ṣatāṁ* Ms.

7 *yata* conj.] *ya* Ms.; *ya*<*d*> Hahn

8 *duṣprāpam* em. Hahn] *duṣprāyam* Ms.

9 °*laṣatām* | *tvadbhakter* conj. Hahn] °*laṣatā* . . .. .. *kter* Ms.

यदि कश्चित्[1] **संयतैरिन्द्रियैः क्वचिद्गिरिगुहादिप्रदेशे । आदरेण स्तिमिता** विक्षेपाभावान्निश्चला **धीर्यस्य** तथाभूतः सन् **भवतः कलाम्** †अचलाद्यवस्थां[2] **ध्यायति । किमपी**ति क्रियाविशेषणम् । तदा **अचिरात् ध्रुवं** निश्चित**मेनं जनं वसुधा स्वयम**प्रार्थिता **वरयति** स्वयंवरत्वेनोपतिष्ठत इति यावत् । किंभूता । **जलधिः शक्करी**व शक्करी मेखला सा **भूषणं** यस्याः । 'शक्करी मेखलाच्छन्दः' इति रभसः ॥

वृत्तपक्षे शक्करीच्छन्दोभेदं भूषयतीति **शक्करीभूषणा** वसुधा । सा च **इन्द्रियैः** प(22a)ञ्चभिः **संयतै**रासादितपाठोपरतिभिरुपलक्षिता ॥

स्वेदेत्यादि ॥

स्वेदपूरविलसत्पुलकोच्छ्वसितैस्त्रुटत्-
कञ्चुकं दधति निर्धुतमप्यमरस्त्रियः ।
कान्तिकम्रमिव ते समितावतिशक्करी-
बन्धसारमुरुकम्पमनङ्गविजृम्भितम् ॥ ८१ ॥

ते तव **समितौ** सदसि । **अमरस्त्रियो ऽनङ्गविजृम्भितं दधति** । किंभूतम् । **त्रुटत्कञ्चुकं** यत्र । कैः । **स्वेदपूरेण विलसन्ति**[3] कमनीयानि **पुलकानामुच्छ्वसितान्यु**द्भेदास्तैः । तथातिक्रान्तं **शक्करीबन्धस्य सारं** बल**मुरुकम्पं** च । पुनः किंभूतम् । **ते** त्वया **निर्धुतमपि** तासामेव **कान्त्या कम्रमिव**[4] । यत् किल निःशेषेण ध्वस्तं तत् कान्तं न भवतीतीवशब्दः । अथवा **तवैव कान्त्या कम्रमिव** । उभयानुरागे हि मन्मथविचेष्टितस्य कम्रता । भगवतश्च[5] विरक्तत्वादमरयोषित एव भगवत्कान्तिसंदर्शनात् कम्रमिव तद्बिभ्रति ॥

वृत्तपक्षे **ऽतिशक्कर्या**[6] पञ्चदशाक्षरेण च्छन्दसा यो **बन्धस्तेन सार**मुत्कृष्ट**मनङ्गविजृम्भितं**[7] नाम । **अतिशक्करीबन्धसार**मित्यधिकारो गुणमणिनिकरं यावत् ॥

अनुपमेत्यादि ॥

---

1 *kaś cit* conj. Hahn, though not reported] .. *ś cit* Ms.

2 *acalādyavasthāṁ* conj. Hahn] *acalāṃdyavasthāṃ* or *acalāṃ vyavasthāṃ* Ms. Reading uncertain.

3 *vilasanti* conj. Hahn] .. .. *santi* Ms.

4 *kāntyā kamram* conj. Hahn] *kā(ntyā)* .. *mram* Ms.

5 *bhagavata(ś ca)* Ms.

6 *vṛttapakṣe 'tiśakvaryā* conj. Hahn] *vṛttamapakṣe śakvaryā* Ms.

7 *anaṅgavijṛmbhitaṁ* conj. Hahn] *ana* .. .. *jṛmbhitaṁ* Ms.

अनुपमरमणीया भङ्गिरङ्गेषु यस्या
हरति रतिमुदाराशेषरूपान्तरेषु ।
जयति तनुरखण्डाखण्डलेष्वासलक्ष्मी-
विजयपरमधामव्यामरुग्मालिनीयम् ॥ ८२ ॥

यस्या भगवत्तनोरङ्गेषु अवयवेष्व**नुपमत्वेन रमणीया**[1] **भङ्गि**र्भक्तिः कर्त्री[2] **उदाराणि** महान्ति[3] भगवत एव यान्य**शेषाणि** यमार्यादि**रूपाणि** हरिहरा[4]दिरूपविशेषा वा । **तेभ्यः**[5] सकाशाद्**रतिं हरति** । .. .. (22b)रेणात्रैवाभिरतेः । **सेयं** महाराजलीलादि**तनुर्जयति** । किंभूता । **अखण्डा** या **आखण्डलेष्वासस्य** शक्रधनुषो **लक्ष्मी**स्तस्या **विजय**स्तस्य यत् **परमं धाम** स्थानं तस्य **व्यामा** चासौ[6] **रुक्** च व्यामप्रभा त**न्माला यस्या अस्ति** सा तथा । भगवतो विश्वक्सहजव्यामप्रभत्वात् । सा च **प्रभा** पञ्चवर्णा ॥

वृत्तपक्षे ऽतिशक्करीबन्धसारमिति लिङ्गविपरिणामेनात्र[7] संबन्धात् । अतिशक्करीबन्धसारा **मालिनी**यं जयति[8] ।

अविकलेत्यादि[9] ॥

अविकलतालशालिकलकाकलीकल[10]-
व्यतिकरवल्लकीवलितचारुपञ्चमा ।

---

[1] *ramaṇīyā* conj. Hahn] .. .. .. *yā* Ms.

[2] *kartrī* em. Hahn] *kartrā* (?) Ms.

[3] *mahānti* em. Hahn, though not reported] *mahāti* Ms.

[4] *hariharā°* p.c.] *harihārā°* a.c.

[5] The root text obviously read *°rūpāntarebhyaḥ.*

[6] *tasya vyāmā cāsau* conj.] .. .. Ms.; (t)<asya **vyāmā** ca> Hahn. —Most likely the missing akṣaras contained the dissolution of the karmadhāraya compound *vyāmaruc.*

[7] *liṅgavipariṇāmenātra* conj.] *vibhaktivi(pa)* .. .. *menātra* Ms., The restoration is corroborated by the commentary on the following stanza.

[8] Here Śākyarakṣita forgot to point to the indication of the caesura: *bhaṅgir aṅgeṣu.*

[9] *avikaletyādi* conj. Hahn

[10] The commentary reads *°kākalīrava* instead of *kākalīkala.*

भणति मुदा प्रतीष्टजिनभार भारती
स्वमहिमकामिनी तव सभासु मद्रकम् ॥ ८३ ॥

प्रतीष्टो ऽनुमतो[1] **जिनस्य भारः** परार्थभारो[2] येन स[3] संबोध्यते । **स्वमहिमानं** तव निजं महत्त्वम् । **कामयते** अजा..नोयते ऽतः सा **भारती तव सभासु मद्रकं**[4] रागविशेषं **भणति** । किंभूता । **अविकलः** समस्तालस्तेन **शाली कलो** ऽव्यक्तमधुरो यस्याः सा **काकली**[5] । सामान्यविशेषभावाद्भेदः । सैव रवस्तेन **व्यतिकरा** मिश्रा या **वल्लकी** वीणा तया **वलितं चारु पञ्चमं** स्थानं यया सा ॥

वृत्तपक्षे ऽतिशक्करीबन्धसारा **कामिनी** । रत्नाकरे[6] समुद्रकम् ॥

जयतीत्यादि ॥

जयति नाथ जगज्जयकुञ्जरनिश्चली-
करणश्रृङ्खलजालनिभाङ्गदभूषितः ।
भुजतरुस्तव दुर्गतिमार्गमहार्गलः
प्रमदमन्मथनिर्मथनः सुगतप्रियः ॥ ८४ ॥

हे **नाथ तव** अवस्थाविशेषे **दुर्गतिमार्गमहार्गलो भुज** एव[7] **तरुः** सज्जनविश्रामभूतत्वात् **जयति** । 'अर्गलं त्रिषु' इति रभसः[8] । (23a) किंभूतः । **जगज्जय** एव **कुञ्जरः** । स **निश्चली-क्रियते** येन । एवंभूतं **श्रृङ्खलजालं** यत्त**न्निभमङ्गदं** केयूरं तेन **भूषितः** । तथा **प्रकृष्टो मदो** यस्य स चासौ **मन्मथश्च** तस्य **निर्मथनः**[9] । अत एव **सुगतानां प्रियः** ॥

---

1 *pratīṣṭo 'numato* conj. Hahn. —The restoration is only tentative.

2 *parārthabhāro* Ms.] *paramārthabhāro* em. Hahn, though not reported. He further suggests in a footnote: Read *paramārya°* ?

3 *sa* conj.

4 *madrakaṃ* em. Hahn] *mandrā(..)drakaṃ* Ms.

5 *kākalī* conj. Hahn. This conjucture seems necessary to complete the explanation of the compound.

6 *ratnākare* conj. Hahn] .. *tmākare* Ms.

7 *eva* em. Hahn] *thava* Ms.

8 *rabhasaḥ* conj. Hahn] *rabha .. .* Ms.

9 *tasya nirmathanaḥ* conj. Hahn] *ta .. .. rmathanaḥ* Ms.

वृत्तपक्षे इहापि विभक्तिविपरिणामेन संबन्धादतिशक्करीबन्धसारः **सुगतप्रियो** नाम । पद्यालंकारे 'वृषभ इत्यधुना[1] गदितः सुगतप्रियः[2]' । सूत्रव्याख्यायां वरबुधैरिति रत्नाकरपादैरिति चिन्त्यम् । तैरस्य वृत्तस्य च्छन्दःशास्त्रे ऽनभिधानात् । अधुना गदित .. .. प्रश्लेषाद्बालेयम् ॥

तवेत्यादि ॥

भवशिरसि महितगुणमहिमभुवं
व्यपगतसकलमलशुचिमधिपते ।
तव वरविजयसमुपचितयशसः
श्रियमनुहरति हि शरदि शशिकला ॥ ८५ ॥

हे **अधिपते** । **तव वराणां** सुरश्रेष्ठानां **विजयेन समुपचितं** य**द्यशस्**तस्य **श्रियम्** । **हि**शब्दो ऽवधारणे । **शरदि शशिकलै**वा**नुहरति**[3] । किंभूताम् । **भवशिरसि** संसारमस्तके[4] **महितो गुणमहिमा** तवैव यस्माद्भवतीति ताम् । तथा **व्यपगतसकलमलत्वेन**[5] **शुचिम्** । शशिकलापि[6] भवस्य महेश्वरस्य शिरसि वर्तमाना महितगुणमहिम्नो भूराश्रयः । कलात्वेन व्यपगतसकल[7]कलङ्कमलशुचिश्च । अतस्तया तदनुहरणम् ॥

वृत्तपक्षे ऽतिशक्करीबन्धसारा **शशिकला**[8] ॥

पट्वित्यादि[9] ॥

पटुपरिमलमिलितमधुकरयुव-
भ्रमसहशितिसुगतसमुचितसुखा ।

---

1 *vṛṣabha ity adhunā* conj. Hahn] *(vṛ) .. .. dhunā* Ms.

2 *°priyaḥ* em. Hahn] *°priyāṃ* Ms.

3 *śaradi śaśikalaivānu°* conj. Hahn] *śa(ra) .. .. laivānu°* Ms.

4 *saṁsāra°* em. Hahn] *sāra°* Ms.

5 *°malatvena* em. Hahn] *°mahatvena* Ms.

6 *śaśikalāpi* conj. Hahn] *.. .. .. lāpi* Ms.

7 Here the Ms. contains a lengthy dittography that was deleted: *kalātvena vyapagatasakala[[mahatvena śuddhim | śaśikalāpi bha(va) .. ..* (23b) *śirasi varttamānā mahitaguṇamahimno bhūr āśrayaḥ | kalātvena vyapagatasakala]]-kalaṅkamala śuciś ca* |.

8 *śaśikalā* em. Hahn, though not reported] *śaśaśikal(ā)* Ms.

9 *paṭv ityādi* conj. Hahn] *.. .. .. di* Ms.

विलसति तव शिरसि रसलयवती
स्रगियममरपतियुवतिविरचिता ॥ ८६ ॥

तव शिरसि अमरपतियुवतिविरचिता[1] **स्रगियं विलसति** । **रसस्य** मकरन्दस्य **लयः** श्लेष-स्तद्वती[2] । किंभूता । **पटुपरिमलमिलितस्य मधुकरयूनो भ्रमं**[3] **सहते** यः **शितिसुगतो** ऽक्षोभ्यस्तस्य **समुचितं**[4] वर्धितं **सुखं** यया । तस्यैव साक्षात्तत्र सुपरिमल[5]योगात् सा तथा । तादृशी च स्रक् मधुकरयूनो भ्रममभिभवति[6] ॥

वृत्तपक्षे ऽतिशक्करीबन्धसारा **स्रगियं** विलसति । सा च **रसेषु** षट्सु **लयो** भङ्गस्तद्वती ॥

नेत्यादि ॥

न यतिपदमयसि यदतिदयधियः
प्रथयसि जगति च परहितकृतिनः ।
जनयति हिमचयरुचिरिति भवतो
वियदुपहतनिजमणि गुणनिकरः ॥ ८७ ॥

अतिक्रान्ता दयां धीर्येषां तान् प्रति **यद्यस्मात्**[7] । **न यतीनां** शान्तरूपाणां **पदमयसि** गच्छसि सौम्यस्वभावं विहाय क्रोधरूपेण दमयस्येवेति[8] भावः । **यच्च परहिते कृतिनः** प्रज्ञावतो **जगति**[9] **प्रथयसि** विस्तारयसि । **इतिस्तस्मात् हिमचयरुचिर्भवतो गुणानां**

---

1 *°viracitā* em. Hahn] *°viravitā* Ms.

2 Hahn suggests in a footnote: Read *leśas.*

3 *°yūno bhramaṁ* conj.] *°(yū) .. ..* Ms.; *°yū<nāṃ bhramaṃ>* Hahn

4 *samucitaṁ* em. Hahn] *mucitaṁ* Ms.

5 *suparimala°* em. Hahn] *saparimala°* Ms.

6 *°yūno bhramam abhibhavati* conj.] *°yū(no) .. .. vati* Ms.; *°yū(n)(ā)<ṃ bhramaṃ abhi>vati* (sic! *abhibhavati*) Hahn. The restoration is uncertain.

7 *prati yad yasmāt* conj.] *pra .. .. ta* Ms.

8 *eveti* em. Hahn] *evati* Ms.

9 *prajñāvato jagati* conj. Hahn] *pa .. .. ti* Ms. The restoration is uncertain. Because of the basic text, *°ti* has to be completed to *jagati*, while the word beginning with *p<r>a°* seems to be a synonym of *kṛtinaḥ*. Elsewhere *kṛtin* is explained as bodhisattva or *vibudha*.

निकरो वियदाकाशं **जनयति** । कीदृशम् । **उपहत**[1]स्त्वद्गुणरत्ननिकरै[2](24a)र्मलिनीकरणा**न्निजो मणिः** सूर्यो यस्य तत्तथा ॥

वृत्तपक्षे ऽतिशक्वरीबन्धसारो[3] **मणिगुणनिकरः** । **अयो** लोहमष्टधा प्रसिद्धम् । तत्र **पदं यतिः** ॥

अतीत्यादि[4] ॥

अतिरतिकरकथ कथमिव समिया-
दविरतनवनवनव तव परमैः ।
गुणगणपरिमितिमुदधिषु यतिभिः
सुयतिभिरगणितगुण मणिनिकरः ॥ ८८ ॥

अतिरतिकरी[5] **कथा** यस्य । **अविरतो** विच्छेदाभावात्[6] । **नवनवो** ऽन्यान्यः । **नवः** स्तुतिर्यस्य । तथा**गणिता गुणा** यस्येति त्रयमपि संबोधनपदम् । कैरगणिता इत्याह । **परमैर्यतिभिः**[7] । किंभूतैः । **शोभना यतिः** संयमो येषां तैः । **तव गुणगणस्य परिमितिमुदधिषु**[8] वर्तमानो **मणिनिकरः**[9] **कथमिव समियात्** समेतु । अपरिमाणत्वाद्गुणानां[10] नैवासादयतीत्यर्थः ॥

वृत्तपक्षे ऽतिशक्वरीबन्धसारो **गुणमणिनिकरः** । **उदधिष्वि**ति बहुवचननिर्देशात् एकशेषाद्वा प्रतिचतुष्कं यति[11].. .. .. लक्षितो द्रष्टव्यः । तथा पद्यालंकारः 'जलधिषु जलधिषु

1 *upahatas* em. Hahn] *uṣahatas* Ms.

2 °*nika(rai~)* Ms.

3 *atiśakvarī*° em. Hahn, though not reported] *atiśakvarīma*° Ms.

4 *(bhā)tītyādi* Ms.

5 *atiratikarī* conj. Hahn] *a .. .. tikarī* Ms.

6 *vicchedā*° em. Hahn, though not reported] *vicchadā*° Ms.

7 *paramair yatibhiḥ* conj. Hahn] *para(mai) .. .. bhiḥ* Ms.

8 *parimitiṃ* em. Hahn] *paramitiṃ* Ms.

9 *vartamāno maṇinikaraḥ* em. Hahn] *vartamāno vṛttapakṣe maṇinikaraḥ* Ms.

10 *aparimāṇatvād* conj. Hahn] *apa .. .. ṇatvād* Ms.

11 *ya(ti)* Ms.

गुणमणिनिकरः' इति । पूर्वस्मादस्य यतिमात्रेण[1] भेदः । पाठशोभया तु तस्य जित्वरत्वम्[2] । अतिशक्करीबन्धसारमिति[3] निवृत्तम्[4] ॥ १५ ॥[5]

जयतीत्यादि ॥

जयति तव तनुरियमुरुतरकरुण
निखिलजगदुचितपरिभुगवनिरिव ।
शिशुमतिकलितसकलजनबहुविध-
विमतिलडितविधिभिरचलधृतिरिह ॥ ८९ ॥

हे **उरुतरकरुण**[6] । **तवेयं तनुरिह जयति** । किं बत **निखिलस्य जगत उचिता परिभुक्** परिभोगस्तस्या **अवनि**.. .. .. (24b) **तद्वत्** । तथा**चलाधृति**र्धैर्यं यस्याः । कैरचला । **शिशु**रल्पा **मति**स्तया **कलितो** यः **सकलो जन**स्तस्य **बहुविधं विमते**र्विप्रतिपत्तेर्**ललितं** यत्तस्य **विधिभिः** ॥

वृत्तपक्षे ऽष्टाविति[7] वक्ष्यति । अष्टौ षोडशाक्षरे च्छन्दसि **अचलधृति**र्नाम । परेषां मात्रासमकजातावेतदुदाहरणम् ॥

प्रतीत्यादि ॥

प्रति जडधियमिह समधिकगुरुदय
मृदुमतिरपि तव शुभमयसमुदय ।
करतलविनिहितकुवलय कलयति
जिनकुलकुवलयमविषमभरमिति ॥ ९० ॥

जडधियं प्रति लक्ष्यीकृत्य **समधिकगुर्वी दया** यस्य[8] तस्यामन्त्रणम् । **शुभमयः** शुभहेतुकः **समुदयो** यस्य । तथा **करतले विनिहितं कुवलय**मिन्दीवरं येन । एतदपि द्वयमामन्त्रण-

---

1 *yati°* em. Hahn] *pati°* Ms.

2 *jitvaratvam* em. Hahn] *(ji)tvara* Ms.

3 *°bandhasāram iti* conj. Hahn] *°.. .. .. .., m iti* Ms.

4 *nivṛttam* em. Hahn] *vṛttam* Ms.

5 The numeral between the two double daṇḍas indicates the end of the *atiśakvarī* category.

6 *°karuṇa* em. Hahn, though not reported] *°karaṇa* Ms.

7 *°pakṣe 'ṣṭāv iti* conj. Hahn] *°pakṣe '.. .. .. ..* Ms.

8 *°gurvī dayā yasya* conj.] *°gura .. .. .. sya* Ms.; *°guru<dayā ya>sya* Hahn

पदम् । **इह** जगति **मृदुमतिरपि**[1] जनो[2] **जिनकुवलयं**[3] मुदितादिभूवलयं **तवाविषमभरमदु-र्वहभरमिति कलयति** । यतस्त्वं[4] करतलविनिहितकुवलय इति शब्दच्छलः ॥

वृत्तपक्षे ऽष्टौ **कुवलयमपूर्वम्**[5] । तच्च डलयोरैक्यात् **जलधिं प्रति यमो** यतिरस्यास्तीति तथा ॥

व्योमेत्यादि ॥

व्योमविकीर्णकीर्तिमदपरिमलकलना-
भङ्गुरतुङ्गवादिमदकलकरिनिकरम् ।
विश्वनोदरे ऽत्र रवयतिजितजलदं
नाथ दधास्युदारमृषभगजविलसितम् ॥ ९१ ॥

हे **नाथ** । **ऋषभः** श्रेष्ठः । स चासौ गजश्च । ऋषभशब्दो भद्र[6]श्रेष्ठपर्यायः[7] । तथा च 'आर्षभं सिंहनादं नदामि' इति प्रयोगः । न भूपमानमन् यथा गजर्षभेति स्यात् ।[8] तस्य **विलसितमुदारमत्र विश्ववनोदरे**[9] **दधासि** । किंभूतम्[10] । (25a) **व्योम्नि विकीर्णा कीर्तिरिव मदपरिमलस्य कलनया** आघ्राणेन **भङ्गुरस्तुङ्गवादिमदकलकरिनिकरो**[11] यस्मात् । गन्ध-गजस्य हि मदगन्धमाघ्रायान्ये मत्ता अपि करिणो लक्ष्यन्ते[12] । पुनः किंभूतम् । **रवो** गर्जितम् । तत्र **यतिः** प्रयत्न इक्कस्यादिभ्यः[13] । तया **जितो जलदो** येन ॥

---

1 °*mati* seems to have been omitted by inadvertency.

2 *jano* conj.] *ja* .. Ms.; *ja<nas t>e* Hahn

3 One expects *jinakulakuvalayaṃ*. Again omitted by inadvertency?

4 *tvaṃ* em. Hahn] *taṃ* Ms.

5 *apūrvam* | conj. Hahn] *apūrva* . . Ms.

6 *bhadra°* em. Hahn] *madra°* Ms.

7 °*paryāyaḥ* conj. Hahn] °*pa* .. *yaḥ* Ms.

8 meaning unclear!

9 *viśvavanodare* em. Hahn] *viśvavadanodare* Ms.

10 *kiṁbhūtam* | conj. Hahn] *kiṁbhū(ta)* . . Ms.

11 *tuṅgavādimadakalakarinikaro* em. Hahn] *tuṅgaṃyadimadakalaṃkarinikaro* Ms.

12 *lakṣyante* conj. and em. Hahn] .. *kṣante* Ms.

13 meaning unclear!

वृत्तपक्षे ऽष्टौ **ऋषभगजविलसितम्** । **रवाः** स्वरास्ते च सप्त तत्र **यति**र्यस्य तत्तथा[1] ॥

क इत्यादि ॥

कस्त्वयि बद्धवर्मणि जगद्धितधानधिया
निर्विहतप्रतिज्ञ परितापकणः क्व चन ।
मारवधूजनस्य कमनीयकपोलतले
यन्नवपत्त्रभङ्गरचनालस एव करः ॥ ९२ ॥

जगद्धितस्य धानमाधानम् । तद्धितधान**धिया**[2] **बद्धवर्मणि** बद्धवीर्यसंनाहे **त्वयि क्व चन**[3] परार्थविषये **परितापस्य कणो** लवो ऽपि । तस्य मम[4] .. .. हितत्वात् । अत एव **निर्विहत-प्रतिज्ञे**त्यामन्त्रणम् । **निर्नि**षेधे ऽत्र । अविहतप्रतिज्ञत्वमेव[5] । कुतः । **यद्** यस्मान्**मारवधू-जनस्य कमनीयकपोलतले नवा** या **पत्त्रभङ्गरचना**[6] तत्रा**लस एव करो** वर्तते मारस्य जितत्वात् ॥

वृत्तपक्षे ऽष्टौ **पत्त्र**[7]**भङ्गरचना** नामापूर्वम् ॥

निरुपमेत्यादि[8] ॥

निरुपमरम्यरूप जिनजातदृश्वनो ऽष्टौ
मदयति ते ऽधिकं विधुतशोक लोकपालान् ।
सदुपधिपुण्डरीकनखराजिराजितेयं
विरचितपञ्चचीररुचिरा कुमारलीला ॥ ९३ ॥

हे **निरुपमरम्यरूप** । **विधुतशोक**[1] । **ते** तव **जिनजातदृश्वनः**[2] सुगतसमूहं दृष्टवत इयं **कुमारी लीलाष्टौ लोकपालान्मदयति** हर्षयति । **अधिक**मत्यर्थम् । **जिनजात**[3]**दृश्वनो** ऽपि

---

1 *yasya tat* conj. Hahn] *ya(sya) .. t* Ms.

2 *taddhitadhānadhiyā* em., VMST (~*blo yis*)] *taddhidhāyā* Ms.; *tadvidhānadhiyā* Hahn

3 *cana* em. Hahn] *ca* Ms.

4 *ma(ma)* Ms.

5 Read °*pratijñas tvam eva* ?

6 *patrabhaṅga*° conj. Hahn] .. .. .. *ṅgā*° Ms.

7 *(pa)tra*° Ms.

8 *nirupa*° em.] *nirūpa*° Ms.

कुमारली(25b)**लेयमतिरुचिरे**त्य**त्यर्थ**मदहेतुः[4] । कीदृशी । **विरचितपञ्चचीरत्वेन रुचिरा** । पुनः किंभूता । **सन्** शोभन **उपधिरु**पाधिरिह[5] स्वर्णं यस्याः । सा चासौ **पुण्डरीकस्य** व्याघ्रस्य **नखराजिश्चे**ति[6] ताभ्यां **राजिते**ति[7] ॥

वृत्तपक्षे **ऽष्टौ कुमारलीला** नाम । **अष्टा**वितीत ऊर्ध्वं नाधिक्रियते ॥

गुणानामित्यादि ॥

> गुणानामत्यष्टिः कथमिह ममेवास्तु जगता-
> मिति च्छन्दः स्वैरं परिणतिमवापत्तव तथा ।
> यथा त्वय्येवास्मिन् परमरसभेदप्रणयनी[8]
> समुद्भूता भूतिर्निखिलसुखशाखाशिखरिणी ॥ ९४ ॥

इह जगति । **मम** या **गुणानाम**[9]**त्यष्टि**रतिव्याप्तिः । .. .. सैव[10] **जगतामाशिषे**[11] **कथमस्त्विति** । **च्छन्दो** ऽभिलाष**स्तव स्वैरं** शनैः **परिणतिं** परिपाकं **तथावापत्** अगमत् **यथास्मिन्** जगति **निखिलानां सुखानां शाखा** पारमिता[12] तस्याः **शिखरं** पर्यन्तस्तद्वती

---

1 *vidhutaśoka* conj.] .. .. .. *śoka* Ms.

2 *°jāta°* em., Edition, VMST (*tshogs*)] *°śata°* Ms., Hahn. This reading is metrically incorrect.

3 *°jāta°* em.] *°śata°* Ms., Hahn

4 *kumāralīleyam atirucirety atyartha°* conj.] *ku .. .. .. leyam atiruciretyartha°* Ms.; *kum<āralī>leyaṃ atirucirātyartha°* Hahn

5 *upādhir iha* em. Hahn] *ūpāviraha* Ms. The restored text is uncertain. As evinced by VMST (*gser bzaṅ*), *sadupadhi°* here is meant to designate «wrought gold».

6 *vyāghrasya nakharājiś* conj. Hahn] *vyā(ghra) .. .. .. rājiś* Ms.

7 *tābhyāṁ rājiteti* conj.

8 *°praṇayiṇī* (sic! *nī*) Edition

9 *guṇānām* em. Hahn] *guṇām* Ms.

10 *saiva* conj. Hahn] .. .. Ms. The restoration is only tentative.

11 Thus tentatively for the unclear *aśāṣi* of the Ms.

12 *sukhānāṁ śākhā pāramitā* conj. Hahn] *sukhā .. .. ramyarā* or *rasyarā* Ms. Nevertheless it seems quite clear that *pāramitā* was used as explanation of *śākhā*.

गुणानां विभूतिः **त्वय्येव** भगवति **समुद्भूता** । परार्थपरत्वेन स्वार्थसंपद्विशेषावाहकत्वात् प्रणिधिप्रस्थानयोर्द्वयोः[1] । किंभूता । **परमस्य रसभेदस्य** शृङ्गारादिरसविशेषस्य **प्रणयनी**[2] ॥

वृत्तपक्षे **ऽत्यष्टिः** सप्तदशाक्षरं च्छन्दस्तथा[3] परिणतिमवापद्यथा **शिखरिणी**[4] समुद्भूता । सा च **रसाः** षट् तत्र **प्रभेदो** भङ्गस्तत्प्रणयनी । अत्यष्टिच्छन्दस्तथा परिणतिमवापद्यथा **समुद्भूतेति** मन्दाक्रान्तापर्यन्तमधिकृतं वेदितव्यम्[5] ॥

(26a) **जयतीत्यादि** ॥

> जयत्यमरमन्दिरोपलविशालवक्षःस्थलः
> स्थलीकमलकाननप्रतिमपादकन्दप्रभः ।
> प्रभाकरशताधिकप्रकटतेजसालंकृतः
> कृतान्तमदमर्दनस्त्रिभवनाथपृथ्वीधरः ॥ ९५ ॥

त्रिभवनाथा बुद्धास्तेषां **पृथ्व्यो** मुदितादिभूमयस्ता**धरतीति**[6] तथा । स **जयति** । किंभूतः । **अमरमन्दिरं** मेरुः । तदु**पलवद्विशालं वक्षःस्थलं** यस्य । एतेन हेमाभत्वमपि[7] सूचितम् । तथा **स्थलीकमलकाननप्रतिमापादकन्दप्रभा** यस्य । कमलान्यपि कन्दादुद्भवन्ति प्रभापि पादकन्दादुद्यती शोणत्वाद्वितततत्वाच्च कमलवनेनोपमीयते[8] । **प्रभाकरशतं**[9] बहव आदित्याः । तद**धिकेन तेजसालंकृतः** । सूर्यसहस्रातिरेकप्रभत्वात् । **कृतान्तमदमर्दन**त्वेन मृत्युमारजय उक्तः ॥

वृत्तपक्षे ऽत्यष्टिच्छन्द[10]स्तथा परिणतिमवापद्यथा[1] **पृथ्वी** वृत्तभेदः समुद्भूता । स च वृत्तभेदो **मदा** मदनास्ते चाष्टौ तत्र **मर्दनं** छेदो यस्य तथा । पृथ्वीविशेषणत्वे तु मदमर्दनेति[2] स्यात् ॥

---

1 *°prasthānayor dvayoḥ* conj.] *°prasthāna .. .. yoḥ* Ms.; *°prasthānaṃ | <ana>yoḥ* Hahn

2 *praṇayanī* em. Hahn] *praṇayaṇī* Ms.

3 *°cchandas* em. Hahn] *°cchandaḥs* Ms.

4 *yathā śikhariṇī* conj. Hahn] *ya .. .. khaṇī* Ms.

5 *veditavyam* conj. Hahn] *vedita .. .* Ms.

6 One expects the resolution *tāsāṃ dhara iti* as a genitive *tatpuruṣa* compound and not as an *upapada tatpuruṣa* as the commentator explains.

7 *hemābhatvam api* conj. Hahn] *hemābha .. .. pi* Ms.

8 *°vanenopa°* conj. Hahn] *°va .. .. pa°* Ms.

9 *°śataṃ* em. Hahn, though not reported] *°śaṃta* Ms.

10 *°pakṣe 'tyaṣṭi°* conj. Hahn] *°pa .. .. . ṣṭi°* Ms.

विमोहेत्यादि ॥

विमोहबहलान्धकारपटलावनद्धैर्मुधा
रसातलगुहातिशायिभवसंकटेषु स्थितम् ।
त्वदङ्घ्रिकमलाश्रयोत्सवसुखं न चेदादृतं
चिरस्य जिनवंशभास्कर कुमार मारैर्जितम् ॥ ९६ ॥

हे **जिनवंशभास्कर** बुद्धवंशालोककर । **कुमार** । **विमोहबहलान्धकारपटलावनद्धैः** प्राणिभिः । **त्वदङ्घ्रि**[3]**कमलाश्रयोत्सव**लक्षणं[4] **सुखं**[5] **चे**द्यदि **नादृतम्** । तदा **रसातलं** पातालं तदेव **गुहा** अनालोकत्वात् । तद**तिशायिषु भवसंकटेषु मुधा** निष्फलं **स्थितम्** । तदा च **चिरस्य मारैर्जितं** जीयते[6] ॥

(26b) वृत्तपक्षे ऽत्यष्टिच्छन्दस्तथा[7] परिणतिमवापद्यथा **रमे**ति पृथिवी समुद्भूता । पूर्वा[8] पृथ्वी इयं च पृथिवी यतिरहिता चेति भेदः ॥

कल्पेत्यादि ॥

कल्पशतोपपादितमहाफलमिव विहितं
चञ्चलमेतदायुरधिप त्वदवनतिपरैः ।
भूषणभव्यभावगमितं श्रितगुरुकरुणा-
दिग्यतिवंश पत्त्रपतितं कमिव जलरुहः ॥ ९७ ॥

एतद**ति**च**ञ्चलमायुस्त्वदवनतिपरै**[9]**र्विहितम्** । किमिव । **कल्पशतेनोपपादितं** संपादितं यन्**महाफलं** त**दिव** । यथा **जलरुहः** पद्मस्य **पत्त्रे पतितं कं** पानीयं चञ्चलमपि[10]

1 *avāpad* em. Hahn] *avād* Ms.

2 *mardaneti* conj.] *mar(da) .. ti* Ms.

3 *tvadaṃghri°* em. Hahn] *tvadaṃhri°* Ms.

4 *kamalāśrayotsava°* conj. Hahn] *kamalā .. .. .. va°* Ms.

5 {{*sukhaṁ*}} Ms.

6 *jīyate* conj. Hahn] .. .. .. Ms. The restoration is uncertain.

7 *tathā* em. Hahn] *taṃthā* Ms.

8 *°bhūtā | pūrvā* em. Hahn] *°bhūtātpūrva°* Ms.

9 *āyus tvadavanatiparair* conj. Hahn] *ā .. .. parair* Ms.

10 *caṁcalam* em.] *cacalam* Ms.; *calam* Hahn

भूषणभव्यभावं[1] दे .. .. **गमयती**ति[2] तथोक्तमाश्रयविशेषात् । तदुक्तम् 'तोयमम्बुजपत्त्रस्थं धत्ते मुक्ताफलश्रियम्' इति । तद्वदायुरपि । **गुर्वी करुणा** यत्र **दिशि** मार्गे सा तथा । **श्रिता गुरुकरुणा**[3] **दिक्** यैर्यतिभिर्मुनिभिस्तेषां **वंशः** । इतः **श्रितगुरुकरुणादिग्यतिवंशो** येनैतत् संबोधनपद**मधिपे**ति च ॥

वृत्तपक्षे ऽत्यष्टिश्छन्दस्तथा परिणतिमवापद्यथा[4] **वंशपत्त्रपतितं** समुद्भूतमिति लिङ्गविपरिणामेन संबन्धात् । तच्च दिक्षु दशसु यतिरस्येति **दिग्यति** ॥

तवेत्यादि ॥

तव गुणविस्तरप्रणयपूतवचोविभवं
वरद स एक एव सुमुखो मुखमावहति ।
मधुमयसामधाम यजुषा सजुषानुगतं
श्रवणसुधाभिमानभवनर्क्कुटकं च विधिः ॥ ९८ ॥

हे **वरद** । **तव गुणानां प्रणयेन** परिचयेन[5] **पूतो वचोविभवो** यस्य तादृङ्**मुखं स एवैको विधिरावहति**[6] नान्यः । अत एव **सुमुखः** । ननु त्रयीपरिचयादेव तस्य सुमुखत्वमस्तीत्याह । **मधुमयस्य**[7] गा(27a)नमाधुर्यात्[8] । **साम्नो** वेदविशेषस्य[9] **धाम** स्थानमपि । अप्यर्थस्य **च**स्य प्रत्येकाभिसंबन्धात् । तथा**नुगत**मपि । केन । **यजुषा** । किंभूतेन । **सजुषा** प्रीतिकरेण । तथा **श्रवणसुधा**[10]रूपेणाभिमनन**मभिमान**स्तस्य **भवनम्** । क्व चित् श्रवणसुधाभिधानेति[11] पाठः । तत्रापि **श्रवणसुधे**त्यभिधानस्य **भवन**मभिधेयत्वेनाश्रयः ।

---

1 *bhūṣaṇabhavyabhāvaṁ* em.] *bhūṣaṇabhāvaṁ* Ms., Hahn

2 *de .. .. gamayatīti* conj. Hahn] *de .. .. tīti* Ms. The restoration is quite uncertain. One expects an explanation of °*gamitaṃ*. Read *deśayati* or *deśitaṁ bhavatīti ?*

3 *gurukaruṇā* conj. Hahn] *gu .. ..* Ms.

4 *pariṇatim avāpad yathā* conj. Hahn] *pariṇati .. .. thā* Ms.

5 *paricayena* conj. Hahn] *.. .. cayena* Ms.

6 *vidhir* em. Hahn, though not reported] *vivir* Ms.

7 *madhumayasya* em. Hahn, VMST (*sbraṅ rtsi raṅ bźin*)] *madhupasya* Ms.

8 *gāna*° conj. Hahn] *.. na*° Ms.

9 *vedaviśeṣasya* p.c.] *vedasya viśeṣasya* a.c.

10 *śravaṇasudhā*° conj. Hahn] *śrava .. .. dhā*° Ms.

11 °*sudhābhidhāneti* em.] °*sudhāneti* Ms., Hahn

तादृशा**मृचां कुट**मिव[1] कुटम् । स्वार्थे कः । 'कुटनिपावस्त्री' इत्यमरः । घट इवाधार इत्यर्थः । एवंभूतमपि मुखं सुमुखतया तदा आवहति यदा त्वद्गुणविस्तरप्रणयेन पूतं वचोविभवं[2] भवति ॥

वृत्तपक्षे ऽत्यष्टिश्छन्दस्तथा परिणतिमवापद्यथा **नर्कुटकं** समुद्भूतम् ॥

त्रिभुवनेत्यादि ॥

> त्रिभुवनसंमदप्रदजिनव्यवसायमधौ
> स्फुटसहकारतामहितमीहितमीश[3] तव ।
> प्रवचनमञ्जरीस्रुतशमामृतपानमुदा-
> भृत यतिषद्वदं कलकणत्कृतिकोकिलकम् ॥ ९९ ॥

हे **ईश** । **त्रिभुवन**स्य **संमदप्रदो** यो **जिनस्य व्यवसायो**[4] बोधिसत्त्वावस्थायां जगदुद्धरणोद्यमः स एव **मधु**र्वसन्तः । तद्विषये सहकरणं **सहकारः** । स **स्फुटो** यस्य तद्भावस्तत्त्वं **सहकारता**[5] । तया **महितं** तवे**हितं**[6] चेष्टितं कर्तृ **यतिषद्वदमभृत** पुष्टवत् । तथा **कलं क्कणन् कृति**जन एव **कोकिलः** । स्वार्थिकः कन् । तमप्य**भृत** । उभयत्र जातावेकवचनम् । कयाभृत । **प्र**(27b)**वचनमञ्जर्याः**[7] **स्रुतस्य**[8] स्यन्दितस्य **शमामृतस्य** तस्य पानात् या **मुत्** तया । आर्यमञ्जुघोषस्य हीच्छाप्रतिबद्धबोधः चेष्टितमशेषबुद्धानां हेत्ववस्थायां जगदुद्धरणस्य सहकारिभावं[9] भजदभिवर्धमानं क्रमेण तानभिसंबुद्धीकृत्य तद्धर्म[10]देशनानिष्यन्दनिर्वाणसुधास्वादप्रीत्या यतिजनश्रावकान् कृतिनश्च बोधिसत्त्वान् बिभर्ति[11] । तथा त्रि-

---

1 *kuṭam iva* em.] .. .. *m iva* Ms.; <*kuṭaka*>*m iva* Hahn

2 *pūtaṁ vacovibhavaṁ* conj.] .. .. *vibhavaṁ* Ms.; <*pūtavaco*>(4)*vibhavaṃ* Hahn

3 *īśa* em. Hahn, VMST (*dbaṅ po*)] *eti* Edition

4 *yo jinasya vyavasāyo* conj. Hahn] *yo* .. .. *vasāyo* Ms.

5 *sahakāratā* conj.

6 *mahitaṁ tavehitaṁ* conj. Hahn] *ma* .. .. *taṁ* Ms.

7 *kayābhṛta* | *pravacana°* conj. Hahn] *kayā* .. .. .. *vacana°* Ms.

8 *srutasya* em. Hahn] *śutasya* Ms.

9 *°uddharaṇasya sahakāri°* conj. Hahn] *°uddhara* .. .. .. *hakāri°* Ms. The restoration is only tentative.

10 *taddharma°* em. Hahn] *tarddharma°* Ms.

11 *bibharti* conj. Hahn] .. .. .. Ms.

जगत्प्रमोदप्रदे ऽपि[1] मधौ विकसच्चूततरुशालितया चेष्टितमुचितमलीनां[2] कलक्वण-त्काराणां कोकिलानामभिनवोद्भिन्नमञ्जरीनिर्यन्मकरन्दपानानन्देनैव[3] तान् बिभर्ति नान्यथा विघातैकरसत्वाच्छमस्य[4] ॥

वृत्तपक्षे ऽत्यष्टिश्छन्दस्तथा परिणतिमवापद्यथा **कोकिलकं** समुद्भूतम् । तच्च **यतयश्च षट्**[5] च तत्र **पदं** यतिर्यस्य तथा ॥

क चिद् इत्यादि ॥

> क चिदपि भवद्भीत्या भूरिप्रवादिमदद्विपो-
> द्दलन सुगतस्वान्तक्ष्माभृद्गभीरगुहागृह ।
> त्रिभवनवनाधीश क्रीडारसार्णवसंयता
> द्रवति हरिणीवारं मारप्रचण्डमहाचमूः ॥ १०० ॥

वने ऽधीशो **वनाधीशः** । सामान्यशब्दत्वे ऽप्यत्र सिंहाभिधानं मदद्विपोद्दलनतया[6] क्ष्माभृ-द्गम्भीरगुहागृहाधिवासात्[7] हरिणीविद्रावणाच्च[8] । भगवानपि **त्रिभवने**[9] **वनाधीश** इव वनाधीशः[10] । **सुगतानां स्वान्तं** मनः । तत्क्ष्माभृद्गम्भीरगुहा सैव **गृहं** यस्य । **भूरिवादि**[11]-(28a)**मदद्विपानामुद्दलनश्च**[12] । त्रयमेतदामन्त्रणपदम् । **कचिदप्यवस्थाभेदे भवतो भीत्या**

---

1 *°jagat°* em. Hahn, though not reported] *°jat°* Ms.

2 *ucitam alīnāṁ* em. Hahn] *ucita alīnā* Ms.

3 *°makararandapānānandenaiva* conj. Hahn] *°makara .. ... nandenaiva* Ms.

4 *°cchamasya* em. Hahn, though not reported] *°cchramasya* ? Ms.

5 *ṣaṭ* conj. Hahn] .. *ṭ* Ms.

6 *°dvipoddalana°* em. Hahn, VMST (*'joms mdzad*)] *°dvipodvalana°* (?) Ms.

7 *°guhāgṛhādhi°* conj.] *°.. .. gṛhādhi°* Ms.; *°guhādhi°* Hahn

8 *°vidrāvaṇāc* em.] *°vidrāvanāc* Ms.

9 *tribhavane* em. Hahn] *tribhuvana°* Edition; VMST (*srid pa gsum*)

10 *vanādhīśaḥ* em. Hahn] *vacanādhīśaḥ* Ms.

11 *bhūrivādi°* conj. Hahn] *bhū .. vādi°* Ms.

12 *uddalanaś* em. Hahn] *udalanaś* Ms.

मारस्य प्रचण्डमहाचमूरं शीघ्रं **हरिणीव द्रवति** पलायते । किंभूता । **क्रीडारस**[1] एव विस्तरत्वा**दर्णव**स्तत्र[2] **संयता** तदायत्तेत्यर्थः ॥

वृत्तपक्षे ऽत्यष्टिश्छन्दस्तथा परिणतिमवापत् यथा **हरिणी** समुद्भूता । सा च **रसेषु** षड्षु **अर्णवेषु** च चतुर्षु[3] **संयता** यतियुक्ता ॥

दुर्दान्तानामित्यादि ॥

दुर्दान्तानां दमनविधये क्वापि कारुण्यवेगाद्
धत्से मूर्तिं चरणशिखया ख्यातविक्रान्त यस्याः ।
त्रैलोकीयं श्रुतिरसभिदाक्रन्दनादैकवृत्ति-
र्मन्दाक्रान्ता व्रजति विलयं नाथ न स्वास्थ्यमाशु ॥ १०१ ॥

हे **नाथ ख्यातविक्रान्त** । **दुर्दान्तानां दमनविधये क्वापि** विषये **कारुण्यस्य वेगा**दुद्रेका**न्मूर्तिं धत्से यस्याश्चरण**[4]**शिखया इयं त्रैलोकी मन्द**मप्या**क्रान्ता** सती **विलयं** विशेषेण लीनतां **व्रजति** मज्जतीति यावत् । तथा सती **न आशु स्वास्थ्यं** व्रजतीति योज्यम् । किंभूता[5] । **श्रुतिरसं** श्रवणाभिलाषं **भिनत्तीति** क्विप् । स चासाव**ाक्रन्दनाद**श्च । तत्र**ैका वृत्तिः** प्रवृत्ति-र्यस्याः[6] ।

वृत्तपक्षे ऽत्यष्टिश्छन्दस्तथा परिणतिमवापत्[7] यथा **मन्दाक्रान्ता**[8] समुद्भूता । श्रुतिर्वेदा-श्चत्वारो रसाः षट् । तत्र भिद्भेदो यस्याः सा तथा । इत ऊर्ध्वमत्यष्टिर्नाधिक्रियते[9] ॥

शोभेत्यादि ।

शोभासंपत्तिः शिरसि गुरुणैकेन सैवोपजाता
या स्यात्कल्पद्रोः शुभफलनिभं बिभ्रतो भद्रकुम्भम् ।

---

1 *krīḍārasa°* conj. Hahn] *krī .. rasa°* Ms.

2 *arṇavas* em. Hahn] *avarṇavas* Ms.

3 *caturṣu* conj. Hahn] *ca .. .. * Ms.

4 *yasyāś caraṇa°* conj. Hahn] *ya .. .. .. ṇa°* Ms.

5 *yojyam | kiṁbhūtā |* conj. Hahn] *yojya . . ..* Ms.

6 Or *pravṛddhi<r>*. However, this is not in accordance with the explanation of the *vṛtti*.

7 *avāpat* em. Hahn] *apād* Ms.

8 *yathā mandākrāntā* conj. Hahn] *ya(thā) .. .. krāntā* Ms.

9 *atyaṣṭir* em. Hahn] *atyaṣṭi* Ms.

व्याख्यान[1]प्रेङ्खत्करकररुहोद्भासिनी भाति भर्तु-
दोर्वल्ली चेयं कुसुमितलता वेल्लितेवानिलेन ॥ १०२ ॥

या स्याच्छो[2]**भासंपत्तिः कल्प**(28b)**द्रोः**[3] कल्पवृक्षस्य । किंभूतस्य । **शुभफलनिभं** सर्व-सत्त्वसाधारणपुण्यफलप्रायं **शिरसि भद्रकुम्भं बिभ्रतः** । **सैव भर्तुर्**मञ्जुश्रियः **शिरसि** स्थितेन **गुरुणा** अक्षोभ्येण**ोपजाता** भवति[4] । भर्तुः कल्पतरुकल्प**स्येयं दोर्वल्ली**[5] **अनिलेन वेल्लिता**[6] कम्पिता **कुसुमितलतेव भाति** । कथम् । **व्याख्यानेन प्रेङ्खन्ती** चासौ **कर**संबन्धिनः **कररुहा** नखास्तै**रुद्भासिनी**[7] च । यस्मात् विशेषणयोरपि विशेष्यमपेक्ष्य[8] विशेषणविशेष्यभावविवक्षायां समासः ॥

वृत्तपक्षे यैव मन्दाक्रान्ता या यत्यादिः **शोभासंपत्तिः**[9] **सैव शिरसि** आदौ **एकेन गुरुणा** कृतेनोपजाता यस्यामियं **कुसुमितलतावेल्लिता** धृतौ वक्ष्यमाणायामष्टादशाक्षरे च्छन्दसि ॥

वृत्तमित्यादि[10] ।

वृत्तमेतदशेषबुद्धकुलाकलङ्ककलानिधे-
राहितं हृदि चेन्महाजड हारहारितवानसि ।
जिह्वया प्रणयीति चेद्धनसारसारमदेन किं
कर्णपूरमकारि चेत् खलु[11] खण्डितं मणिकुण्डलम् ॥ १०३ ॥

अशेषबुद्धकुलस्याह्लाददानादिभि**रकलङ्ककलानिधे**र्भगवत **एतदुक्तं** वक्ष्यमाणं च[12] **वृत्तं हृदि चेत् आहित**[1]**मा**रोपितम् । वक्ष्यमाणे**नेति**ना[2] संबन्धादित्यतः । हे **महा**[3]**जड** मुक्ता**हार-**

---

1 *vyākhyāna°* em. Hahn] *khyāna°* Edition

2 *cchobhā°* em.] *chabhā°* Ms.

3 *°saṁpattiḥ kalpadroḥ* conj. Hahn] *°saṁpa .. . . droḥ* Ms.

4 *°jātā bhavati* conj. Hahn] *°jā .. ..* Ms.

5 *dorvallī* em. Hahn] *rdovallī* Ms.

6 *vellitā* em. Hahn] *velli* Ms.

7 *nakhās tair udbhāsinī* conj. Hahn] *na .. .. .. dbhāsinī* Ms.

8 *viśeṣyam apekṣya* em. Hahn] *viśeṣyānapekṣya* Ms.

9 *yatyādiḥ śobhāsaṁpattiḥ* conj. Hahn] *yatyādi . .. . ttiḥ* Ms.

10 *ityādi* conj. Hahn] *i .. ..* Ms.

11 *khalu* conj. Hahn

12 *ca* conj. Hahn

हारितवानसि[4] । अस्यैव परमनिर्वृति[5]हेतुत्वेन महाशीतलस्यापि भवतो हारो ऽहार्येवे-त्यर्थः[6] । **जिह्वया प्रणयि चेत् कृतम्** । इ .. .. .. घनः सारो ऽस्य[7] (29a) **घनसारः** कर्पूर-**सारमदेन किम्** । न किंचित् । अस्यैव सुस्वादत्वात् । **कर्णपूरम्** । कर्णभूषण**मकारि**[8] **चेत्** । अत्रापीतियोगात् । अतः **खलु** निश्चितं **मणिमयकुण्डलं खण्डितं** जितम्[9] । एतस्यैव श्रोत्र[10]भूषणभूतत्वात् ॥

वृत्तपक्षे धृतौ **कर्णपूरं** नाम दृष्टलक्ष्यमेव ॥

उपचितेत्यादि ।

> उपचितपुण्यसंचय शचीकरतलसुखदैः
> परिचरणैरतृप्तिगमिव स्वमसममहिमन्[11] ।
> मणिमयपादपीठफलकं स्फुटयति भवतः
> कलिततमालपत्त्रमलिकान्नमति शतधृतौ ॥ १०४ ॥

हे **उपचितपुण्यसंचय** । **असममहिमन्** । **भवतो मणिमयं पाद**[12]**पीठफलकम्** । **शचीकर-तलेन** क्रियमाणत्वात् **सुखदैर**पि शचीकरतलस्य वा सुखदैः **परिचरणैः** परीष्टिभि**रतृप्ति-गमि**वातृप्तमिव यत्तदधुना **नमति**[13] **शतधृतौ** शतमखे **अलिकाल्ल**लाटात्[14] सकाशात् ।

---

1 *āhitam* conj. Hahn. This addition is only tentative. Śākyarakṣita might have omitted the *pratīka*.

2 °*māṇeneti(nā)* Ms.

3 *mahā*° conj. Hahn] .. *hā*° Ms. The akṣara *hā* rather looks like *rā*.

4 °*hāritavān* em. Hahn] °*hārītavān* with mark of deletion above the *ī* Ms.

5 °*nirvṛti*° em. Hahn] °*nirvṛtti*° Ms.

6 *bhavato hāro 'hāry eva* em. Hahn] *bhavato hārir eva* Ms. The addition of the subject *hāro* is absolutely necessary.

7 (*sāro 'sya*) or (*sāro me*) Ms

8 *karṇa*° em. Hahn] *kaṇa*° Ms.

9 *jitam* conj. Hahn] .. .. *m* Ms.

10 *śrotra*° em. Hahn] *śotra*° Ms.

11 °*mahiman* em. Hahn] °*mahima* Edition

12 °*mayaṁ pāda*° conj. Hahn] °*ma* .. .. .. *da*° Ms.

13 *adhunā namati* conj. Hahn] *adhu* .. .. *mati* Ms.

14 *lalāṭāt* em. Hahn] *laṭalāṭāt* Ms.

तद्वा प्राप्यं[1] **कलितं तमालस्य**[2] तापिञ्छस्य[3] तिलकीकृतं **पत्त्रं** येन । तत्तादृशं **स्वमा**त्मानं **स्फुटयति**[4] । तृप्तं प्रकाशयतीति यावत् । भो/भाक्षभुजो[5] ऽपि कमनीयकामिनीकर-तलविहितैः[6] सुखहेतुभिरपि परिवेशादिभिस्तर्पितस्यापि ललाटतिलकमेव[7] तृप्तिमावेदयते । तथा भगवतो ऽप्युपचितपुण्यसंभारस्यासममहिम्न[8]स्तादृङ्मणिमयपादासनं[9] शचीनाम्नो योषितः करतलसु(29b)खदै[10]रुपस्थानैर्नैव[11] तृप्तिमाविष्करोति । यदा तु नमतः क्रतूनां शतस्य कर्तुर्ललाटादुत्तमाङ्गात् संक्रान्ततमालपत्त्रं स्यात्तदाविष्क्रिया ॥

वृत्तपक्षे **तमालपत्रमपूर्वं स्फुटयति**[12] । कुत्र । भवा रुद्रा एकादश तेषु **भवतः** । **धृताविति** निवृत्तम् ॥

परार्थे इत्यादि ॥

> परार्थे स्थास्नूनामतिधृतिमतामीश विश्वानुकम्पा-
> मुखोन्मीलन्नानारसरसपदाकर्णयावेदयामि ।
> दशां तामाधेहि क्षणमपि गुरो पावनीं पावनानां
> समन्तध्वान्तानि प्रहरसि यया मे ऽघविस्फूर्जितानि ॥ १०५ ॥

हे **परार्थे स्थास्नूनामतिधृतिमतां** बोधिसत्त्वानाम**मीश** । **नाना**प्रकारो **रसो**[13] ऽभिलाषो येषु **रसेषु** ते । तथा **विश्वानुकम्पैव**[1] **मुखं** द्वारं ते **उन्मीलन्तो**[2] ये नानारसास्तेषां **पद** । इद-

---

[1] One expects something like *tac ca prāptaṃ*. — For the meaning of *kalita*, see pw under *kalita* 9): "a) *versehen mit* (im Comp. vorangehend)." VMST (*thob ste*) follows the interpretation of the commentary. Possibly the Ms. reads *prāpya*.

[2] *tamālasya* em. Hahn] *tāmalasya* Ms.

[3] This word is attested in various spellings: *tāpiccha, tāpiñcha*, and *tāpiñja*.

[4] *ātmānaṁ sphuṭayati* conj. Hahn] *ātmā .. . . ti* Ms.

[5] *bhokta°* or *bhokṣa°* Ms. The word has to be an epithet of Indra.

[6] *kamanīyakāminīkaratala°* em. Hahn] *kāmanīyakāminīkaratavala°* Ms.

[7] *lalāṭatilakam* conj. Hahn] *la .. .. tilakam* Ms.

[8] *asamamahimnas* em.] *asamasamamahimnas* Ms., Hahn

[9] *°pādāsanaṃ* em. Hahn] *°pādāśanaṃ* Ms.

[10] *karatalasukhadair* conj. Hahn] *karata .. .. khadair* Ms.

[11] *upasthānair naiva* em. Hahn] *upasthanenaiva* Ms.

[12] *sphuṭayati* conj. Hahn] *.. ṭayati* Ms.

[13] *°prakāro raso* conj.] *°pra .. .. .. so* Ms.; *°prakāraraso* conj. Hahn

मप्यामन्त्रणम् । **आकर्णय** शृणु । **आवेदयामि**[3] । किमावेदयसीत्याह । हे **गुरो पावनानां** मध्ये **पावनीं दशां तामपि क्षणमप्याधेहि । ययाघानां** पापानां **विस्फूर्जितानि मे हरसि ।** किंभूतानि[4] । **समन्तं** सर्वं **ध्वान्तं** येभ्यस्तानि ॥

वृत्तपक्षे **ऽतिधृतौ** ऊन[5]विंशत्यक्षरे च्छन्दसि सतां संमता **मेघविस्फूर्जिता । रसेषु रसेषु पदं** यतिर्यस्याः ॥

पायादित्यादि ॥

पायाद्वो वरबुद्धवंशजलधेर्वृद्धौ सुधादीधिति-
मञ्जुश्रीः परिभूतमन्मथकथः प्रज्ञाङ्गनासंगमे ।
भीमभ्रान्तिविभावरीपरिभवे बिभ्रद्यतिं भास्वतो
विश्वक्लेशकुरङ्गसङ्गरविधौ शार्दूलविक्रीडितम् ॥ १०६ ॥

वरबुद्धवंशः । स एव विस्तरत्वादिना **जलधिस्तस्य वृद्धौ सुधादीधितिर्मञ्जुश्रीर्वो** युष्मान् **पायात् । प्रज्ञा** याद्बया धीः **सैवाङ्गना तत्सङ्ग**(30a)**मे** ऽपि[6] **परिभूतमन्मथकथ** इति विरोधाभासः । पुनः किंभूतः । **आदित्यस्य यति**[7]माचारं **बिभ्रत्** । किंनिमित्तम् । **भीमा** भयावहा[8] या **भ्रान्तिरविद्या सैव विभावरी** तस्याः **परिभवे**[9] तथापि[10] **विश्वस्य** विश्वे वा **क्लेशास्त** एव **कुरङ्गास्तेषां सङ्गरविधौ शार्दूलस्य** द्वीपिनो **विक्रीडितं** बिभ्रदिति संबन्धः ॥

वृत्तपक्षे लिङ्गविपरिणामेन[11] संबन्धा**दतिधृतिमतं शार्दूलविक्रीडितम् । भास्वतो** भास्वति द्वादश**यतिं** बिभ्रत् ॥

अन्तरित्यादि ॥

---

1 °*kampaiva* em.] °*kampai* Ms.; °*kampaiḥ* Hahn

2 *te unmīlanto* em. Hahn] *tenmīlanto* p.c.] *tonmīlanto* a.c. —Read *tata unmīlanto* ?

3 *āvedayāmi* conj. Hahn] *ā .. ..* Ms.

4 *harasi | kiṁbhūtāni* conj. Hahn] *hara(si) . .. bhūtāni* Ms.

5 *'tidhṛtau ūna°* em. Hahn] *'tivṛtau una°* Ms.

6 *tatsaṅgame 'pi* conj. Hahn] *tatsa .. me 'pi* Ms.

7 *yatim* em. Hahn] *patim* Ms.

8 *bhayāvahā* em. Hahn] *bhayāvattā* Ms.

9 *tasyāḥ paribhave* conj. Hahn] *ta .. . . ve* Ms.

10 *tathāpi* em. Hahn] *tatathāpi* Ms.

11 °*vipariṇāmena* conj. Hahn] °*vipa .. .. .. na* Ms.

अन्तस्त्रासाङ्कुराभोत्पुलक[1]तनुरुहैस्त्रैलोक्यविजया-
वस्थां ते वीक्ष्य भग्नं सुरमुनिविसरैरुग्रग्रहनुदः ।
कारुण्यादुद्यतस्याप्यमलतरशरज्ज्योत्स्नापरिकरा-
दिन्दोर्बिम्बादनर्घस्मितवसुवदनाशेषप्रियकृतौ ॥ १०७ ॥

स्मितमेव वसु द्रव्यं यस्य तत्तथा । **अनर्घं स्मितवसुवदनं**[2] यस्य तस्यामन्त्रणम् । कस्मात् सकाशात्तथा[3] त्वमित्याह **अमलेत्यादि** । किंनिमित्तं तदित्याह । **अशेषस्य** सत्त्वनिकायस्य **प्रियकृतौ**[4] । **ते** तव **उग्रग्रहनुदस्त्रैलोक्य**[5]**विजया** याचलक्रोधा**द्यवस्था**[6] तां[7] त्रैलोक्यविजयरूपां[8] वा **वीक्ष्य भग्नम्** । कैः । **सुरमुनिविसरै**र्देवर्षिसंघैः । किंभूतैः । **अन्तस्त्रास**बीजस्या**ङ्कुराभा उत्पुलका**[9] हृषितास्**तनुरुहा** येषां तैः । कथंभूतस्य तव । **कारुण्या**ज्जगदर्थ**मुद्यतस्यापि** कृपयोद्युक्तस्य जगत्प्रीतिविधानार्थं स्मितमुखस्य चेयमवस्था विरोधिनीति[10] (30b) चेन्न । आहत्य भयोपदर्शने पर्यन्ते निःश्रेयसावहनादिति[11] ॥

वृत्तपक्षे **कृतौ** विंशत्यक्षरे च्छन्दसि **सुवदना** । तत्र च **मुनीनां विसरै**र्निवहै**र्भग्नं** भङ्गः प्रतिसप्तकं यतिरित्यर्थः[12] । **कृता**विति वृत्तं यावदधिकृतम् ॥

भयेत्यादि ॥

भयभग्नैरतिदूरतो विरहिणां पत्त्रैः श्रयायायता-
ममराणां गुरुभक्तिनिर्भरमनोव्यक्तौ सहायोपमम् ।

---

1 *°ābhotpulaka°* em.] *°ābhotpalita°* Edition, Hahn

2 *smitavasuvadanaṁ* conj. Hahn] *smi .. .. .. vadanaṁ* Ms.

3 *kasmāt sakāśāt* em. Hahn] *kasmāc chakāśāt* Ms.

4 *°kṛtau* em. Hahn] *°kṛte* Ms.

5 *°nudas trailokya°* conj. Hahn] *°nu(?)da .. .. kya°* Ms.

6 *avasthā* em. Hahn] *avasthāṃ* Ms.

7 *tāṁ* conj. Hahn

8 *trailokya°* em. Hahn] *trailoka°* Ms.; *°rūpāṃ* p.c.] *°rūpaṃ* a.c.

9 *°rābhā utpulakā* conj.] *°rābh(ā ū).. .. kā* Ms.; *°rābhā* (..)<*li*>*kā* Hahn

10 *virodhinīti* conj.] *viro .. .. ..* Ms.; *°viro<dha iti>* Hahn. The restoration is uncertain.

11 *niḥśreyasāvahanād iti* em. Hahn] *niśśreyasāvahanādi* Ms.

12 *yatir ity arthaḥ* conj. Hahn] *yati .. .. rthaḥ* Ms.

गगनामेयरयं युगान्तजलदध्वानाधिकक्ष्वेडितं
परितः खण्डितमारमस्तु जगतस्त्वत्सिंहविक्रीडितम् ॥ १०८ ॥

तव सिंहस्य विक्रीडितं परितः खण्डितो मारो येन तादृशं **जगतो ऽस्तु**[1] भवतु[2] । किंभूतम् । **भयेन**[3] **भग्नैः पत्त्रै**रित्यैरावणादिभि[4]र्वाहनै**र्विरहिणाम्** । यतस्ते **त्वदाश्रयायागच्छन्तः सुरा दूरादेव** त्वत्सिंहविक्रीडितभयभ्रष्टवाहनाः । अतो भग्नाहंकारतया त्वय्यभिव्यक्त[5]**गुरुतरभक्तयः** संवृत्ताः । ततस्तेषां **भक्तिनिर्भरमनो ऽभिव्यक्तौ** त्वत्सिंहविक्रीडितस्यैव **साहाय्यम्** । गुरौ वा वाहनादिपरिहारेणागमनाद्भक्ति[6]निर्भरं मनो भवतीति तदभिव्यक्तिरूपोपदेशे तस्यैव सहकारितेत्यभिप्रायः[7] ॥

वृत्तपक्षे कृतौ **सिंहविक्रीडितम्** । तच्च खण्डिता मारास्त्रयोदश[8] यत्र तादृक् । नन्वष्टौ वस्वङ्गमदना[9] इति पठ्यते । सत्यम् । किं तु प्रतिपदमारभ्य मदनत्रयोदशीं[10] यावत् स्मराणामुदयो[11] भवतीति त्रयोदशैवोक्ताः । यथा[12] (31a) च पद्यालंकारे 'इदमीशानमतं कृतौ स्मरयति स्यात् सिंहविक्रीडितम्' इत्यस्य व्याख्याने स्मरास्त्रयोदशेति । एतच्च वृत्तं शार्दूलविक्रीडितस्याद्यगुरोः स्थाने लघुद्वये[13] सतीति भेदः ॥

व्याप्तेत्यादि ॥

व्याप्तविश्वया शरन्नभस्तलातिशुद्धया धियाधियात
दुःसहार्तिविक्लवाप्रमेयसत्त्वधात्वधीनसत्कृपाढ्य ।

---

1 *astu* conj. Hahn. This addition may not be necessary.

2 *bhavatu* p.c.] *bhavātu* a.c.

3 *bhayena* conj. Hahn. This addition may not be necessary.

4 *pattrair ity airāvaṇādibhiḥ* conj. Hahn] *pattrai .. .. .. vaṇādibhiḥ* Ms.

5 *abhivyakta°* conj. Hahn] *a .. .. kta°* Ms.

6 *āgamanād bhakti°* conj.] *āgama .. .. kti°* Ms.; *°gama(śa?)<..bha>kti°* Hahn

7 *sahakāritety* p.c.] *sahikāritety* a.c.

8 *mārās trayodaśa* em. Hahn] *mārā daśa* Ms.

9 *°madanā* em. Hahn] *°mandanā* Ms. *vasu*, *aṅga*, and *madana* are symbolic designations for the number 8.

10 *°trayodaśīṁ* em.] *°trayodaśīr* Ms., Hahn

11 *smarāṇāṃ* em. Hahn] *svarāṇāṃ* Ms.

12 *°daśaivoktāḥ | yathā* conj.] *°daśaivo .. ..* Ms.; *daśaiva | <tathā>* Hahn

13 *laghudvaye* conj. Hahn] *.. .. ..* Ms.

संसृतौ च निर्वृतौ च शश्वदप्रतिष्ठ वादिनां[1] वरिष्ठ
वृत्तमीदृशं तु नामतो ऽपि नापरस्य सिद्धिमभ्युपेति ॥ १०९ ॥

हे **व्याप्तविश्वया शरन्नभस्तलातिशुद्धया धियाधियात** अध्याश्रित । **दुःसहा आर्तिस्तया**[2] **विक्लवो** व्याकुलो यो **ऽप्रमेयसत्त्वधातुस्तदधीना**[3] या **सती कृपा** तया **आढ्य** । **संसृतौ** संसारे । **निर्वृतौ च** निर्वाणे **शश्वन्न विद्यते प्रतिष्ठा येषां** ते च ते **वादिनश्च** तेषां **वरिष्ठे**तीद-मपि[4] द्वयमामन्त्रणम्[5] । **ईदृशमुक्त**वक्ष्यमाणं[6] भवतो **वृत्तं नामतो ऽपि** नाममात्रेणाप्य-**परस्य सिद्धिं** निश्चयं **नाभ्युपैति** ॥

वृत्तपक्षे कृतौ **वृत्तं** नाम । कृताविति निवृत्तम् ॥ २० ॥[7]

तीव्रेत्यादि[8] ॥

तीव्रतापविद्रुतायसच्छटासदृक्कटाक्षसंयमक्षणा-
धीनविश्वसंचयैश्चतुर्दिगीश्वरैः प्रकृत्युदञ्चितात्मभिः ।
स्फारविभ्रमप्रपञ्चपञ्चपञ्चबाणजिष्णुभिर्दशात्मना
सुन्दरीजनेन चातनोषि कामपि प्रकामविस्मयां श्रियम् ॥ ११० ॥

तीव्रतापेन[9] **विद्रुता** या **आयसी** आयसस्य[10] वा **छटा तत्सदृशानां**[11] **कटाक्षाणां**[12] **संयम-क्षणे ऽधीनो विश्वस्य संचयः** सृष्टिर्येषां तै**श्चतसृणां दिशामीश्वरै**र्यमान्तकादिभिश्चतुर्भिः[1]

---

1 *śaśvadapratiṣṭha vādinām* em., commentary] *śaśvadapratiṣṭhavādinām* Edition, Hahn

2 *ārtis tayā viklavo* conj. Hahn] *ā viklavo* Ms. The correction seems to be cogent.

3 *°dhātus tadadhīnā* conj. Hahn] *°.. .. .. dadhīnā* Ms.

4 *variṣṭhe°* em. Hahn] *pariṣṭhe°* Ms.

5 *dvayam āmantraṇam* conj. Hahn] *dvaya . .. . ṇam* Ms.

6 *ukta<ṃ> vakṣyamāṇaṁ* Hahn

7 The figure 20 marks the end of the category of metres consisting of 20 syllables per line.

8 *tīvretyādi* conj. Hahn] .. .. *tyādi* Ms.

9 *°tāpena* em. Hahn] *°tāyena* Ms.

10 *āyasasya* em. Hahn] *āyasya* Ms.

11 *tatsadṛśānāṃ* em. Hahn] *tatsadṛśāṇāṃ* Ms.

12 *kaṭākṣāṇāṃ* em. Hahn] *kaṭākṣaṇāṃ* Ms.

क्रोधैः करणभूतैः **कामपि प्रकामविस्मयां श्रियमातनोषि** । किंभूतैः । **प्रकृत्यैव उदञ्चितो** महत्त्वेनोत्थापित **आत्मा तैः**[2] (31b) तथा । **स्फारो विभ्रमस्य** भ्रान्तेर्विलासस्य वा **प्रपञ्चो** वैचित्र्यं तस्य पञ्चनं **पञ्चो** विस्तारणं यस्य । स चासौ **पञ्चबाणश्च** तस्य **जिष्णुभिः** । न केवलमेतैरेव । लोचनादयः पञ्च देव्यो[3] वक्रादयः[4] षड्वेति **दशात्मना सुन्दरीजनेनापि** उपलक्षणमेतन्माण्डलेयकथनम्[5] । अन्ये ऽपि द्रष्टव्याः ॥

वृत्तपक्षे **प्रकृतौ** एकविंशत्यक्षरे च्छन्दस्युदञ्चिता **सुन्दरी** नाम ॥

उत्कीर्णत्यादि[6] ॥

> उत्कीर्णोन्निद्रकुन्दप्रकरमिव दृशां चारुभङ्गैस्त्रिभागैः
> स्वेदस्रस्ताङ्गरागस्नपितमिव मुहुः कान्तकान्तिच्छटाभिः ।
> व्याप्तं व्योम त्वदर्चारुचिभिरभिहताविद्य विद्याधरीभिः
> सौरभ्याकृष्टहृष्टक्वणदलिपटलोल्लासितस्रग्धराभिः ॥ १११ ॥

स्रजामेव **सौरभ्येणाकृष्टं**[7] पश्चादिष्टार्थलाभाद्**धृष्टमत**[8] एव **क्वणत् यदलिपटलं** तेनो**ल्लासिताः स्रजः** पूजार्थं **धरन्ती**ति ताभिः । **त्वदर्चारुचिभिर्विद्याधरीभिर्व्योम**[9] **व्याप्तं** सत् **उत्कीर्ण** उप्त ऊर्ध्वं क्षिप्तो वा **उन्निद्राणां कुन्दानां प्रकरो** यत्र तदि**वा**भातीति गम्यम् । कैर्व्याप्तं तथाभाति । तासामेव **दृशां त्रिभागैः** कटाक्षैः स्फुरण[10] .. .. .. दृशैः **चारुर्भङ्गो**[11] वलनं येषां तैः । तथा ताभिरेव विद्याधरीभिः **कान्तकान्तिच्छटाभिर्व्योम** व्याप्तम् । भगवद्दर्शनजनित-सात्त्विक**स्वेद**वशात् **स्रस्तेनाङ्गरागेण**[12] विलेपनेन **स्नपितं**[1] मृषित**मिवा**भाति[2] ॥

---

1 *diśām īśvarair yamāntakādibhiś caturbhiḥ* em. Hahn] .(*i*) .. *m īśvarair yamāntakādi catubhiḥ* Ms.

2 *ātmā taiḥ* conj. Hahn] *ā* .. .. . Ms.

3 *devyo* conj. Hahn] .. .. Ms.

4 Or *vaktrādayaḥ*?

5 *upalakṣaṇam* em. Hahn, though not reported] *upalakṣanm* Ms.

6 *utkīrṇetyādi* conj. Hahn] *utkī* .. .. *di* Ms.

7 °*kṛṣṭaṃ* em. Hahn] °*kaṣṭaṃ* Ms.

8 *i(scchā)rtha*°. The conjunct letter is very indistinct.

9 °*dharībhir vyoma* conj. Hahn] °*dha* .. .. .. *ma* Ms.

10 (*sphu*)*raṇa* Ms.

11 *cārur* em. Hahn, though not reported] *cāra* Ms.

12 °*rāgeṇa* conj. Hahn] °*rā* .. .. Ms.

वृत्तपक्षे प्रकृत्युदञ्चिता **स्रग्धरा** । सा च **चारुभङ्गो** यतिर्येषां तै**स्त्रिभिः**[3] **भागैः** प्रत्येकं सप्त-काक्षरैर्लक्षिता । प्रकृत्युदञ्चितेति निवृत्तम्[4] ॥

आकृ(32a)**तीत्यादि**[5] ॥

आकृतिजन्मवृत्तविभवक्रमातिशयसंपदः सुखमिया-
दीश दिगन्तगीतममलं यशश्च शरदिन्दुसुन्दरतरम् ।
गायति यस्त्वदाह्वयमयं[6] सदैव भगवन्भवाध्वगजनो
नूनमगम्यगौरव गिरां गुरो गुणसमुद्र मद्रकमिदम् ॥ ११२ ॥

हे **भगवन् ईश** । **गिरामगम्यगौरव गुरो गुणसमुद्र** । **यो भवाध्वगजन इदं त्वदाह्वयमयं**[7] त्वन्नामगर्भं **मद्रकं** रागविशेषं **सदैव गायति** सः । **आकृतिश्च** रूपम् । **जन्म** च[8] देवादि-जातिः । **वृत्तं** च सच्चरितम्[9] । **विभवश्च** धनादि । **क्रमश्च** विक्रमः । एषा**मतिशयसंपदः** **सुखं** यथा भवति त**थेयादा**सादयेत् । **दिगन्ते गीतं शरदिन्दुसुन्दरतर**त्वादेवा**मलं**[10] **यश-श्चे**यात् ॥

वृत्तपक्षे **आकृतौ** द्वाविंशत्यक्षरे च्छन्दसि जन्म यस्य त**न्मद्रक**मिदं वृत्तम् । तच्च **दिक्षु** दशसु **अन्तो** विरामस्तेन गीतम्[11] । आकृतिजन्मेति निवृत्तम्[12] ॥

मध्वासारेत्यादि ॥

मध्वासारस्नातोद्भ्रान्तप्रबलमदमुखरमधुकरनिकरं
प्रीतेरेकं लीलावासं विदितबलमपि मुनिहृदयविकृतौ ।

---

1 *snapitaṁ* conj. Hahn. This addition is not absolutely necessary.

2 Hahn suggests in a footnote: Read *mṛśitam*?

3 *tais tribhiḥ* em. Hahn] *taibhiḥ* Ms.

4 *nivṛ(ttam)* Ms.] *nirvṛ(ttaṃ)* Hahn

5 *ākṛtītyādi* conj. Hahn] .. .. *tītyādi* Ms.

6 *tvadāhvaya*° em., commentary] *tavāhvaya*° Edition, Hahn

7 *tvadāhvaya*° em. Hahn] *tadāhvaya*° Ms.

8 *rūpam | janma ca* conj. Hahn] *rū* .. . . Ms.

9 *saccaritaṃ* p.c.] *sāccaritaṃ* a.c.

10 °*sundaratvād* conj. Hahn] °.. .. .. *tvād* Ms.

11 *gītaṃ* em. Hahn] *gātaṃ* Ms.

12 *nivṛttam* conj.] *ni* .. .. . Ms.; *nir(v)<ṛttam* ||> Hahn

वागीशान त्वय्येकान्तं वसुविषयविरतिसमुपचितबलिः
संभोगश्रीमत्ताक्रीडं वरद दिवि नियतमनुभवति ॥ ११३ ॥

हे **वागीशान** । **वरद** । **त्वयि एकान्तं वसुविषये विगता रतिर्यत्र** समुपचयने तद्यथा भवति वसुविषये वादृष्टतया **समुपचितो बलिः** उपहारो[1] येन स सुधीः । **संभोगश्रीमत्तया** क्रीडनं **क्रीडं दिवि नियतमनुभवति** । किंभूतम् । **मधुनः** सुधाया **आसारेण स्नातस्तदनु उपरि भ्रान्तः प्रबलमदेन मुखरो**[2] **मधुकराणां निकरो** यस्मिन् । **प्रीतेश्च एकमसाधारणं लीलावासम्** । अत एव **मुनीनां हृदयविकारायापि बलं** यस्य **विदितं**[3] तत्तथा । इह त्वयि सर्वस्वेन पूजाविधा(32b)नात्[4] स्वर्गसुधापान[5]क्रीडासुखमनुभवतीत्यर्थः ॥

वृत्तपक्षे **वसवो**[6] ऽष्टौ । **विषयाः** पञ्च । तेषु यति[7]र्यस्य त**न्मत्ताक्रीडं विकृतौ** त्रयोविंशत्यक्षरे च्छन्दसि ॥

मदेत्यादि ॥

मदगुरुगण्डगर्जितजितोन्नताम्बुदगजेन्द्रवृन्दमलिनं
निशितसमस्तशस्त्रकिरणप्रभाम्बरपिनद्धपत्तिनिवहम् ।
प्रवररथाधिरूढसुभटं बलं बलनिधे त्वदेकशरणं
श्रयति नरं मनोहरयतिप्रवेशवशगोत्तमाश्वललितम् ॥ ११४ ॥

हे **बलानां** स्थानास्थानज्ञानबलादीनां दशानां **निधे** । **त्वदेकशरणं नरं बलं** चतुरङ्गं **श्रयति** । कीदृशम् । **मदेन गुरुगण्डानां गर्जितेन जितोन्नताम्बुदानां गजानां**[8] **वृन्देन मलिनम्** । तथा **निशितसमस्तशस्त्रकिरणानां**[9] **प्रभा** विस्फुरणं सैव**ाम्बरं** वस्त्रं तेन **पिनद्धः पत्तिनिवहो** यत्र । क्वचित् **प्रभास्वरे**ति पाठः । तत्र **किरणैः** प्रभास्वरादेव[10] **पिनद्धः पत्तिनिवहो** यस्मिन्

---

1. *upahāro* conj. Hahn] .. *pahāro* Ms.
2. °*madena mukharo* conj. Hahn] °*made* .. .. *kharo* Ms.
3. *viditaṁ* conj. Hahn
4. *pūjāvidhānāt* em. Hahn] *pūjā* .. .. *nāta* Ms.
5. °*pāna*° em. Hahn] °*yāna*° Ms.
6. *vasavo* em. Hahn] *vasavau* Ms.
7. *yatir* Ms.] <*viratir*> *yatir* conj. Hahn
8. *gajānāṃ* conj. Hahn] *gajān* . . Ms. —Read *gajendrāṇāṃ* ?
9. °*śastra*° em. Hahn] °*śatra*° Ms.
10. *prabhāsvarād* conj. Hahn] .. *bhāsvarād* Ms.

तत्तथा । **प्रवररथाधिरूढसुभटं** च । **मनोहरा** उचितानतिक्रमा च **यति.. ..**परमो[1] येषाम् । तथा **प्रकृष्टो**[2] **वेशो** येषामत एव ते सुशिक्षितत्वाद्वाहक**वशगा उत्तमाः** । जात्युत्कर्षा**दश्वास्तैर्ल्लडितम्** ।

वृत्तपक्षे **हरा** एकादश । तेषु **यतिर्यस्य तदश्वललितं** विकृतौ[3] । विकृताविति निवृत्तम् ॥ २३ ॥[4]

प्रीतीत्यादि ॥

प्रीतिनिवासं कृतिभुवि विदितोदारवरप्रदवरिवसनं त्वां
यः स्मरतीश प्रतिहतविमतिः संततमन्तिमपदमुदितेषु ।
यौवनलीलासचिवसमुदयत्पञ्चमकस्वरयतिरमणीया
स्यादिह तन्वी हिमकरवदना तद्वशगा सह नरपतिलक्ष्म्या ॥
११५ ॥

हे ईश[5] । **कृतिनां** बोधिसत्त्वानां **भुवि** मुदितादिभूमौ **विदित** । **उदारवरप्रदं वरिवसन**माराधनं[6] यस्य । यतः **उदि**(33a)**तेषु** उक्तपदशालिषु[7] मध्ये **ऽन्तिमं** पर्यन्तवर्ति **पदं** यस्य तथा भवानतस्तं **त्वां प्रीतेर्निवासं यः प्रतिहतविमतिः संततं स्मरति** तस्य पुंसो **वशगा हिमकरवदना तन्वी**[8] संमता **नरपतिलक्ष्म्या सह स्यात्**[9] । कीदृशी । **यौवनेन** या **लीला** सैव **सचिवो** यस्य स चासौ **समुदयन्पञ्चमकस्वरश्च** तस्य **यति**र्मूर्च्छा तया **रमणीया** युवती । .. .. .. ॥

---

1 The two akṣaras after *yati* are difficult to read. *yati(r vyu)paramo* Hahn

2 *prakṛṣṭo* conj. Hahn] *prakṛ* .. Ms.

3 *vikṛtau* conj. Hahn] .. *kṛtau* Ms.

4 The figure 23 indicates the end of the category of the metres of 23 syllables per line.

5 *īśa* conj. Hahn

6 *vari°* em. Hahn] *vara°* Ms.

7 *yataḥ uditeṣu uktapadaśāliṣu* conj. Hahn] *yata(ḥ)..* .. *(teṣu u)kta(pada)śāliṣu* Ms. The upper parts of the first eleven akṣaras are broken off. The readings are uncertain.

8 *tanvī* conj. Hahn] *ta* .. Ms.

9 *syāt* em. Hahn] *syā* Ms.

वृत्तपक्षे **संकृतौ** चतुर्विंशत्यक्षरच्छन्दः सैव भूस्तत्र विदिता **तन्वी** । किंभूता । **पञ्चमकं** पञ्चमं स्थानं **स्वराः** सप्त । तेषु **यतिः** । तया रमणीया ॥ २४ ॥[1]

विश्वेत्यादि[2] ॥

विश्वहितैकासङ्गसहान्तःकरणकरण वसुपदमिव परमं[3]
यो ऽधिप गृह्णातीह तवाख्यां तमभिकृतिवसतिरपि भुवि सरसी ।
सिध्यति मज्जद्दिग्गजगण्डच्युतमदपरिमलसुरभितसलिला[4]
सारसहंसक्रौञ्चपदाङ्कोत्कनककमलवनरणदलिपटला ॥ ११६ ॥

विश्वहिते[5] **एकमद्वितीयमासङ्गं सहते** तदनुगुणत्वात् यत्तादृशम**न्तःकरणस्य करणं** प्रवर्तनं यस्य तस्य संबोधनम् । तथा **अधिपे**ति । यथा वसूनां द्रव्याणां पदमु[6]त्पत्तिस्थानं किंचित्प्रसिद्धम् । तथा **तवाख्या**प्यभिमतादतिशयसिद्धिहेतुत्वात् **वसुपदमिव परमम्** । वसूनां पदमिव वाचकमिव **इह** जगति **यो गृह्णाति तमभि**लक्ष्यी[7]कृत्य **कृतिनां** विबुधानां **वसतिरपि सरसी भुवि सिध्यति** । कीदृशी । **मज्जद्दिग्गजगण्डच्युतमदपरिमलसुरभितसलिला**[8] । तथा **सारसहंसक्रौञ्चपद**(33b)**मङ्को**[9] यत्र । तथा उद्गतेषु **कनककमलवनेषु रणदलिपटलं** यस्यां सैवंरूपा सरसी देवानामपि क्रीडाश्रयः ॥

---

1 The figure 24 indicates indicates the end of the category of the metres of 24 syllables per line.

2 *viśvetyādi* conj. Hahn] *vi* .. .. .. Ms.

3 *paramaṃ* em., commentary] *paramāṃ* Edition, Hahn

4 °*salilā* em. Hahn] °*sarit* (sic! °*salit*) Edition, unmetrical! VMST translates *rol pa can*, which points to the wrong reading (or wrong interpretation) °*sa-līlā* instad of °*salilā*.

5 *viśvahite* conj. Hahn] .. *śvahite* Ms.

6 *dravyāṇāṁ padam* conj. Hahn] *dra* .. .. *dam* Ms.

7 *gṛhṇāti tam abhilakṣyī*° conj. Hahn] .. .. *m abhilakṣī*° Ms.

8 *majjaddiggaja...salilā* em. Hahn] *majjadiggaja...salino* Ms. See the note on the main text.

9 °*krauñcapadam* conj. Hahn] °*krauñca* .. .. *m* Ms.

वृत्तपक्षे **ऽभिकृतिः** पञ्चविंशत्यक्षरं च्छन्दो वसतिर्यस्याः सा **क्रौञ्चपदा**[1] । सा च **करणानि** च **वसव**श्च तेषु **पदं** विश्रामं **गृह्णाति**[2] । करणानि पञ्च ॥ २५ ॥[3]

ध्वान्तेत्यादि ॥

ध्वान्तध्वंसिन् माराराते हतवृजिन जिनतनयभूविभूषण मुत्कृतौ
प्रौढोन्मीलल्लावण्यश्रीः स्थितिजनक गिरि भवभिदामुदार-
पराक्रम ।
त्वय्यारब्धावन्ध्याराधो विधुरयति वरद सुधियां विराजतया
स्फुरन्
भोगासक्तो ऽपीह स्वैरं विषमतमविषयतनुभृद्भुजङ्ग-
विजृम्भितम् ॥ ११७ ॥

हे **ध्वान्तध्वंसिन्** । **माराराते हतवृजिन**[4] क्षतपाप[5] । **जिनतनयभूविभूषण** । **मुत्कृतौ** प्रमोद[6]जननेन **प्रौढा उन्मीलन्ती लावण्यश्री**र्यस्येदमपि संबोधनम् । तथा **भवभिदां** बुद्धानां **गिरि** वाग्विषये **स्थितिजनक** सद्धर्मधूर्धर । **उदारपराक्रम** भगवन् । **त्वय्यारब्धो**[7] **ऽवन्ध्य आराध** आराधनं[8] येन स पुमान् । हे **वरद स्वैरं** स्वच्छन्दं **विधुरयति** दमयति । किम् । **विषमतमा** विनोपायं भुज्यमानत्वेनानिष्टावाहकत्वाद् **विषया**[9] रूपादयो येषां ते च ते **तनुभृत**श्च त एव भयहेतुत्वा**द्भुजङ्गा**स्तेषां[10] **विजृम्भितम्** । किंभूतः । **भोगेष्वासक्तो ऽपि** । **सुधियां** मध्ये **विशेषेण राजत** इति विराजता तया स्फुरन्[11] .. ..रे .. । **वीनां** पक्षिणां

---

1 *krauñcapadā* conj. Hahn] *krau .. .. dā* Ms.

2 *gṛhṇāti* em. Hahn] *gṛhnāti* Ms.

3 The figure 25 indicates the end of the category of the metres of 25 syllables per line.

4 *°vṛjina* em. Hahn] *°vṛjana* Ms.

5 *kṣatapāpa* em. Hahn] *kṣatayāya* Ms.

6 *mutkṛtau pramoda°* conj. Hahn] *.. .. .. .. moda°* Ms.

7 *tvayy ārabdho* conj. Hahn] *.. .. .. bdho* Ms.

8 *ārādha ārādhanaṁ* em.] *ārādhanam ārādho* Ms., Hahn

9 *°vāhakatvād viṣayā* conj. Hahn] *°vāhaka .. ..* Ms.

10 *°tvād* p.c.] *°tvad* a.c.

11 *virājatā tayā sphuran* conj.] *virā(ja) .. ..* Ms.; *virāj<atā tayā ..> <.. .. .. .. >re (..)* Hahn

राजतया गरुडो ऽपि । अहीनां **भोगेषु** देहेष्वासक्तः । **विषमतमं विषं याति** श्रयति स चासौ **तनुश्च** तद्भूतो ये **भुजङ्गास्तेषां विजृम्भितं वि**(34a)**धुरयति**[1] ॥

वृत्तपक्षे उत्कृतौ षड्विंशत्यक्षरे च्छन्दसि **भुजङ्गविजृम्भितम्** । तच्च **गिरयो** ऽष्टौ कुलपर्वता **रुद्राश्चैकादश**[2] तेषु **भिदा** भङ्गेन लक्षितम् । नन्वन्यत्र सप्तैव कुलाचलाः .. ..[3] राजः 'वसुकुल[4]गिरिभिः स्यान्मालिनी नौ मयौ य' इति । सत्यम् । इह त्वष्टौ द्रष्टव्याः । तथा चानर्घराघवः 'मूर्तीरष्ट महेश्वरस्य दलयन्नष्टौ[5] कुलक्ष्माभृतः' इति । रत्नाकरे[6] 'वसुमदन-दहनमुनिभिर्भुजङ्गविजृम्भितम्[7]' इत्यत्र वसुभिर्मदनै[8]र्दहनैर्मुनिभिरस्येति विवरणं तल्लेखक-प्रमादायातम् । मदनदहनो रुद्र एव हि तत्राभिमत.. .. ..[9]राजः 'वसुमनसिजरिपुतुरगै-र्भुजङ्गविजृम्भितम्[10]' इति ॥

तन्वदित्यादि ॥

> तन्वत्सुस्फुटमविरतममितममृतरसकणमिव परितो ऽङ्गेषु
> प्रत्यालोचनसमुदयिनवरसरसपदमसदृशमतुलश्रीकम्[11] ।
> यत्कृच्छ्रैरपि न सुलभमपरविविधसुकृतविधिभिरभियुक्तात्मा
> त्वत्सेवातरुफलमिह समनुभवति तदखिलविपद्-
> प्रवाहाख्यम् ॥ ११८ ॥

---

1 *vijṛmbhitaṁ vidhurayati* conj. Hahn] .. .. *dhurayati* Ms.

2 *rudrāś caikā°* em. Hahn] *rūpāś caika°* Ms.

3 An unknown number of akṣaras is broken off.

4 *vasukula°* em. Hahn] *kula°* Ms.

5 *aṣṭau* em. Hahn] *eṣṭau* Ms.

6 *ratnākare* or *chandoratnākare* conj. Hahn] .. .. .. *re* or .. .. *re* Ms.

7 *°madanadahanamunibhir* em. Hahn] *°vadanamunibhir* Ms. The text of the commentary shows that we have to read *°madana°* instead of *°vadana°* and that *°dahana°* was omitted as already observed by Śākyarakṣita. The text thus corrected is the latter part of Ratnākaraśānti's definition (*Chandoratnākara* 2.80). The omitted first part runs: *mau gvau nau lkau sujair vaḥ syād .....* .

8 *madanair* em. Hahn] *mardanair* Ms.

9 An unknown number of akṣaras is broken off.

10 *manasijariputuragair* em. Hahn] *manasiriṣṭajñāturagair* Ms. Our restoration is tentative. The source could not be identified.

11 *°śrīkaḥ* Edition

अखिला विपदो ऽपवहत्यधिक्रामत्यणि । **अखिलविपदपवाहमाख्या** यस्य तत् **त्वत्सेवा-तरुफलमिह**[1] जगत्य**भियुक्तात्मा** पुरुषो **ऽनुभवति**[2] । किंभूतम् । **यत्कृच्छ्रैरपि** कष्ट-साध्यैरपि **अपरैः सुकृतविधिभिर्न सुलभम्** । अत एवा**सदृशमतुलश्रीकं**[3] च । पुनः किं-भूतम् । .. ..[4] **आलोचनमालोचनं प्रति समुदयिन**श्च ते **नवरसा**श्च[5] शृङ्गारादयः । तेषु **रसो** ऽभिलाषो येषाम् ।[6] तेषां **पदम्** । अत एव **सुष्ठु स्फुटमविरतममितममृतरसकणमिवाङ्गेषु**[7] **परितस्तन्वत्** । सुधारसपृषद्भिः परितो ऽङ्गानि सिञ्चदिति यावत् । अथवाङ्गेषु परितः स्फुटमविरतममितम[8]मृतरसकणमिव[9] तन्वत्सु सत्सु । यथोक्तं तत् त्वत्सेवा[10]तरुफल-मनुभवतीत्यर्थः ॥

वृत्तपक्षे उत्कृता**वपवाह** इत्याख्या यस्य तद्वृत्तम् । **नव** च **रसा**श्च तेषु **पदं** यस्य तत्तथा । इयता यतिशरीरसंज्ञोपेतैः सच्छन्दोभेदैर्भगवतः[11] स्तुतिरुक्ता[12] । इत ऊर्ध्वं **दण्डक**भेदै-र्वक्तव्येति ॥ ॥

चपलेत्यादि ॥

चपलचरणपीडितागाधिपोपेतपातालतालूच्छलद्व्यालपालस्तुतं
जयति जयति चारुकारुण्यकेलिस्फुरत्पद्मनर्तेश्वराकारलीला-
यितम् ।
अनिभृत[13]भुजदण्डषण्डप्रचण्डानिलोल्लासितः श्रान्तिशान्तिं

---

1 *°taruphalam* conj. Hahn] *°.. .. .. lam* Ms.

2 *'nubhavati* em. Hahn] *'nubhāvati* (?) Ms.

3 *evāsadṛśam* em. Hahn] *evaśadṛśam* Ms.

4 (34b) *raso 'bhilāṣo yeṣāṃ* added inadvertently in the Ms.

5 *te ca te rasāś ca* added inadvertently in the Ms.

6 *śṛṅgārādayaḥ | teṣu raso 'bhilāṣo yeṣāṁ | teṣāṁ* conj.] *śṛṅgārādayaḥ teṣāṁ* Ms.

7 *ivāṅgeṣu* conj. Hahn] *i .. .. ṣu* Ms.

8 *aviratam amitam amṛta°* conj. Hahn] *aviratam amṛta°* Ms.

9 *°kaṇam* em. Hahn] *°kaṣaṇam* Ms.

10 *tvatsevā°* conj. Hahn] *ta . .. vā°* Ms.

11 *sacchandobhedair* em. Hahn] *saccha .. .. dair* Ms.

12 *uktā* em. Hahn] *uktāḥ* Ms.

13 VMST translates *nipatita°*.

तनोतीव ते
प्रलयसमयशङ्कया यत्र लोकत्रयीदण्डकश्चण्डवृष्टिप्रयातो
ऽम्बुदः ॥ ११९ ॥

पद्मनर्तेश्वरो[1] मञ्जुवज्रस्याम्नायविशेषः । **कारुण्यक्रीडया स्फुरच्चारुपद्मनर्तेश्वराकार**[2]**लीलायितं**[3] तव **जयति जयती**ति संभ्रम आभीक्ष्ण्ये[4] वा द्विरुक्तिः । किंरूपम् । **चपलचरणाभ्यां पीडितेन अगानामधिपेन** मेरुणा तदुपरि नतेनात **उपेतस्य पातालस्य**[5] (35a) भयात् **तालुना**[6] **उच्छलता व्यालपालेन**[7] भुजगपतिना **स्तुतम्**[8] । **यत्र** पद्मनर्तेश्वराकारलीलायिते[9] नृत्यत्वरया **अनिभृतानां भुजदण्डानां षण्डेन**[10] संदोहेन **उल्लासितश्चण्डया वृष्ट्या**[11] **प्रया(?)तो**[12] ऽनुगतो[13] **ऽम्बुदस्ते** ताण्डव**श्रान्तेः**[14] **शान्तिं तनोतीव** । नृत्यतो हि श्रमो भवति स चानिलोल्लासितेन[15] वर्षता पयोदेनापोह्यत[16] इति भगवतो ऽपि तथैवोत्प्रेक्ष्यते[17] । कीदृशः[18]। **प्रलयसमयशङ्कया लोकत्रयीं दण्डयति** पीडयति तथा । विनेयविशेषमनु-

---

1 °*narteśvaro* em. Hahn] °*nateśvaro* Ms.

2 °*padmanarteśvarākāra*° conj. Hahn] °*pa .. .. kāra*° Ms.

3 °*līlāyitaṁ* em. Hahn] °*līlāpite* Ms.

4 *ābhīkṣṇye* em. Hahn] *ābhīkṣṇe* Ms.

5 *upetasya pātālasya* conj. Hahn] *u .. ..* Ms.

6 *bhayāt tālunā* em. Hahn] *bhayāta tā tālu | nā* Ms.

7 *vyālapālena* em. Hahn] *vyālapālaina* Ms.

8 *stutam* em. Hahn] *tutaṃ* Ms.

9 °*līlāyite* em. Hahn] °*līlāpite* Ms. —Between *te* and the following *nṛ*° stands a small raised character that looks like *ga*.

10 *ṣaṇḍena* em. Hahn] *daṇḍena* Ms.

11 *vṛṣṭyā* em. Hahn] *dṛṣṭyā* Ms.

12 *prayāto* conj. Hahn] *pra .. to* Ms.

13 The strange paraphrase *anugato* for *pra<yā>to* is confirmed by VMST (*rab tu ldan pa'i*).

14 °*śrānteḥ* em. Hahn] °*śrānte* | or °*śrānto* Ms.

15 *cānilollāsitena* em. Hahn] *cānilollāsite* Ms.

16 *apo(hya)ta* Ms.

17 *utprekṣyate* em. Hahn] *utprekṣate* Ms.

18 *kīdṛśaḥ* conj. Hahn] *kīdṛ .. .* Ms.

जिघृक्षोः खलु भगवतः कृपाकेलिनिर्भरताण्डवारम्भे ऽत्यद्भुतोद्भटविकटभुजदण्ड[1]-मण्डलप्रभवप्रभञ्जनजवैरुज्जृम्भितः ससंरम्भमम्भोभृदकाण्डप्रचण्डवारिधारान्धकारारब्ध-दुर्दिनः संवर्तः संवृत्त इति चेतसि त्रासमातन्वानः पीडयत्याहत्य[2] जगत्त्रयं पर्यन्ते तु पर-हितैकपरिणाममधुर एव॥

वृत्तपक्षे **चण्डवृष्टिप्रपातो**[3] नाम प्रथमो **दण्डकः** । दीर्घत्वाद्दण्ड इव दण्डकः ॥ २७ ॥

प्रतीत्यादि[4] । ....

प्रतिपदमिह जातशुद्धेः समाधेस्त्रयस्याक्षरस्याभिसंवर्धनादन्त्य-
रूपस्पृशः
समधिगमवशाज्जयत्यार्यवर्यैः प्रभूतप्रमोदैः प्रगीतः प्रभाव-
प्रकर्षस्तव ।
वरद यदनुमोदनावादसाराविणातृप्तचित्तैः सुरैर्वाद्यमाना न यान्ति
श्रम-
मपरिमपरमोपकारोत्तमर्णार्णवव्यालजीमूतलीलाकरोद्दाम-
शङ्खादयः ॥ १२० ॥

हे[5] **वरद** । **अपरिमो** ऽनुत्तरः **परमोपकार**स्तत्रो**त्तमर्ण** इवोत्तमर्णस्तस्य संबोधनम् । **प्रभूत-प्रमोदैरार्यवर्यैः प्रगीतस्तव प्रभावप्रकर्ष इह** जगति **जयति** । कस्मात्[6] (35b) स तथाभूतः । **त्रयस्य** शून्यानिमित्ताप्रणिहितलक्षणस्य **समाधेः समधिगमवशात्** । किंभूतस्य । **प्रतिपद-मभिसंवर्धनाज्जातशुद्धेः** प्रहीणमलस्या**क्षरस्या**विचलस्य[7] । अ .. .. **न्त्यरूप**[8]**स्पृशः** प्रकर्षपर्यन्तगतस्वभावस्य । यस्य च प्रगीतस्वभावस्या**नुमोदनावादेन यत्साराविणं** संभूय

---

1 °*vikaṭabhujadaṇḍa*° conj. Hahn] °*vika* .. .. .. *daṇḍa*° Ms.

2 *pīḍayaty* conj. Hahn] .. .. .. *ty* Ms.

3 Hahn suggests in a footnote: Read °*prayāto* in accordance with the earlier explanation? Should we also read °*prayāte* instead of °*prapāte* in the Vivṛti on the following two verses? Cf. Jayadeva 7.32.

4 *pratītyādi* conj. Hahn] *pratītyā* .. Ms.

5 *he* conj. Hahn] .. Ms.

6 *jayati* | *kasmāt* conj. Hahn] *jaya* .. . . The restoration is uncertain.

7 *akṣarasyāvicalasya* em. Hahn] *akṣarasya vācālasya* Ms.

8 *a* .. .. *ntyarūpa*° em. Hahn] *a* .. *rūpa*° Ms.

रवणं तत्रा**तृप्तचित्तैः सुरैर्वाद्यमानाः श्रमं**[1] विश्रामं[2] **न यान्ति** । के । **अर्णवस्य व्याला** इव कार्ष्ण्यात् ये **जीमूतास्तेषां** मनोज्ञध्वनित्वेन **लीलाकरा** ये **उद्दामशङ्खादयस्ते** ॥

वृत्तपक्षे इह चण्डवृष्टिप्रपाते ऽन्त्यानां त्रयाणाम[3]क्षराणां गुरुलघुक्रमेण यद्रूपं तत्स्पृश-स्त्रयस्याक्षरस्य प्रतिपदं प्रतिपादमभिसंवर्धनात् । **अर्णार्णवव्यालजीमूतलीलाकरोद्दाम-शङ्खादयो** ये ते[4] दण्डकभेदाः श्रमं विश्रामं पर्यन्तं न यान्ति अपर्यन्ता इति यावत् । तत्रा-**र्णस्ये**[5]दमेवोदाहरणम् । अर्णवादीनामूहितव्यानीति ॥ २७ ॥

प्रविकचेत्यादि[6] ॥

> प्रविकचकनकपङ्कजसौभाग्यभागङ्ग दत्तेनभावाश्रितेभ्यस्तमःसु
> त्रिभुवनशमविधानार्थ[7]निर्वाणनीवृत्तमालाकृतावात्तभक्ते भवारौ ।
> दशबलतनयवर्गाग्रिमेण त्वया नाथ निर्माथिदुःखापहेन स्तुतेन
> प्रचित इति शुभराशिर्महान् यस्ततः स्ताज्जनौघे समृद्धिः समग्रे
> ऽपि सैव ॥ १२१ ॥

प्रविकचकनकपङ्कजसौभाग्यभागङ्गं[8] यस्य । **इन** आदित्यः । **तमःसु** अज्ञानतिमिरविषये तन्नाशार्थम् । **आश्रितेभ्यो**[9] **दत्तमिनत्वं**[10] येन । **त्रिभुवनस्य शमो**[11] (36a) निर्वाणं **तद्विधा-नार्थं निर्वाणनीवृन्नि**वरणं[12] यस्य । तथा **तमालाकृतौ** श्यामे **भवारौ**[13] भगवत्यक्षोभ्ये[14]

---

1. *śrama(ṃ)* Ms. For the restoration, see the following metrical explanation.
2. *viśrāmaṃ* em. Hahn] .. .. Ms.
3. *antyānāṁ trayāṇām* conj. Hahn] *antyā* .. .. *ṇām* Ms.
4. °*śaṅkhādayo ye te* conj. Hahn] °*śaṅkhāda* .. .. .. Ms.
5. *arṇasya* em.] *arṇavasya* Ms., Hahn
6. °*vikacetyādi* conj. Hahn] °*vikace* .. *di* Ms.
7. °*vidhānārtha*° em. Hahn] °*vidhānāya* Edition
8. °*bhāg aṅgaṃ* em. Hahn] °*bhāg āṅgaṃ* Ms.
9. *āśritebhyo* em. Hahn] *āśritabhyo* Ms.
10. *inatvaṃ* em. Hahn] *inantaṃ* Ms.
11. *śamo* conj. Hahn] *śa* .. Ms.
12. *nirvāṇanīvṛn* em. Hahn] *nirvāṇānīvṛn* Ms.
13. *bhavārau* em. Hahn] *bhavādau* Ms.
14. *bhagavaty* em. Hahn] *bhagaty* Ms.

आत्ता भक्तिर्येन स तथा । चतुष्टयमिदमामन्त्रणम् । हे **नाथ** । **दशबलतनयवर्गस्य** बोधिसत्त्वगणस्याग्रिमेणादिमेन । **निर्माथिदुःखापहेन त्वया** । **इति** यथोक्तक्रम**स्तुतेन यो** मया **महान् शुभराशिः प्रचितस्ततः** शुभराशेर्भगवतो[1] या **समृद्धिः सैव जनौघे ऽपि समग्रे स्ताद्भ**वतु ॥

अपरो ऽर्थः । **मित्रपादानां गङ्गदत्त** इति गृहस्थनाम[2] । तत्पितु**र्दशबल** इति । तत्काल एव चैको .. .. णम् । **दशबलतनयवर्गस्याग्रिमेण** ज्येष्ठेन मया **गङ्गदत्तेन** निर्वाणं नयतीति **निर्वाणनीर्वृत्तमालेयं कृता** । इत्यतः **प्रचितो यो महान्शुभराशि**रित्यादि व्याख्यातार्थम्[3] ॥

वृत्तपक्षे **प्रचितो** नाम । **समृद्धिः सैवे**ति यैवान्त्याक्षरत्रयस्य चण्डवृष्टिप्रपाते संतत्या वृद्धिः[4] सैव **प्रचिते** ऽपि । केवलं[5] मध्यलघुत्रय[6].. .. .. इह त्वादिलघुत्रयस्येति भेदः । तत्र चण्डवृष्टिप्रयात[7]प्रचितस्येदमुदाहरणम् । 'अर्णप्रचितादीनामुन्नेयानि[8] यथेष्टं वा नामानि' इति पद्यालंकारः । **समग्रे**[9] .. .. (36b) सर्वत्र दण्डके न त्वत्रैव । तेन वक्ष्यमाणे ऽपि **प्रवृत्ताख्ये प्रचित**वदक्षरत्रयस्य वृद्धौ[10] नामान्तरम् ॥

अहमित्यादि ॥

अहमपि तव पादपद्माभिसंराधनाधीनधीसंनिरुद्धान्तर-
ध्वान्तजातः
समधिगतसमस्तवस्तूत्करव्यापिनैसर्गिकस्वप्नमायामयाद्वैत-
तत्त्वः ।
अकरुणकरुणाबलावार्यवीर्योदयारब्धनानाविधव्यापृतिध्वस्त[11]-

---

[1] *°rāśer bhagavato* conj.] *°rāśe .. .. vato* Ms.; *°rāśe<r bha>vato* Hahn

[2] *gṛhastha°* p.c.] *gṛhasthā°* a.c.

[3] *ityādi vyākhyātārtham* conj. Hahn] *i .. .. .. khyātārtham* Ms.

[4] *vṛddhiḥ* em. Hahn] *vṛrddhiḥ* Ms.

[5] *traya°* added inadvertently in the Ms.

[6] *°traya* conj. Hahn] *°tra(ṃ)ya* Ms.

[7] *°prayāta°* em. Hahn, though not reported] *°prayāt°* Ms.

[8] *unneyāni* em.] *unneyā* Ms., Hahn

[9] *samagre* conj. Hahn] *sama ..* Ms.

[10] *vṛddhau* em. Hahn] *vṛddho* Ms.

[11] *°dhvasta°* em. Hahn] *°vyasta°* Edition

मार-
स्त्रिजगति परमोपकारैककृत्यप्रवृत्तश्चरेयं जनो यावदेको ऽप्य-
मुक्तः ॥ १२२ ॥

न केवलं जनौघे ऽपि सैव समृद्धिः स्ताद**हमपि त्रिभुवनस्य परमोपकार**[1] **एवैकं कृत्यं** तत्र[2] **प्रवृत्तश्चरेयं** जन्मवशितया[3] ताव**द्यावदेको ऽपि सत्त्वो न मुक्त** इत्यार्यमञ्जुश्रिय इव प्रणिधानं विधत्ते । किंभूतश्चरेयम् । **तव पादपद्मयोरभि**[4]**संबोधने**[5] **ऽधीनया धिया सम्यग्निरुद्धमान्तरं ध्वान्तजातं** यस्य । अत एव **सम्यगधिगतं समस्तवस्तु** विसरणशीलमबाधितत्वात्[6] **नैःसर्गिकं**[7] **स्वप्नमायामयमद्वैत**[8] एव ग्राह्यग्राहकाभावादद्वैत[9]**तत्त्वं** येन । **अकरुणेषु** या **करुणा** तस्या **बलं** चा**वार्यवीर्योदयश्च** ता**भ्यामारब्धया नानाविधया व्यापृत्या** चर्यया **ध्वस्ता मारा** येन स तथा[10] । अथवा **अकरुणकरुणाबले**त्यामन्त्रणम्[11] ॥

वृत्तपक्षे **प्रवृत्तो** ऽयं नाम । प्रचिते प्रथमं षड् लघवस्तत आदिलघुकानि त्रिकाणि सप्त । इह गुर्वन्तषल्लघुभ्य आदि[12]लघुत्रयाणि सप्त । वृद्धिरुक्तैव ॥

स्फारेत्यादि ॥

स्फारफुल्लस्थलाम्भोजनिर्भासभृत्पादपीठान्तविश्रान्तकान्तामर-
व्यालदैत्येन्द्रचूलोपलार्चिश्चयो
दुःसहोद्दामदुःखानलग्रस्तपर्यस्तशक्तित्रिलोकीविशोकीक्रिया-
निर्विरामश्रमाश्चर्यचर्यानिधिः ।

---

1 *paramopakāra* conj. Hahn] .. .. .. *pakāra* Ms.

2 *tatra* em. Hahn] *tātra* Ms.

3 °*vaśitayā* em. Hahn] °*vaśitāyā* Ms.

4 °*padmayor abhi*° conj. Hahn] °*padma* .. .. *bhi*° Ms.

5 °*saṃrādhana*° Edition

6 *abādhitatvāt* em. Hahn] *abādhitatvā* Ms.

7 *naiḥsargikaṃ* Ms.] °*naisargika*° Edition, VMST (*'dris pa*)

8 *advaita* conj. Hahn] *a* .. .. Ms.

9 *grāhyagrāhakābhāvād* conj. Hahn] *grāhyabhāvād* Ms.

10 *ta*(*thā*) Ms.

11 *āmantraṇam* em. Hahn] *āmantram* Ms.

12 *ādi*° conj. Hahn] .. *di*° Ms.

शुद्धसंबुद्धवंशावतंसप्रकाशस्फुरत्कीर्तिकीर्णान्तरालप्रसारः
कुमारो जयत्येष वागीश्वरः
सर्वदुर्वारमारप्रवीरध्वजिन्युद्धवध्वंसबद्धाभिरामासमप्रौढि-
निर्व्यूढ[1]गाढप्रतापोदयः ॥ १२३ ॥

सर्वदुर्वारमारप्रवीराणां ध्वजिन्याः सेनाया **उद्धवस्योत्सवस्य ध्वंसे या बद्धा अभिरामासमप्रौढिस्तस्या** (37a) **निर्व्यूढ्या**[2] **गाढो** ऽत्यर्थतीव्रः **प्रतापोदयो** यस्य स एव **वागीश्वरः कुमारो जयति** । किंभूतः । **स्फारफुल्लस्थलाम्भोजस्य निर्भासं** सादृश्यं बिभर्ति **यत्पादपीठं** तस्यान्ते **विश्रान्तः**[3] **कान्तो ऽमरेन्द्रव्याडेन्द्रदैत्येन्द्राणां चूडोपलस्य** चूडारत्नस्या**र्चिश्चयो** यस्य स तथा । **दुःसहोद्दामदुःखानलेन ग्रस्ता** अत एव **पर्यस्ता** व्याकुला **शक्तिर्**यस्याः सा चासौ[4] **त्रिलोकी**[5] च तस्या **विशोकीक्रियायां निर्विरामश्रमत्वादेवाश्चर्या** या[6] चर्या तस्या **निधिः** । **शुद्धसंबुद्धवंशस्यावतंसो**[7] भूषणं तद्वत्**प्रकाशते** या **स्फुरन्ती कीर्ति**स्तया[8] **कीर्णो** व्याप्तो **ऽन्तरालप्रसारो** येनासौ तथा ॥

वृत्तपक्षे द्वादशभिर्मध्यलघुत्रयैरयं **प्रतापोदयो** मन्तव्यः । अन्यत्रास्य मत्तमातङ्गलीलाकर इति नाम[9]। इदमेव लक्ष्यं दृष्टम् । जयदेवेशानरत्नाकरेषु[10] **प्रवृत्तः प्रतापोदयश्च** न स्तः[11] ॥

प्रौढेत्यादि ॥

प्रौढवरवज्रवनिताङ्गपरिरम्भविलसत्पुलकजालकजगज्जयतनुत्रं
सान्त्र[12]सवसास्रमधुपानमदमुक्तविकटाट्टहसितत्रसदशेषसुर-

---

1 *°nirvyūḍhi°* em.] *°nirvyūḍha°* Edition, Hahn

2 *nirvyūḍhyā* em.] *nirvyūrḍhyā* Ms.; *nirvyūḍho* em. Hahn

3 *viśrāntaḥ* conj. Hahn] *viśrā* .. . Ms.

4 *sā cāsau* conj. Hahn] (*sā*) .. *sau* Ms.

5 *trilokī* em. Hahn] *trikokī* Ms.

6 *yā* em. Hahn] *yāḥ* Ms.

7 *°syāvataṁso* em. Hahn] *°svāvataso* Ms.

8 *kīrtis tayā* conj. Hahn] *kī* .. .. *yā* Ms.

9 *nāma* conj. Hahn] .. .. Ms.

10 *°ratnākareṣu* em. Hahn] *°ratnākare* Ms.

11 *na staḥ* em.] *nāsti* Ms., Hahn

12 *sāntra°* em., commentary, VMST (*rgyu mar bcas shing*)] *sāndra°* Edition, Hahn. Both readings can be defended.

दैत्यम् ।
गाढविनिगूढदयविस्मयमयाप्रतिमरौद्रतनुमद्वयमहार्णवनिमग्नं
शुद्धगुणधाम करुणाबलमुदारनवनाट्यरसवल्लितवृत्तमभि-
वन्दे ॥ १२४ ॥

त्वां **करुणाबलमभिवन्दे**[1] । किंभूतम् । **विलसत्पुलकजालकं जगज्जये**[2] **तनुत्रं** संनाहो यस्य । इयता शृङ्गारवीरावुक्तौ । **सान्त्रं वसासहितमस्त्रं**[3] तदेव **मधु** । **तत्पानमदेन**[4] **वि-मुक्तविकटाट्टहसितैस्त्रसदशेषसुरदैत्य**जातं यस्य[5] । (37b) अनेन बीभत्सहास्यभयानकाः । **गाढमत्यर्थं विनिगूढाश्लिष्टा**[6] **दया**[7] **विस्मयमयी** आश्चर्यकरी **अप्रतिमरौद्रा** च **तनुर्यस्य** तम् । अनेन कारुण्यविस्मयरौद्राः । **अद्वयं** ग्राह्यग्राहकादि[8]रहितं तत्त्वम्[9] । तन्मये[10] **महार्णवे निमग्नम्** । तथा **शुद्धानां गुणानां** दशबलादीनां **धाम** स्थानम् । अनेन शान्तः । अत एत[11] **उदारा नव नाट्यरसा** यस्य सन्तीति[12] **मतुप्** । तथाभूतं[13] **ललितं वृत्तं** यस्य । कर्मधारयमत्वर्थीयाद्बहुव्रीहिरेवेष्टव्यो लाघवार्थमित्यस्य समासमत एवाभिमतत्वात् । व्यासवादिमते तु मत्वर्थीयो ऽपि । यथा 'बिसकिसलय[14]च्छेदपाथेयवन्तः' इति ॥

---

1 °*vande* em. Hahn] °*vandya* Ms.

2 °*pulakajālakaṁ jagajjaye* conj. Hahn] °*pulaka .. .. ye* Ms. The restoration is very uncertain because only 3-4 akṣaras seem to be broken off.

3 *vasā*° em. Hahn] *vaśā*° Ms.

4 *tatpāna*° em. Hahn] *tatayāna*° Ms.

5 °*vikaṭāṭṭahasitais trasadaśeṣasuradaityajātam* conj. Hahn] °*vikaṭāṣṭahasitais tad-aśeṣutāra(d)aitya .. ..* Ms. The restoration is very uncertain because 5 to 6 akṣaras seem to be broken off.

6 This is a remarkable explanation of *vinigūḍha*. VMST translates it by *sbyor ba*.

7 *dayā* em. Hahn] *daryadayā* Ms. *darya*° seems to be a wrongly written *dayā* which the copyist forgot to delete.

8 *advayaṁ grāhyagrāhakādi*° conj. Hahn] *a .. .. grāhakādi*° Ms.

9 *tattvam* em. Hahn] *tatve* Ms.

10 *tanmaye* em. Hahn] *tanmayena* Ms.

11 *ata eta* conj.] *ata e* Ms.; *ata* Hahn. —Should we read *ata eva* ?

12 *santīti* conj.] *astīti* Ms., Hahn

13 *matup* | *tathābhūtaṁ* conj. Hahn] *matu . . .. .. bhūtaṁ* Ms.

14 *yathā bisakisalaya*° conj. Hahn] *ya(thā) kisalaya*° Ms.

वृत्तपक्षे **ललितवृत्तं** नाम । अत्रादिगुरुलघुत्रयाणि सप्त गुरुद्वयं च । अस्य लक्षणमीशानेन दर्शितम् ॥ ३० ॥

॥ इति दुष्करप्रभेदवृत्तमाला[1]स्तुतिविवृतौ समवृत्तानि ॥

इदानीं यथोद्देशमर्धसमवृत्तैर्भगवतः स्तुतिमाह । **इद**मित्यादि ॥

इदमर्धमबालशशिप्रभं
बालरविप्रभमादधदर्धम् ।
करुणावशवर्ति भवद्वपुः
कस्य मनो न करोत्युपचित्रम् ॥ १२५ ॥

करुणावशेन वर्तितुं शीलं यस्य तदिदं **भवतो**[2] **वपुः कस्य**चित् द्रष्टु**रुपचित्रं मनो न करोति** । **उपगतं चित्रमा**श्चर्यम् । अत्यादयः क्रान्ताद्यर्थे द्वितीययेति[3] समासः । कथं तथा करोति यस्माद**बालशशिप्रभ**(38a)**मर्ध**[4]**मादधाति** । **बालरविप्रभं**[5] **चार्धम्** । अबालग्रहणेनात्यन्त-धावल्यमुक्तम् । बालग्रहणेन लौहित्यम् । एतच्च नामसंगीतावाम्नायान्तरं द्रष्टव्यम् ॥

वृत्तपक्षे इदं यथोक्तं पूर्वार्धमिदं चापरार्धमादध**दुप**[6]**चित्र**मर्धसमं वृत्तम् । इदमर्धमादधदर्ध-मित्यधिकारो विपरीताख्यानिकां यावत् । यत्र च लिङ्गान्तरं[7] तत्र लिङ्गविपरिणामेन संबन्धनीयम् । अर्धयोरक्षरसाम्ये ऽपि लघुगुरुकृतो भेदः ॥

तत्त्वेत्यादि ॥

तत्त्वसुधारसतृप्तिविशेषात्
सकलसमीहितसिद्धिवशाद्वा ।
त्वच्चरणानुभुवा[8] भवितव्यं
भवमथनश्रुत न द्रुतमध्या ॥ १२६ ॥

---

1 *°vṛttamālā°* conj. Hahn] *°vṛ .. mālā°* Ms.

2 *bhavato* conj. Hahn] *bhava ..* Ms.

3 *dvitīyayeti* em.] *dvitīyeti* Ms., Hahn

4 *°prabham ardhaṃ* conj. Hahn] *°prabha .. ddhaṃ* Ms.

5 *bālaraviprabhaṁ* em.] *bālārāpi prabha* Ms.

6 *aparārdham ādadhad* em. Hahn] *aparordham ādhad* Ms.

7 *liṅgāntaraṁ* em. Hahn] *liṅgāntaṁ* Ms.

8 *°caraṇānubhuvā* em. Hahn] *°caraṇārdhabhuvā* Edition

भवस्य संसारस्य **मथनं श्रुतं** यस्य **भवमथने**[1] वा **श्रुतो** विदितः । तस्यामन्त्रणम् । **त्वच्चरण**माराधा .. .. [2]नो **ऽनुभवति** यस्तेन पुंसा । **नास्ति धीर्यस्य** तथा **न भवितव्यम्** । असुधिय इति निषेधादिह[3] यणादेश एव । कथ**मध्या न भवितव्यं द्रुतं** शीघ्रम् । **तत्त्वसुधा-रसतृप्ति**[4]**विशेषात् सकलसमीहितसिद्धिवशाद्वे**त्युभयसंपदुक्ता । '**त्वच्चरणानु**चरेण[5] न भाव्यं **भवमथनश्रुत न द्रुतमध्ये**[6]' इति पद्यालंकारसूत्रम् । तत्र **अध्या**[7] **त्वच्चरणानु**[8]चरेण न न भाव्यमित्यर्थः ॥

वृत्तपक्षे यथोक्तमिदमर्धमादधती **द्रुतमध्या** ॥

किमित्यादि ॥

किमुशन्ति बुधा अधिकं विभो
यदि जनीय तदीयतनुर्भवेत्[9] ।
तव दृष्टिसुधारसधारया
स्फुरितहाररुचा हरिणप्लुता ॥ १२७ ॥

हे **विभो जनीय** जनेभ्यो हित । **बुधाः**[10] **किमधिकं उशन्ति**[11] कामयन्ते[12] । (38b) न किंचित् । **यदि तव दृष्टिसुधारसधारया स्फुरितहाररुचा**[13] **तदीया**[14] तेषां **तनुर्हरिणी** चासौ

---

1 *bhava°* em. Hahn] *bhavaṃ°* Ms.

2 One or even two letters are broken off. The expression remains unclear.

3 *iti niṣedhād* Ms.] *itiniṣedhād* Hahn

4 *°sudhārasatṛpti°* conj. Hahn] *°sudhā .. .. tṛpti°* Ms.

5 *°caraṇānucareṇa* em. Hahn] *°caraṇānucaraṇena* Ms., unmetrical! There is a mark of deletion above the *ā mātrā* in *°cā(raṇena)*.

6 *°śruta na druta°* em. Hahn] *°śrutamadruta°* Ms.

7 *adhyā* em. Hahn] *adhiyā* Ms.

8 *tvaccaraṇānu°* conj. Hahn] *.. .. .. ṇānu°* Ms.

9 *tadīya°* em. Hahn, commentary (*teṣāṃ*), VMST (*de rnams kyi*)] *tanīya°* Edition

10 *budhāḥ* em. Hahn] *buddhāḥ* Ms.

11 *uśanti* em. Hahn] *usanti* Ms.

12 *kāmayante* conj. Hahn] *kā .. .. ..* Ms.

13 *sphurita°* p.c.] *sphurite* a.c.; *°hārarucā* em. Hahn] *°hārūrucā* Ms.

14 *tadīyā* conj. Hahn

प्लुता चेति तादृशी भवति । हरिणशब्दो ऽत्र शुक्लपर्यायः । हारेणापि हृदि स्फुरता तनुः विमला व्याप्ता[1] च भवति ॥

वृत्तपक्षे **हरिणप्लुता** ॥

इयमित्यादि ॥

इयमुरुकरुणारसा मुखश्रीः
समधिगता निजधीश्रियो रसेन ।
स्फुरदधरदलातिहारिहेमा-
म्बुजकलिकेव विभाति पुष्पिताग्रा ॥ १२८ ॥

तवेति वक्ष्यमाणेनाभिसंबन्धा**दियं**[2] तव **मुखश्रीः पुष्पिताग्रा** विकसितपर्यन्ता । **अतिहारि-हेमाम्बुजकलिकेव**[3] **विभाति** । यतो धर्मदेशनादिना **स्फुरदधरदला** । तथा **उरुकरुणारसा** । बहलकारुण्यमकरन्दा **निजधीश्रियो रसेना**नुरागेण **समधिगता** संबद्धा । **निज**[4]**धी-श्रिये**ति तु यदि पाठः स्यात्स्यादर्थस्य समीचीनता । कनकपङ्कजकलिकाप्युरुरसा श्रियो रसेनानुगता च भवति ॥

वृत्तपक्षे **पुष्पिताग्रा** औपच्छन्दसिका[5]प्रभेदः ॥

मुखमित्यादि ॥

मुखमिदमपरं तवोत्पल-
प्रकररुचामिव भाति संचयः ।
समुदितमिव कैरवश्रिया
हरति मनो ऽपरवक्त्रमीदृशाम् ॥ १२९ ॥

इदं तव दक्षिणं मुखं[6] नीलत्वा**दुत्पलप्रकररुचां संचय इव भाति** । **अपरं** च वाम**वक्त्रं** शुक्ल-त्वात् **कैरवस्य श्रियेव समुदितं**[7] समुत्पन्नमीदृशामतिसुन्दरं **मनो हरति** ॥

वृत्तपक्षे **ऽपरवक्त्रं** वैतालीयप्रभेदः ॥

---

1 *vimalā vyāptā* conj. Hahn] *vi .. .. .. ptā* Ms.

2 *tava* occurs in stanza 129.

3 *°hemāmbujakalikeva* conj. Hahn] *°hemāmbuja .. .. keva* Ms.

4 *nija°* conj. Hahn] *.. ja°* Ms.

5 *aupacchandasikā°* conj. Hahn] *aupacchanda .. ..°* Ms.

6 *dakṣiṇaṁ mukhaṃ* em. Hahn] *dakṣiṇāmukhaṃ* Ms.

7 *samuditaṁ* conj. Hahn] *sa .. ditaṁ* Ms.

इदमित्यादि ॥

इदमर्धसमं समीक्ष्यते ते
बत वृत्तं जयिनो जगत्त्रयस्य ।
क्वचिदर्थविधौ विधूतविश्वा
शिशुलीला ललितापि यत्तवेयम् ॥ १३० ॥

तव जगत्त्रयजयिन[1] **इयं ललितापि शिशुलीला यद्य**(39a)स्मात्[2] । **क्वचिदर्थविधौ** पर[3]-प्रयोजनसंपादननिमित्तं **विधूतविश्वा** रूपान्तरेण कम्पितजगत्त्रया भवति । अत **इदं वृत्त-मर्धसमं** यस्य तथा **समीक्ष्यते** । **बत**शब्द आश्चर्ये[4] ॥

वृत्तपक्षे **शिशुलीला** ॥

पदमित्यादि ॥

पदमेकमवेक्ष्य ते क्षणं
प्रसभाक्रान्तजगत्त्रयीशिखम् ।
कथमस्तु न विश्वभारती
निजदासीव तव प्रियंवदा ॥ १३१ ॥

क्षणमेकस्मिन् क्षणे **प्रसभं** हठात्[5] । **आक्रान्ता जगत्त्रय्याः शिखा** शिखरं ब्रह्माण्डं येन तादृशं **ते** तव **पदमवेक्ष्य** जितस्य[6] एकपादतलाक्रान्तरूपस्य **विश्वस्य भारती निजदासीव प्रियंवदा न कथमस्तु** । भवत्येव । सापेक्षत्वे ऽपि गमकत्वात्समासः । त्रिविक्रमस्या-प्युक्तरूपं[7] पदमेकमवलोक्य सरस्वती चतुरानना नलिनवनराजहंसी[8] दासीव[9] प्रियंवदा संवृत्ता ॥

---

[1] *°jayina* em. Hahn] *°japina* Ms.

[2] *yady asmāt* conj. Hahn] *ya .. smāt* Ms.

[3] *para°* em. Hahn] *prara°* Ms.

[4] *āścarye* conj. Hahn] *ā .. rye* Ms.

[5] *prasabhaṁ* em. Hahn] *prabhavaṃ* Ms. The paraphrase *haṭhāt* supports *prasabha°*, the reading of the edition.

[6] *jitasya* conj. Hahn] *.. tasya* Ms.

[7] *uktarūpaṁ* conj. Hahn] *ukta .. paṁ* Ms.

[8] *nalina°* em. Hahn] *nanalina°* Ms.

[9] *dāsīva* em. Hahn, though not reported] *dāśīva* Ms.

वृत्तपक्षे **प्रियंवदा** । वैतालीयप्रभेदः ॥

स्वरसेत्यादि[1] ॥

स्वरसोपनतां शमशय्यां
किं नु[2] विधूय धियो ऽप्यतिदुर्गैः ।
अतिचित्रचरित्रशतैस्ते
वेगवती करुणा यदि न स्यात् ॥ १३२ ॥

यदि ते तव **करुणा वेगवती** दुःखार्ते जगति विश्वगाणुप्रचारा **न भवे**त्तदा **शम**[3] एव **शय्या** शमे वा शयनम् । तां **स्वरसोपनतां विधूय**[4] **अतिचित्रचरित्र**[5]**शतैस्ते किम्** । प्रयोजनं नास्तीत्यर्थः । किंभूतैः । **धियो ऽप्यतिदुर्गैः** । मनोरथस्याप्यविषयैः[6] ।

वृत्तपक्षे **वेगवती** नाम ॥

सर्वेत्यादि ॥

सर्वातिशयस्य धाम धाम्नः
सर्वाङ्गीणसुलक्ष्यलक्षणश्रीः ।
लोकस्य गतापि हि स्मृतिं ते
भद्रं भद्रविराङ्तनुस्तनोति ॥ १३३ ॥

भद्रेण विराज(39b)त[7] इति **भद्रविराट्** तव **तनुः** सर्वस्य **लोकस्य स्मृतिं गतापि** स्मरण-विषयभूतापि न केवलमेवंभूता[8] **भद्रं तनोति** । किंभूता । **हि**शब्दो भिन्नक्रमे यस्मात् । **सर्वातिशयस्य**[9] **धाम्न**स्तेजसो **धाम**[10] । तथा **सर्वाङ्गीणा** सर्वावयवव्यापिका[1] **सुलक्ष्या**[2] सुव्यक्ता **लक्षणानां श्रीः** संपत्तिर्यस्याः ॥

---

1 *svarasetyādi* conj. Hahn] *svara .. .. di* Ms.

2 *kiṃ tu* Edition

3 *śama* em. Hahn] *sama* Ms.

4 *vidhūya* em. Hahn] *vidhūpa* Ms.

5 *aticitracaritra°* conj. Hahn] *ati .. .. caritra°* Ms.

6 *°rathasyāpy-* em. Hahn] *°rathasāpy-* Ms.

7 *virājata* conj. Hahn] *.. .. .. ta* Ms.

8 *kevalam evaṁ°* em. Hahn] *kevam eva°* Ms.

9 *sarvātiśayasya* conj. Hahn] *sarvā .. ..* Ms.

10 *dhāma* em. Hahn, VMST (*gnas*)] *nāma* Ms.

वृत्तपक्षे **भद्रविराट्** ॥

परित[3] इत्यादि ॥

> परितः स्फुरद्भिरभिरामै-
> रंशुमयैः परार्थपरमार्थैः ।
> पविपद्मखड्गमणिचक्रैः
> केतुमती विभाति तव मूर्तिः ॥ १३४ ॥

परार्थ[4] एव **परमो ऽर्थः** प्रयोजनं येषां तैः । **पविपद्मखड्गमणिचक्रै**रक्षोभ्यामिताभामोघसिद्धिरत्नसंभववैरोचनचिह्नैः **केतुमती तव कीर्तिः**[5] पञ्चात्मिकसमाजमण्डले **विभाति** । किंभूतैः । **परित** इत्यादि सुगमम् ॥

वृत्तपक्षे **केतुमती** । 'केतुमती स्वरेषु चरमे ऽङ्गे' इति पद्यालंकारसूत्रादत्र प्रथमे पादे रसेषु चरमे[6] स्वरेषु यतिरिष्टा । अन्यैस्तु ते यती न दर्शिते ॥

चैत्तेत्यादि ॥

> चैत्तमात्र[7]भावभाजि[8] भाव्यते क्व
> परा परार्थसंपदीदृशी दयायाम् ।
> सेयमेतदाकृतिच्छलादतो ऽव-
> यवध्वनेर्मतुप्स्त्रिया समाभिधाना ॥ १३५ ॥

चित्तस्य विशेषावस्था **चैत्तम्** । तदेव तन्**मात्रम्** । तद्**भाव**स्तत्त्वम् । तद्**भाजि** चैत्तस्वभावायां **दयायां** दयाविषये **ईदृशी** सर्वाकारप्रवृत्ता **परा परार्थसंपत् क्व संभाव्यते** । तस्या अमूर्तत्वेन तादृक्परार्थसंपादनासामर्थ्यात्[9] । **अतः सेयं** दयैषोक्त(40a)लक्षणा या भगवदाकृतिस्तदेव **च्छलं** ततः । **अवयवध्वने**रवयवशब्दान्**मतुप्** । स एव **स्त्री** । स्त्रीप्रत्ययान्ता-

---

1 °*vyāpikā* em. Hahn, VMST (*kun khyab*)] °*vyāyikā* Ms.

2 *sulakṣyā* em. Hahn] *sulakṣā* Ms.

3 *parita* em. Hahn] *parata* Ms.

4 *parārtha* conj. Hahn] *pa .. rtha* Ms.

5 Hahn suggests in a footnote: Read *mūrtiḥ*, in accordance with VMST (*sku*).

6 *carame* conj. Hahn] *ca .. me* Ms.

7 °*mātra*° em. Hahn, commentary, VMST (*tsam gyis*)] °*śobhi*° Edition

8 °*bhāji* em. Hahn, commentary, VMST (*bsten pa'i*)] °*bhāvi* Edition

9 °*saṁpādanā*° em. Hahn] °*saṁpadanā*° Ms.

वस्थापरिग्रहात् । **तया** अनुकरणमात्ररूपया **सममभिधानं** यस्या अनुकार्यरूपायाः । अवयववतीत्यर्थः ॥

वृत्तपक्षे **यवध्वनेर्मतुप्स्त्रिया समाभिधाना यवमती** । मादुपधायाश्च[1] मतोर्वो ऽयवादिभ्य इति यवादिप्रतिषेधात् वत्वाभावः । ऋजुना क्रमेण संज्ञाप्रवेशो न निर्वहतीति[2] पूर्वेषामेवैष वाक्यविन्यासः । अत इहैवोद्धार्यशब्दरूपवैषम्ये ऽपि श्लेषो ऽभिमतः । तत्र प्रियंवदावेगवती[3]भद्रविराड्केतुमतीनां प्रत्येकमयुक्पादौ दशाक्षरौ युक्पादावेकादशाक्षरौ । द्रुतमध्याहरिणप्लुतापरवक्त्रशिशुलीलानामयुक्पादौ एकादशाक्षरौ[4] युक्पादौ द्वादशाक्षरौ । पुष्पिताग्रायवमत्योरयुक्पादौ[5] द्वादशाक्षरौ युक्पादौ त्रयोदशाक्षराविति द्रष्टव्यम् ॥

उदयदित्यादि ॥

> उदयदरुणकिरणनिकरपरिकर-
> कनकमयविमलहिमकरजयनी ।
> जयति निखिलजगदभिरुचि[6]कृतिपटु-
> रतिभव तव तनुरियमतिरुचिरा ॥ १३६ ॥

हे **अतिभव तव**[7] **तनुरियमतिरुचिरा** सती **निखिलजगदभिरुचिकृतौ पटुर्जयति** । रुचिरत्वमेव कृतिः[8] । **उदयंश्चासौ**[9] **अरुणकिरणपरिकरो** यः **कनकमयः** कनक(40b)विकारः[10] **हिमकरश्च**[11] तयो**र्जयनी** वर्णाह्लादकारित्वाभ्याम् ।

---

1 *upadhāyāś* em. Hahn] *upadhāc* Ms.

2 *na nirvahatīti* em. Hahn] *narnivahatīti* Ms.

3 *°vegavatī°* conj. Hahn] *°vega .. tī°* Ms.

4 *°daśākṣarau* conj. Hahn, though not reported] *°da .. kṣarau* Ms.

5 *°matyor ayuk°* em. Hahn] *°matyo yuk°* Ms.

6 *°abhiruci°* em. Hahn, commentary] *°abhirati°* Edition. VMST has *mṅon par dga bar byed la*, which can translate both words.

7 *tava* conj. Hahn] *.. va* Ms.

8 *ruciratvam eva kṛtiḥ* em. Hahn] *rucirātvam eva kṛtaḥ* Ms. Unclear!

9 *sāyam* Ms. adds inadvertently.

10 *kanakavikāraḥ* conj. Hahn] *ka .. .. vikāraḥ* Ms.

11 *udayaṃś cāsau [sāyam] aruṇakiraṇa<nikara>parikara<ś ca> yaḥ kanakamayaḥ ka<naka>(40b)vikāraḥ <sūryaś ca vimala>himakaraś ca* Hahn. The reconstruction suggested by Hahn is not mandatory since the Ms. makes good sense, if we just take out the word *sāyam*.

वृत्तपक्षे **ऽतिरुचिरा** । अर्धार्धे[1] इति एकत्रिंशदक्षरमखण्डमेवार्धम् । अर्धेन युक्तमर्धमर्धार्धं तस्मिन् सति । द्विवचनान्तत्वे तु एकशेषः स्यात् । अविहित[2]चरणविभागत्वेनेय**मति-रुचिरा**[3] परमते ऽर्धद्वयेनैव वेदितव्येत्यर्थः । एतन्मते तु प्रथमः पादः षोडशाक्षरो द्वितीयः पञ्चदशाक्षर इति चतुष्पदीय**मति**[4]**रुचिरा** । तथा च पद्यालंकारसूत्रम् 'अचलधृतिरथ तिथिरपरमत इति यमविरतचरणयतिरतिरुचिरा[5]' इति ॥

त्रिभुवनेत्यादि ॥

त्रिभुवनदुरधिगमचरणपरिचरणगुरुविभवभगवदसितसुगत-
प्रतिकृतिसचिवविमलमणिनिचयखचितसुपरिघटनगुण-
वसतिः ।
निज[6]नयगदनरवलयलवसमनुकृतिरसिकनिभसुरभिसुरसुमनः-
परिमलमिलदलिकुलकणितनिधिरधिगमजलद जयति तव
शिखा ॥ १३७ ॥

हे **अधिगमजलद**[7] । **तव शिखा** चूडा **जयति** । कीदृशी । **त्रिभुवनेन दुरधिगमं** त्वदेक-लभ्यत्वात् । **चरणपरिचरणं** यस्य । अत एव **गुरुविभवः** । तादृशस्या**सितसुगतस्या**क्षोभ्यस्य[8] या **प्रतिकृति**र्निर्माणकायः[9] । तस्याः **सचिवानां** तादृशानां **विमलमणीनां नि-चयेन**[10] **खचितत्वात् सुपरिघटन**लक्षणस्य **वसतिः** । तथा **निजनयस्य** बोधि[11]सत्त्वनीतेर्यो **गदनरव**स्तस्य **लयो** ऽनुत्कटता तस्य **लवः** । तत्**समनुकृतौ रसिकनिभं** रसिकप्रायं च[12]

---

1 *vṛttapakṣe 'tirucirā* conj. Hahn

2 *syāt | avihita°* conj. Hahn] *(syā) . ..vihita°* Ms.

3 *°tveneyam* em. Hahn] *°tvaneyam* Ms.

4 *catuṣpa(dī)yam ati°* Ms.

5 *°yatir* em. Hahn] *°viratir* Ms., which has one syllable in excess.

6 *nija°* em. Hahn, VMST (*rang gi*)] *jina°* Edition

7 *°jalada* conj. Hahn] *°ja .. da* Ms.

8 *akṣobhyasya* conj. Hahn] *akṣobhya ..* Ms.

9 *nirmāṇa°* em. Hahn] *nirvāṇa°* Ms.

10 *nicayena* em. Hahn, though not reported] *nicāyena* Ms.

11 *(bo)dhi°* Ms.

12 *°prāyañ* em. Hahn] *°prāpañ* Ms.

तत् । **सुरसुरभिसुमनसां**[1] तदापीडचूडानाम् । **परिमलेन मि**(41a)**लदलिकुलं** च तस्य यत् **क्वणितं** गुञ्जितं **तन्निधिः** ॥

वृत्तपक्षे **शिखा** । तत्रायुक्पादयोः प्रत्येकं त्रिंशल्लघूनि गुर्वन्ते । युक्पादयोरष्टाविंशल्लघूनि गुरु चान्ते ॥

समुदयेत्यादि ॥

समुदयदिशि समुपनतरुचिषु विविधसमुदयकरणमभिदधती
प्रशमसुखरसरसिकमतिषु निरुपमशमसुखपथकथनपृथुनिरतिः
।
अपरिमितसुकृतफलमधिप तव जयति सकलजिनननयनयनगी-
र्ऋजुमतिषु नियतमृजुरमृतकुट कुटिलमतिषु निरतिशयकुटिल
पदा ॥ १३८ ॥

हे **अधिप** । **अमृतकुट** प्रवचनाश्रय । **जिननयस्य** प्रकाशकत्वान्**नयनभू**ता **तव गीर्जयति** । **जिननयनयने**[2]त्यामन्त्रणपदं वा । किंभूता । **समुदय** एव **दिक्** पुरुषार्थैकदेशत्वात् । तत्र **समुपनतरुचिषु**[3] विनेयेषु **विविधं समुदयस्य करण**मुपाय**मभिदधती प्रशमसुख**लक्षणे **रसे**[4] **रसिकमतिषु निरुपमस्य शमसुखपथस्य कथने पृथुनिरति**स्तत्परता यस्याः सा **तथा** । **अपरिमितस्य सुकृतस्य** पुण्यज्ञानसंभारस्य **फलं** निष्यन्दभूता । पुनः कीदृशी । **ऋजु-मतिषु** सत्त्वेषु **नियतमृजु**रवक्रपदा **कुटिलमतिषु** तु **निरतिशयकुटिलपदा** ॥

वृत्तपक्षे **कुटिलपदा** । परेषां खञ्जेति मुख्यं नाम कुटिलपदाघु[5]क्त्या व्याख्यायते । तद्विपर्यय इति ।[6] शिखाया विपर्ययः । तेन तत्र[7] यौ[8] युक्पादौ ताविहा(41b)युक्पादौ[1] यौ चायुक्पादौ तौ युक्पादौ ॥

---

1 Is this a mistake for *surabhisurasumanasāṁ°*? The reading of the edition is meaningful and supported by the Tibetan translation: *lha yi me to dri bzaṅ po.*

2 *jinanayanayanety ā~* em.] *jinanayety ā~* Ms., Hahn

3 *samupanataruciṣu* em. Hahn] *samuparuciṣu* Ms.

4 *rase* conj. Hahn

5 The unclear letter looks like *ghu.*

6 Something seems to be missing before this sentence.

7 *tatra* em. Hahn] *tra* Ms.

8 *yau* em. Hahn, though not recorded] *yo* Ms.

आख्यनिकेत्यादि ॥

आख्यानिकेयं भवतो गुणाना-
मिति स्तुवंस्त्वामभिमन्यते यः ।
नूनं स गण्डूषजलोपयोगान्
मया निपीतो ऽम्बुधिरित्यवेति ॥ १३९ ॥

त्वां स्तुवन् भूतगुणैरभिव्याहरन्[2] **भवतो गुणानामियमाख्यानिका**[3] सामस्त्येनाख्यान**मिति**[4] **यो** महान् **मन्यते**[5] । **नून**मित्यादि सुबोधम् ॥

वृत्तपक्षे **आख्यानिका** ॥

यद्याख्यानिका न भवति किं तर्हि भवतीत्याह । **अपि त्वि**त्यादि ॥

अपि त्वशेषस्मरवैरिणाम-
प्याख्येयताख्यातिमनाश्रितेषु ।
गुणेषु ते नाथ वृथाभिमान-
स्याख्यानिकासौ विपरीतपूर्वा ॥ १४० ॥

किं तु[6] हे **नाथ** । **अशेषाणां स्मरवैरिणां** बुद्धाना**माख्येयताख्यातिं** निर्वचनीयताव्यपदेश[7]-**मनाश्रितेषु गुणेषु** या **आख्यानिकासौ वृथाभिमानस्य** मिथ्याभिमानिनो जनस्य **विपरीत-पूर्वा आख्यानिका** । अनाख्याने ऽप्याख्यानाभिमानात् ॥

---

1 *ihāyukpādau* em.] *ihāyuyukpādau* Ms.

2 °*vyāharan* em. Hahn, though not reported] °*vyāharaṇ* Ms.

3 *iyam* em. Hahn] *imam* Ms.

4 *iti* em. Hahn] *itita* Ms.

5 *manya(te)* Ms.

6 A remarkable paraphrase of *api tu*.

7 *ākhyeyatākhyātiṁ nirvacanīyatā°* em. Hahn, VMST (*brjod bya~*)] *akhyeyatā-khyātir nivacanīyatā | vyapadeśam* Ms.

वृत्तपक्षे **आख्यानिका विपरीतपूर्वा**[1] । आख्यानिकाद्वयमुपजातिप्रभेदः । चतुर्दशप्रकारासूपजातिषु द्वे अर्धसमे अन्या विषमाः । तत्रार्धसमे **आख्यानिकाविपरीताख्यानिका**ख्ये । एते च पद्यालंकारे उपजातिप्रस्ताव एव दर्शिते इति[2] ॥

॥ इति दुष्करप्रभेदवृत्तमालाविवृतावर्धसमवृत्तानि ॥

संप्रति यथोद्देशं विषम(42a)वृत्तौ भगवन्तं स्तौति । **अष्टाभि**रित्यादि ॥

अष्टाभिरक्षरैः पादो
ऽसोढस्तद्गाढमज्जनादनुवृद्धैः ।
गुणसागर सागरैरपूरिताङ्गुरीगर्तो
विषमं दशान्तरे दयां पदचतुरूर्ध्वं नयति भावम् ॥ १४१ ॥

हे **गुणसागर दशान्तरे** वज्रभैरवादिदशायाम्[3] । **न पूरितो ऽङ्गुरीणां गर्तो** यस्य स तव **पादो ऽसोढः** सोढुमशक्यः । जातावेकवचनम् । पादा इत्यर्थः । कैः । **अक्षरै**रशोष्यै**रष्टाभिः**[4] **सागरैः** । किंभूतैः[5] । **तस्य** पादस्य **गाढमज्जनादनुवृद्धै**रपि सुमेरुपरिवेष्टिकाः सप्त बाह्यश्च महोदधिरित्यष्टौ सागरा[6] इति **विषमं** रूपं **दयां** तव **भाव**मभिप्रायं **नयति** प्रापयति । किंभूतम् । **पादाश्चत्वार ऊर्ध्वा** यत्र ॥

वृत्तपक्षे **पदचतुरूर्ध्वं** नाम **विषमं** वृत्तम् । तत्र प्रथमः पादो ऽष्टभिरक्षरैः । इत ऊर्ध्वमपरे पादाः सागरैश्चतुर्भिरक्षरैरनुक्रमेण वृद्धैर्ज्ञेयाः ॥

इतीत्यादि ॥

इति निगदितजातौ
कृतविषमचरणरचनायाम् ।
लघुगुरुनियतिभृति भयमयति को न
भवसि न यदि नियतमभिविधिवचनमनु पीडः ॥ १४२ ॥

---

1 *vṛttapakṣe ākhyānikā viparītapūrvā* conj. Hahn

2 *iti* em. Hahn] *ti* Ms.

3 *°daśāyāṃ* em. Hahn] *°daśānāṃ* Ms.

4 *aśoṣyair* em. Hahn] *aśeṣair* Ms.

5 *kiṃbhūtaiḥ* em. Hahn] *kiṃbhūte* Ms.

6 *sāgarā(ḥ)* Ms.

इत्यनन्तरोक्तप्रकारेण **निगदितायां जातौ** स्वभावविषमे तव **को न भयमयति** गच्छति । कीदृश्याम् । **कृतविषमचरणरचनायाम्** । विहितोर्ध्वाधःपादविन्यासायाम् । पुनः कीदृशि । **लघुगुरुनियतिभृति** । विनेया[1]नुरोधात् क्वचिल्लाघवं च क्वचिद्गौरवं च बिभ्रत्याम् । इह तु गौरवमेवाभिप्रेतम् । सर्व एव भयमासादयति **यदि** त्वं **नियतमभिविधिवचनमनु पीडो न भवसि** । अभिविधिवच(42b)नमाङ्[2] । तमनु तेन सह पीड **आपीडः** । समन्ताद्दयावान् यदि न भवसीत्यर्थः ॥

वृत्तपक्षे निगदितायां पदचतुरूर्ध्वजातौ[3] कृतविषमचरणरचनायामेतच्छ्लोकप्रस्तारक्रमेण लघुगुरुनियमं दधत्यां सत्याम् । अभिविधिवचनमनु पीडो व्याख्यातार्थः । अत्रान्तिम-द्वयद्वयं[4] गुरु शेषं लघु । पद्यालंकारे तु पदचतुरूर्ध्वमनियत् (?) पाठसौभाग्याभावाद-स्मात् पृथक् दर्शितम् । इह तु पूर्वाम्नायानुसारेणोक्तम् ॥

सुचिरेत्यादि ॥

> सुचिरनिहितहितमति[5]कन्दा-
> ङ्कुर इव तव भाति ।
> विषमजनदमनघटितविकटमूर्ते-
> स्त्रिपुरहरमुकुटमणिसदृशदशनकलिकेयम् ॥ १४३ ॥

विषमजनदमनी घटिता विकटा मूर्तिर्येन तस्य **तव** । **त्रिपुरहरस्य** महेश्वरस्य **मुकुटमणिः** शशिकला तत्**सदृशी दशनकलिकेयं भाति** । अत्रापीडप्रथमपादस्य द्वितीयत्वं द्वितीयस्य प्रथमत्वम् । शेषं पूर्ववत् ॥

प्रसरदित्यादि ॥

> प्रसरदुरुदहनघनघोर-
> च्छटमिव गगनतलमनवधि दधाना ।
> प्रसभमभिमुखं ते
> प्रशमयति शमनमपि नयनवलनलवलीला ॥ १४४ ॥

---

1 *vineyā°* em. Hahn] *vineye°* Ms.

2 *°vidhiva(ca)nam āṅ* Ms. — Hahn suggests in a footnote: Read *abhividhivacana āṅ*?

3 *°ūrdhva°* em. Hahn] *°ūrdhvaṃ°* Ms.

4 *atrāntimadvayadvayaṃ* Ms.] *atrāntimadvayaṃ* Hahn

5 One expects rather *sucirahitanihitamati°*.

ते तवानन्तरोक्तरूपस्य **नयनस्य** यो **वलनलवो** मनागावर्जनं तस्य **लीलाप्रसभमभिमुखागतं** **शमनमपि** यममपि **प्रशमयति** । किंकुर्वाणा । **प्रसरन्ती**[1] **उरुदहनस्य घनत्वात् घोरा च्छटा** यस्मिंस्तादृश**मनवधि गगनं** कटाक्षज्वालाजटिलत्वा**द्दधाना** ।

वृत्तपक्षे **लवली** । इहाप्यापीडप्रथमपादस्य तृतीयत्वम् । शेषं प्राग्वत् ॥

(43a) **मृद्वित्यादि** ॥

मृदुजनमनु पुनरियमेव
प्रशमितसकलकटुकलुषविषराशिः ।
प्रतिमुहुरभिनवमतुलसुखनिधिमुपनयन्ती
नियतममृतधारा ॥ १४५ ॥

प्रशमितसकलकटुकलुषविषराशिरियमेव तव नयनवलनलवलीला । **मृदुजनं पुन**र्लक्ष्यीकृत्य[2] **नियतममृतस्य धारेव** । किं कुर्वती । **प्रतिमुहुः** पुन**रभिनवमतुलं सुखस्य निधि**माश्रय**मुपनयन्ती** । यथा विनेयाशयं[3] करुणया निर्माणवैचित्र्यात्[4] ॥

वृत्तपक्षे आपीडप्रथमपादस्यैव[5] चतुर्थत्वे ऽमृत[6]धारा ॥

॥ **पदचतुरूर्ध्वप्रभेदाः** ॥

तडिदित्यादि[7] ॥

तडितोज्ज्वलं जलदराशि-
मनिशमुदभारबन्धुरम् ।
घोरघनरसितमीश तनुः
कृपया कुतो ऽपि जयतीयमुद्गता ॥ १४६ ॥

---

1 *prasarantī* em. Hahn] *praśarantī* Ms.

2 *lakṣyī°* em. Hahn] *lakṣī°* Ms.

3 *vineyāśayaṃ* em. Hahn] *vinopāśayaṃ* Ms.

4 *°vaicitryāt* em. Hahn] *°vaitryāta* Ms.

5 *°prathamapādasyaiva* em. Hahn] *°prathamasyaiva* Ms.

6 *caturthatve 'mṛta°* em. Hahn] *caturthe 'mṛta°* Ms.

7 *taḍid ityādi* em. Hahn] *taḍ ityādi* Ms.

हे **ईश इयं** तवानन्तरोदितरूपा **तनुः कृपया**[1] कयाप्यनिर्वचनीयया[2] **निशमुद्धता जलदराशिं जयति** । कीदृशम् । **उज्ज्वलं तडिता** । तथा **उदकस्य भारो** राशिः । भारे उदकस्योद्भावः । तेन **बन्धुरं** नम्रम् । **घोरघनरसितं** च । एभिरुपमान[3]गतैर्विशेषणैरुपमेयस्य भगवतो यथासंख्यं प्रहरणकिरणैरौज्ज्वल्यं श्यामत्व[4] पीनत्वे प्रचण्डनिबिडाट्टहसितं च ध्वनितम् ॥

वृत्तपक्षे उद्गता । अत्र प्रथमद्वितीयपादौ प्रत्येकं दशाक्षरौ । तृतीयचतुर्थावेकादशत्रयोदशाक्षरौ[5] । गुरुलघुनियमः प्रतिरूपप्रस्तारादवधार्यः ॥

अत इत्यादि ॥

अत एव दुष्करतराणि
विलसितशतानि तन्वतः ।
ह्लादयत्यखिललोकमिदं
पटुकीर्तिसौरभकमद्भुतं तव ॥ १४७ ॥

अत एव करुणावशादेव अन्येषां **दुष्करतराणि**[6] **विलसितशतानि तन्वतस्तव** । **पटु** स्फुटं **कीर्ते**(43b)**रिदम**[7]**द्भुतं सौरभकं** सौन्दर्यं परिमलो वा**खिलं लोकमाह्लादयति** । यशो हि शुभ्रं सुगन्धि चेति कविसमयः ।

सुगन्धयद्दिशः शुक्लमम्लानकुसुमं दिवः ।
भूरि तत्रापतत्तस्मादुत्पपात[8] दिवं यशः ॥

इति च माघः ॥

वृत्तपक्षे उद्गताया एव तृतीयपादस्यान्यथात्वे यथादर्शिते **सौरभकम्** ॥

भृकुटीत्यादि ॥

---

1 *kṛpayā* conj. Hahn

2 *anirvacanīyayā* em. Hahn] *anirvacayā* Ms.

3 *upamāna°* em. Hahn] *upamāṇa°* Ms.

4 *(śyā)matva°* Ms.

5 *°daśākṣarau* conj. Hahn] *°daśākṣa* .. Ms.

6 *°tarāṇi* em. Hahn] *°rāśi* Ms.

7 *kīrter* conj. Hahn] .. .. *r* Ms.

8 *apatat tasmād* conj. Hahn, though not reported] *apata* .. *smād* Ms.

भृकुटीकटाक्षदशनेषु
किमपि विकृतानि बिभ्रतः ।
दमयति तव भुवनानि वपु-
र्ललितं च किं तु विकटं यदीदृशम् ॥ १४८ ॥

ललितं च मनोहरमपि **तव वपुर्भुवनानि दमयति** । ननु भयानकस्य भुवनदमनं युज्यत इत्याह । **किं तु भृकुटीकटाक्षेण** युक्तेषु **दशनेषु विकृतानि** । संबन्धिभेदाद्बहुवचनम् । **किमपी**ति क्रियाविशेषणम् । **बिभ्रतस्तव यदीदृशमतो विकटम्** ॥

वृत्तपक्षे उद्गताया एव तृतीयपादस्य यथादर्शितमन्यथात्वे **ललितं** नाम पूर्वेषां किं तु यदीदृशमतो नाम्ना **विकटं** युज्यते ॥

॥ **उद्गताभेदाः** ॥

प्राग्भारेत्यादि ॥

प्राग्भारातिशये ऽपि तादृशे ऽद्भुतभीमे
भुवनाहितहतये समं समन्तात् ।
मरुदनतिशयरयः
प्रचुपितमपि तव न समेति सलीलम् ॥ १४९ ॥

प्राग्भारः सुमेर्वादिपर्वतावनतशिखरभागस्त**स्यातिशयः** पर्यन्त**स्तादृशे ऽप्य**तिदुर्गत्वाद-**द्भुतभीमे समन्तात्** सर्वतो दिक्षु **समं** तुल्यकालं **भुवनानामहितहतये** यत्तव **सलीलं प्रचुपितं** मन्दगमनं तद**पि** । **अनतिशयरयो** महावेगो ऽपि **मरुन्न**[1] (44a) **समेति**[2] ।[3]

किं भूयो भगवन्भवन्तमाश्रयमाप्तः
स्थिरभार[4]मतुलमार्षभं दधानम् ।
तच्छुद्धविराड्विशेषणं ह्य-
परविषमशिरसि पदं विनिधत्ते ॥ १५० ॥

---

1 *marun* em. Hahn] *maran* Ms.

2 *sameti* conj. Hahn] .. .. .. Ms.

3 The last folio of the manuscript is missing.

4 *sthirabhāram* em. Hahn] *sthitabhāvam* Edition; *rlabs po che'i gnas* VMST

आराध्येति भवन्तमाशयैकसमृद्ध्या[1]
कुशलं यदमलमस्ति वर्धमानम् ।
तदिदमखिलमुदञ्चतु भुवनमुरुपदं
त्वदभिमतमतिविविधवृत्तविशेषैः ॥ १५१ ॥

अपि च प्रचयेन भूयसा
कुशलस्यास्य निकामनिर्मलस्य ।
विगलतु सकलस्य देहिनो
भवरजनीप्रभवान्धकारराशिः ॥ १५२ ॥

॥ **सर्वविषमाणि** ॥

किं च प्रौढप्रज्ञाप्रेय-
स्यालिङ्गेनानङ्गक्रीडम् ।
उडुपतिरुचिरनिचयमयमिववपु-
रनतिशयकरुणमिह[2] वहदनुभवतु ॥ १५३ ॥

॥ **अर्धविषमम्** ॥

विचित्रवृत्तैरितिवर्णनेन
यदाचितं चन्द्रकरामलं शुभम् ।
ततो ऽस्तु लोकः परिमुक्तशोकः
स्फुरन्महासौख्यशिखासखीवरः ॥ १५४ ॥

॥ **पादविषमम्** ॥

॥ **आर्यमञ्जुघोषस्य दुष्करप्रभेदा वृत्तमालास्तुतिः समाप्ता** ॥

॥ **कृतिरियं महापण्डितस्थविरज्ञानश्रीमित्रस्य** ॥

---

1 *āśayaika°* em. Hahn, VMST (*bsam pa gcig pa ~*)] *āśrayaika°* Edition

2 *anatiśaya°* em. Hahn] *aniratiśaya°* Edition. The line still has one syllable in excess.

Index of Verses

विश्वचक्रवर्तिनां जिनानाम् ॥ ३३ ॥

विश्वहितैकासङ्गसहान्तःकरणकरण वसुपदमिव परमम् ॥ ११६ ॥

वृणे वरमिमं त्वदेकमतुल- ॥ ६६ ॥

वृत्तं सममर्धसमम् ॥ १ ॥

वृत्तमेतदशेषबुद्धकुलाकलङ्ककलानिधेः ॥ १०३ ॥

व्याप्तविश्वया शरन्नभस्तलातिशुद्धया धियाधियात ॥ १०९ ॥

व्योमविकीर्णकीर्तिमदपरिमलकलना- ॥ ९१ ॥

शरदमृतकरकरश्रेणी- ॥ ३८ ॥

शोभासंपत्तिः शिरसि गुरुणैकेन सैवोपजाता ॥ १०२ ॥

श्रीनिकेत लीलाचतुरं ते ॥ २८ ॥

श्रेयःसंभोगं विषयविरतिमव्यग्राम् ॥ ७९ ॥

संपूर्णो ऽन्तर्गुणगणरत्नैश्चित्रै- ॥ ५६ ॥

संमुखवलन्मुखमृगाधिपतिपृष्ठा- ॥ ७६ ॥

समाश्रय- ॥ ८ ॥

समुदयदिशि समुपनतरुचिषु विविधसमुदयकरणमभिदधती ॥ १३८ ॥

सर्वातिशयस्य धाम धाम्नः ॥ १३३ ॥

सर्वातिशायिगुणनिर्भरलब्धमोदैः ॥ ७५ ॥

साधिगमं समकालम् ॥ २२ ॥

सुखदुःखातिशयादिहेतुजातैः ॥ ६८ ॥

सुचिरनिहितहितमतिकन्दा- ॥ १४३ ॥

स्फारफुल्लस्थलाम्भोजनिर्भासभृत्पादपीठान्तविश्रान्तकान्तामरव्याल- ॥ १२३ ॥

स्फारामोदा मधुनिधिरधिकम् ॥ ४० ॥

स्वरसोपनतां शमशय्याम् ॥ १३२ ॥

स्वेदपूरविलसत्पुलकोच्छ्वसितैस्त्रुटत्- ॥ ८१ ॥

हरति नितान्तमियं तव कीर्तिः ॥ ५९ ॥

Index of Metres

अजयः

१. एवौपम्ये ऽवधारणे ॥ (पृ. १९, २) (वृत्तमाला ७५)

अमरः

१. कुटनिपावस्त्री । (२.९.३२) (वृत्तमाला ९८)

कलिकालसर्वज्ञः रत्नाकरः

१. च्छन्दांसि विदुः षड्भिरारभ्यैकैकवृद्धिभिः पादैः । (१.५) (वृत्तमाला ६)

२. प्रहरणकलिता ननविननवितैः । (२.५१) (वृत्तमाला ७८)

३. मो वा स्त्रौ वा यदि वातोर्मिमाला । (२.२१) (वृत्तमाला ४४)

४. वसुमदनदहनमुनिभिर्भुजङ्गविजृम्भितम् । (२.८०) (वृत्तमाला ११७)

कालिदासः

१. बिसकिसलयच्छेदपाथेयवन्तः । (मेघदूत १.११) (वृत्तमाला १२४)

जयदेवः

१. गायत्रं छन्दसामाद्यम् । (१) (वृत्तमाला ६)

२. प्रहरणकलिता च ननभनलगैः । (७.६) (वृत्तमाला ७८)

३. सिंहललितं च कथितं भजसनो गौ । (वृत्तमाला ७६)

पद्यविवेकः

१. उक्तमत्युक्तकं मध्या प्रतिष्ठा सुप्रतिष्ठया ।
प्रायः प्रयोगबाह्यत्वादभव्यत्वाच्च नाश्रिताः ॥ (वृत्तमाला ५)

पद्यालंकारः

१. इदमीशानमतं कृतौ स्मरयति स्यात् सिंहविक्रीडितम् । (वृत्तमाला १०९)

२. †कुरुयैव† पूर्वानुरोधात्तु दर्शिता । (वृत्तमाला ४४)

३. गायत्र्यादीन्येव च्छन्दांसि दर्शितानि । (वृत्तमाला ६)

४. जलधिषु जलधिषु गुणमणिनिकरः । (वृत्तमाला ८८)

५. जातौ बहुवचने उष्णिहम् । (वृत्तमाला १३)

६. वृषभ इत्यधुना गदितः सुगतप्रियः । (वृत्तमाला ८४)

७. वेदच्छेदे भ्रमरविलसिता । (वृत्तमाला ४०)

पद्यालंकारसूत्रम्

१. अचलधृतिरथ तिथिरपरमत इति यमविरतचरणयतिरतिरुचिरा । (वृत्तमाला १३६)

२. केतुमती स्वरेषु चरमे ऽङ्के । (वृत्तमाला १३४)

३. त्वच्चरणानुचरेण न भाव्यं भवमथनश्रुत न द्रुतमध्या । (वृत्तमाला १२६)

माघः

१. सुगन्धयद्दिशः शुक्लमम्लानकुसुमं दिवः ।
भूरि तत्रापतत्तस्मादुत्पपात दिवं यशः ॥ (१९.२०) (वृत्तमाला १४७)

मुरारिः (अनर्घराघवम)

१. मूर्तीरष्टमहेश्वरस्य दलयन्नष्टौ कुलक्ष्माभृतः । (३.५४) (वृत्तमाला ११७)

रङ्गरचना

१. स्मृतिहेतवे पुरुषोत्तमः । भरतादिषूद्धरते लवम् ॥ (वृत्तमाला ६)

रभसः

१. अर्गलं त्रिषु । (वृत्तमाला ८४)

२. कलधौतं स्वर्णे रूप्ये । (वृत्तमाला ७०)

३. शक्करी मेखलाच्छन्दः ॥ (वृत्तमाला ८०)

राजः

१. वसुकुलगिरिभिः स्यान्मालिनी नौ मयौ यः । (वृत्तमाला ११७)

२. वसुमनसिजरिपुतुरगैर्भुजङ्गविजृम्भितम् । (वृत्तमाला ११७)

Untraced Citations

१. अनन्तः पद्यमार्गो ऽयं विशेषः पाठशोभया । (वृत्तमाला १)

२. च्छन्दसा हि वचसां प्रवृत्तिः । (वृत्तमाला १०)

३. तोयमम्बुजपत्त्रस्थं धत्ते मुक्ताफलश्रियम् । (वृत्तमाला ९७)

४. धीः श्रीः । तेस्ताम् ॥
सर्वैः कार्या । बुद्धे भक्तिः ॥
सौगतं मद्बलम् ।
सूदितं युक्तिभिः ॥
शीलैराढ्याः सर्वे सत्त्वाः ।
सौख्योपेताः संपद्यन्ताम् ॥

सर्वविदाज्ञा यो ऽनुविधत्ते ।
तं च सदर्थाः के न भजन्ते ॥ (वृत्तमाला ६)

५. बोधिसत्त्वरथं प्राप्य सर्वदुष्खाश्रमापहम् ।
एवं सुखात् सुखं गच्छन् को विषीदेत् सचेतनः ॥ (वृत्तमाला २९)

६. मूर्तिरेव तवाचष्टे भगवन् वीतरागताम् । (वृत्तमाला ७१)

७. रूपमहो यथेदमाह्लादि पटे ऽपि हि नाथ तावकम् । (वृत्तमाला ३)

८. विश्रामो ऽर्धे पदे भङ्गः पादांशे वक्ष्यतो यतिः । (वृत्तमाला २)

Bibliography

Ajayapāla

Nānārthasaṃgraha of Ajayapāla. Edited by T. R. Chintamani. University of Madras. Madras 1937.

Amarasiṃha

The Nâmaliṅgânus(!)âsana of Amarasimha with The Commentary T(!)îkâ-sarvaswa of Vandyaghat(!)îya-Sarvânanda. Edited by T. Gaṇapati Sâstrî. The Travancore Government PressTrivandrum 1914.

Jayadeva

Jayadāman. A collection of ancient texts on Sanskrit Prosody and A Classified List of Sanskrit Metres with an Alphabetical Index. Edited by H. D. Velankar. Haritosha Samiti. Bombay 1949.

Kālidāsa

The Megha-dūta of Kālidāsa. Critically edited by Sushil Kumar De. Sahitya Akademi. New Delhi 1956.

Māgha

The Śiśupâlavadha of Mâgha With The Commentary (Sarvankashâ) of Mallinâtha. Edited by Pandit Durgâprasâda and Pandit Śivadatta. Sixth Ed. Revised by T. Śrinivâsa Venkatrâma Śarmâ. Bombay 1914.

Murāri

The Anargharâghava of Murâri. With The Commentary of Ruchipati. Edited by Paṇḍit Durgâprasâd, and Wâsudev Laxmaṇ Śâstrî Paṇśîkar. Nirṇaya Sîgar Press. Bombay 1929 (Fourth edition).

Ratnākaraśānti

Ratnākaraśānti's Chandoratnākara. Edited by Michael Hahn. Nepal Research Centre Miscellaneous Papers. Kathamandu 1982.

Grammatical Discussions in Śākyarakṣita's *Vṛttamālā(stuti)vivṛti*

Mahesh A. Deokar

Lata Mahesh Deokar

S. S. Bahulkar (University of Pune)

Introduction

Jñānaśrīmitra's (first half of the 11th century)[1] *Vṛttamālāstuti* (= VMS) 'Garland of Praise [of Mañjuśrī's Conducts] in [Various] Metres' is an ingenious work of poetry combining devotional sentiments and scientific discussion on classical Sanskrit metres. After an introduction consisting of four *āryā* stanzas (1–4), in which he explains the aim of his composition, Jñānaśrīmitra describes in the following 150 stanzas (5–154), composed in various metres, different conducts of Mañjuśrī. These are classified into the three main categories of peaceful (*sama*), half peaceful, and half angry (*ardhasama*), and angry (*viṣama*). At the same time, using stanzas 5–154 as illustrations of particular metrical structures, he defines these metres along with their names, the categories to which they belong, and their caesuras. These metres are also classified into three divisions of *sama*- 'equal,' *ardhasama*- 'half equal', and *viṣamavṛtta*s 'unequal.' In order to compose such complex verses with parallel structures, the use of ingenious linguistic tools and techniques was inevitable for the author. The names of metres like *meghavisphūrjita, narkkuṭaka,* and *toṭaka* were difficult to use in the praise of Mañjuśrī in a meaningful manner. Still difficult was the task to include the names of metres like *yavamatī* and *āpīḍa,* as they do not fit into the metrical structure of those particular metres. In order to solve these difficulties, Jñānaśrīmitra was forced to use uncommon words or split common words in an uncommon manner, and had to choose such expressions as would suggest the intended name of a metre. Indicating caesura and the metrical genre in a manner that would likewise apply to the description of Mañjuśrī was an equally difficult task. This also has been successfully accomplished by using different synonymic collocations and symbolic terms.

Such a complex structure of the text presents a challenging task before its commentator. It certainly demands a thorough understanding of the main text (*mūlagrantha*) and an in-depth knowledge of grammar, lexicography,

---

[1] Cf. HAHN 1971: 6.

metrics, and Buddhist philosophy, especially the Mahāyāna philosophy, particularly related to Vajrayāna. Śākyarakṣita (between 1050–1150 A.D.),[1] who flourished almost a hundred years after Jñānaśrīmitra, well equipped with all those prerequisites, has successfully explained the complex nature of the verses in his elaborate commentary entitled *Vṛttamālāstutivivṛti*[2] (= VMSV) or *Vṛttamālāvivṛti*.[3] He divides his comment on each verse into two parts. In the first part, the verse is explained with regard to Mañjuśrī whereas in the second, it is analysed from the metrical point of view. This exegesis includes glosses on relatively unknown words, dissolution of compounds, analysis of difficult or irregular word formations and usages, and comments on the syntax of a verse. While explaining the verse from the metrical point of view, he also makes use of some works on metrics. In order to understand Śākyarakṣita's analysis of the text, and to evaluate his scholarship, it is necessary to study all these different aspects of his commentary.

In the present paper, we focus our attention on the grammatical discussions occurring in Śākyarakṣita's VMSV. The scope of these discussions is limited only to those sections of the commentary that directly hinge on rules of grammar, grammatical derivations involving specific verbal roots or suffixes, grammatical terminology, concepts, and maxims.

Sometimes Śākyarakṣita explains the words without referring either to grammatical rules or suffixes. In such cases, a knowledgeable reader can easily deduce the underlying grammatical rule or suffix simply by reading his comments. Two such examples may be cited to clarify the point:

1. *śayanam* 'bed' (verse 40).[4] Śākyarakṣita explains the word as *śayyate 'sminn iti śayanaṃ* | "*Śayana* 'bed' is that on which one sleeps." The explanation clearly indicates that the word is derived from the root *śī śayane* by adding a primary derivative affix *lyuṭ* (= *ana*) in the sense of a

---

1 Cf. HAHN 1971: 8.

2 Cf. the commentary at the end of verse 124: *iti duṣkaraprabhedavṛtta-mālāstutivivṛtau samavṛttāni* |

3 Cf. the commentary at the end of verse 140: *iti duṣkaraprabhedavṛttamālāvivṛtāv ardhasamavṛttāni* |

4 *sphārāmodā madhunidhir adhikaṃ cūrṇaṃ cātuḥsamam iva dadhatī* | *nīlābjaśrīr dalasukhaśayanāsaṃparyāptabhramaravilasitā* ||

location (*adhikaraṇa*). The said suffix is taught by *karaṇādhikaraṇayoś ca* (P III.3.117), and *lyuṭ* (CV I.3.97).

2. *janīya* 'O benefactor of the people!' (verse 127).[1] Śākyarakṣita explains this secondary derivative form in the vocative case as *janebhyo hita* 'O benefactor of the people!' From this explanation, one can easily figure out the underlying suffix and the grammatical rule. The form is derived by adding the suffix *īya* to the word *jana* ending in a dative case in the sense of 'beneficial to it.' The suffix *cha* (= *īya*) is taught by the rule *tasmai hitam* (P V.1.5, CV IV.1.4).

Since such discussions do not have a direct mention of grammatical rules, concepts or maxims, they fall outside the defined scope of this paper. These are not dealt with here for they are general in nature and require no special knowledge of Sanskrit grammatical treatises.

For the convenience of presentation, the grammatical discussions are classified under six main sections. They are as follows:

I. Word Categories

II. Derivation of Words and Morphophonemic Changes

III. Explanation of Unique Usages

IV. Explanation of Peculiar Compounds

V. References to Grammatical Concepts and Maxims

VI. Semantic or Syntactic Interpretations

An attempt is made to elaborate these condensed grammatical discussions by quoting relevant rules or extracts from the commentaries on grammatical works. In all the possible cases, we have also tried to trace back Śākyarakṣita's comments to their probable sources in the grammatical treatises of Pāṇini and Candragomin.

I. Word Categories

Understanding the role of a particular word in a sentence is extremely important for the correct comprehension of the text. In a number of cases where one may have a doubt regarding the grammatical status of a word,

---

1 *kim uśanti budhā adhikaṃ vibho yadi janīya tadīyatanur bhavet | tava dṛṣṭisudhārasadhārayā sphuritahārarucā hariṇaplutā* ||

Śākyarakṣita makes a clear reference to the category to which it belongs. These references are limited to the following word categories:

A. *Saṃbodhana* or *āmantraṇa* 'vocative'

B. *Kriyāviśeṣaṇa* 'adverb'

C. *Kartṛ* 'agent'

There are altogether twenty-three references of this kind, out of which nineteen refer to the vocative forms, three to adverbs, and one to the syntactic category 'agent.'

A. *Saṃbodhana* or *āmantraṇa* 'vocative'

When a vocative form is not easily discernible in a verse or when its boundary is unclear, Śākyarakṣita clearly points it out by referring to its grammatical category. It is, however, somewhat peculiar that he uses two different technical terms, viz. *saṃbodhana* or °*pada* and *āmantraṇa* or °*pada* to refer to the vocative. In the commentary on verses 31,[1] 34,[2] 50,[3] 57,[4] 88,[5] 97,[6] 116,[7] 117,[8] and 120[9], he uses the terms *saṃbodhana* and °*pada* whereas the terms *āmantraṇa* and °*pada* are employed in the commentary on verses 90,[10] 92,[11] 100,[12] 105,[1] 107,[2] 109,[3] 121,[4] 122,[5] 126,[6] and 138.[7] Out of these

---

1 *bhuvanoddyota svāminn iti saṃbodhanadvayam* |

2 *he śuddhavirāḍ iti saṃbodhanaṃ hetubhāvena* |

3 *anantarodbhāvitalakṣaṇeti bhagavataḥ saṃbodhanam* |

4 *paramottameti vā saṃbodhanam* |

5 *agaṇitā guṇā yasyeti trayam api saṃbodhanapadam* |

6 *itaḥ śritagurukaruṇādigyativaṃśo yenaitat saṃbodhanapadam adhipeti ca* |

7 *tādṛśam antaḥkaraṇasya karaṇam pravartanaṃ yasya tasya saṃbodhanam* |

8 *mutkṛtau pramodajananena prauḍhā unmīlantī lāvaṇyaśrīr yasyedam api saṃbodhanam* |

9 *he varada* | *aparimo 'nuttaraḥ paramopakāras tatrottamarṇa ivottamarṇas tasya saṃbodhanam* |

10 *jaḍadhiyam prati lakṣyīkṛtya samadhikagurvī dayā yasya tasyāmantraṇam* | ... *etad api dvayam āmantraṇapadam* |

11 *nirvihatapratijñety āmantraṇam* |

12 *trayam etad āmantraṇapadam* |

nineteen references, seven are that of *saṃbodhana*, two of *saṃbodhanapada*, eight of *āmantraṇa* and two of *āmantraṇapada*. It is noteworthy that although the term *saṃbodhana* is found in Pāṇini's *Aṣṭādhyāyī*,[8] and the *Cāndravyākaraṇa* of Candragomin,[9] the term *āmantraṇa* is altogether missing in both the grammars. The term *āmantraṇa* appears in the *Kātantravyākaraṇa* of Śarvavarman.[10] This choice of technical terms is rather puzzling as it is unusual for an author to use side-by-side two different terms belonging to different traditions.

With regard to verse 34,[11] Śākyarakṣita not only identifies the word *śuddhavirāṭ* as a *saṃbodhana* but also comments that this *saṃbodhana* is used to convey the additional sense of *hetu* 'a cause'.[12] He thereby suggests a conditional interpretation of the same as "O! Since you shine distinctly with your natural appearance without any ornaments."[13] Such subtle comments add new dimensions to the understanding of these already intricate verses.

---

1 *viśvānukampaiva mukhaṃ dvāraṃ te unmīlanto ye nānārasās teṣāṃ pada | idam apy āmantraṇam |*

2 *anarghaṃ smitavasuvadanaṃ yasya tasyāmantraṇam |*

3 *nirvṛtau ca nirvāṇe śaśvan na vidyate pratiṣṭhā yeṣāṃ te ca te vādinaś ca teṣāṃ variṣṭhetīdam api dvayam āmantraṇam |*

4 *catuṣṭayam idam āmantraṇam |*

5 *athavā akaruṇakaruṇābalety āmantraṇam |*

6 *bhavasya saṃsārasya mathanaṃ śrutaṃ yasya bhavamathane vā śruto viditaḥ | tasyāmantraṇam |*

7 *jinanayanayanety āmantraṇapadaṃ vā |*

8 Cf. P II.3.47, III.2.125: *saṃbodhane ca |*

9 Cf. CV II.1.94: *saṃbodhane |*

10 Cf. Kt II.4.18: *āmantraṇe ca |* Also cf. Mahesh Deokar, 2008: 187–190.

11 *nānāratnamarīcimālinī pronmīlan nijakāntisaṃpadā | pratyaṅgaṃ tava bhūṣaṇāvalī nītā śuddhavirāṭ parābhavam ||*

12 *he śuddhavirāḍ iti saṃbodhanaṃ hetubhāvena |*

13 *yasmāt tvaṃ śuddho nirbhūṣaṇo viśeṣeṇa rājasa iti |*

B. *Kriyāviśeṣaṇa* 'adverb'

Another word type identified by Śākyarakṣita is *kriyāviśeṣaṇa* 'adverb.' A mention of this term can be found in the commentary on verses 57,[1] 80,[2] and 148.[3] Out of these three references, in the commentary on verse 57, Śākyarakṣita uses the expression *kriyāyā viśeṣaṇam* 'qualifier of an action' instead of *kriyāviśeṣaṇam*. Here he suggests two different interpretations for the word *drutavilambitam*: first as an adverb and second as an adjective. For a detailed discussion of how these two different interpretations yield two different nuances, readers may refer to section VI, no. 4.

In verses 80[4] and 148,[5] the expression *kim api*, which can also have two possible interpretations, is interpreted as an adverb rather than an adjective. Thus, verse 80 should be construed as *yadi kaś cit saṃyatair indriyaiḥ kva cid ādarastimitadhīr bhavataḥ kalāṃ kim api dhyāyati.*[6] Similarly, verse 148 should be construed as *bhṛkuṭīkaṭākṣadaśaneṣu vikṛtāni kim api bibhratas tava yad lalitaṃ ca kiṃ tu īdṛśaṃ vikaṭaṃ vapuḥ bhuvanāni damayati.*[7]

C. *Kartṛ* 'agent'

In the commentary on verse 99,[8] Śākyarakṣita identifies the syntactic category of the word *īhitam* as *kartṛ* 'agent' of the verb *abhṛta.*[9] The word

---

1 *drutaṃ vā vilambitaṃ vā yad uccāritaṃ vacaḥ | kriyāyā viśeṣaṇaṃ vacaso vā | tad api bahu manyante |*

2 *kim apīti kriyāviśeṣaṇam |*

3 *kim apīti kriyāviśeṣaṇam |*

4 *bhavataḥ kalāṃ kim api saṃyatair indriyaiḥ kva cid ādarastimitadhīr yadi dhyāyati | acirāt svayaṃ varayatīyam enaṃ janaṃ vasudhā dhruvaṃ jaladhiśakvarībhūṣaṇā ||*

5 *bhṛkuṭīkaṭākṣadaśaneṣu kim api vikṛtāni bibhrataḥ | damayati tava bhuvanāni vapur lalitaṃ ca kiṃ tu vikaṭaṃ yad īdṛśam ||*

6 "If someone with his mind being motionless on account of close attention would meditate in whatever manner with restrained faculties upon your spiritual stages at some place."

7 "Your charming form, which is nevertheless of such a terrifying (appearance), tames all the worlds when you are exhibiting in an inexplicable manner scary gestures of frowning, side glances and teeth."

8 *tribhuvanasaṃmadapradajinavyavasāyamadhau sphuṭasahakāratāmahitam īhitam īśa tava | pravacanamañjarīsrutaśamāmṛtapānamudābhṛta yatiṣaṭpadaṃ kalakaṇat-kṛtikokilakam ||*

9 *tavehitaṃ ceṣṭitaṃ kartṛ |*

īhitam ending in the suffix *kta* can be interpreted in two different ways, either as an action noun meaning 'an act' or as a passive participle meaning 'wished, desired.' By explaining the word as *ceṣṭitam* and identifying it as an agent, Śākyarakṣita hints at its status as an action noun. This clarifies the syntactic structure of the verse and thereby helps to understand it without ambiguity. The basic structure of the verse should be now understood as *tavehītaṃ yatiṣaṭpadaṃ tathā ca kalakaṇat kṛtikokilakam abhṛta.*[1]

II. Derivation of Words and Morphophonemic Changes

A. Derivation

Śākyarakṣita's great command over the Pāṇinian and Cāndra grammars can be seen from his derivations of difficult words. These include references to: a. nominal stems or verbal roots along with their meanings as they occur in the *Dhātupāṭha*; b. relevant suffixes; c. the subsequent morphophonemic changes; d. appropriate rules from the *Aṣṭādhyāyī* or the *Cāndravyākaraṇa*; and e. maxims from the grammatical works. All the derivations discussed by Śākyarakṣita are listed below in the sequential order of the verses.

1. *naikabhavīya* (adj.) 'of many lives' (verse 9).[2] The word is a secondary derivative from a compound stem *naikabhava*, which is further derived from two nominal stems *na* and *ekabhava*. Under normal circumstances, before a noun beginning with a vowel, the negative particle *na* is substituted by *a*.[3] In the next step, an augment *na* is added at the beginning of the following word.[4] However, in exceptional cases like *naikabhavīyaḥ*, *na* remains unchanged. After the compounding, the *taddhita* affix *cha* is added to the compound stem *naikabhava* in the sense of

---

1 "O lord! Your acts nurtured bees in the form of ascetics and cooing cuckoos in the form of Bodhisattvas."

2 *naikabhavīyābhyāsavivṛddham | bodhaviśeṣaṃ sādhu dadhānaiḥ ||*

3 Cf. *nalopo nañaḥ* (P VI.3.73), *naño naḥ* (CV V.2.91).

4 Cf. *tasmān nuḍ aci* (P VI.3.74), *tato 'ci nuṭ* (CV V.2.93).

'existing there'.[1] The *taddhita* affix *cha* is further replaced by *īya* to produce the final form *naikabhavīyaḥ*.[2]

Śākyarakṣita explains the whole process as follows:

> As to the word *naikabhava-*, there is no elision of *na* since the word belongs to the class of words beginning with *nakha-*. (Thereafter,) since the word has a *vṛddhi* letter at its initial position, the suffix *cha* in the sense of 'existing there' is added to the word *naika-bhava-* (resulting in the form) *naikabhavīyaḥ*, which qualifies the word *abhyāsaḥ* (meaning 'the practice of many lives').[3]

The probable source of Śākyarakṣita's explanation seems to be the rule *nakhādayaḥ* (CV V.2.95). Note that the corresponding rule in the Pāṇinian grammar is: *nabhrāṇnapānnavedānāsatyānamucinakulanakhanapuṃsakanakṣatranakranākeṣu prakṛtyā* (P VI.3.75).

2. *uṣṇi* (f. loc.) 'in the hot season' (verse 13).[4] This is a locative singular of *uṣan-* 'the hot season, the summer.' The word is derived from the root *uṣ-* by adding the *uṇādi* suffix *kanin*. Śākyarakṣita describes the derivation of the word as follows:

> The root *uṣ-* is in the sense of 'burning.' The *uṇādi* suffix *kanin* is added after it since the word *uṣan* belongs to the class of words beginning with *pūṣan-*.[5]

It is interesting that although *uṣa dāhe* is a clear reference to the *Cāndra-dhātupāṭha*, the source of Śākyarakṣita's comment *auṇādikaḥ kanin, pūṣāditvāt* is certainly not the *Cāndra-uṇādi*. There the relevant rule reads *śvādayaḥ* (CU 3.80).

3. *trailokī* (f. nom.) 'the triple world' (verse 29).[1] This is a feminine secondary derivative derived from the compound stem *triloka* 'the triple

---

1 Cf. *vṛddhāc chaḥ* (P IV.2.114), *ādaijādyacaś chaḥ* (CV III.2.24).

2 Cf. *āyaneyīnīyiyaḥ phaḍhakhachaghāṃ pratyayādīnām* (P VII.1.2), *āyaneyīnīyiyaḥ phaḍhakhachaghāṃ ṣphādyādīnām* (CV V.4.2).

3 *naikabhavo nakhāditvān nalopābhāvaḥ | tatra bhavo vṛddhyāditvāc chaḥ | naika-bhavīyo 'bhyāsaḥ |*

4 *jājvalīti śāsanaṃ tvāṃ sametya saugatam | sūryadhāma duḥsahaṃ sātirekam uṣṇi hi ||*

5 *uṣa dāhe | auṇādikaḥ pūṣāditvāt kanin |* Cf. *uṣa dāhe |* (CDh 1.232)

world' by adding the pleonastic suffix *ṣyañ* (*svārthe*) as it belongs to the class of words beginning with *cāturvarṇya-*.[2] Thereafter the feminine suffix *ṅīṣ*[3] is added to the secondary derivative *trailokya* to form the word *trailokī-* by eliding the *taddhita* affix *ya*.[4] Śākyarakṣita describes this derivation in short without showing inclination to any particular grammatical tradition. He comments:

> *Trailokī* means 'the triple world.' When a *taddhita* suffix *ṣyañ* is added because of the word (*triloka*) being a member of the class of words beginning with *cāturvarṇya-*, (the feminine) suffix *ṅīṣ*, which is indicated by the *it* sound *ṣ*, is added to it, as in case of the word *sāmagrī-*.[5]

4. *nānāratnamarīcimālinī* (f. nom.) 'possessing the garland of rays (emitting) from different jewels' (verse 34).[6] This feminine word is derived from the compound stem *nānāratnamarīcimālā* by adding the possessive *taddhita* affix *ini*[7] with the further addition of the feminine suffix *ṅīp*.[8] Śākyarakṣita's comment is brief. He merely says:

   > (It means) that which has the garland of beams of various jewels. Since the word belongs to the class of words beginning with *vrīhi-*, (the suffix) *ini* is added.[9]

   Here, too, Śākyarakṣita's affiliation to any specific school of grammar remains obscure. Cf. *vrīhyādibhyaś ca* (P V.2.116), and *vrīhyādy ata iniś ca* (CV IV.2.119).

---

1 *tvām udgītakulodayaśailaṃ prajñālokam upāyarathastham | vande jāḍyavikhaṇḍanaśauṇḍaṃ trailokīnalinīsavitāram ||*

2 Cf. the *vārttika cāturvarṇyādīnāṃ svārtha upasaṃkhyānam* on the rule *guṇavacanabrāhmaṇādibhyaḥ karmaṇi ca* (P V.1.124). Also cf. the *gaṇasūtra cāturvarṇyādīnāṃ svārthe* on *guṇavacanabrāhmaṇādibhyaḥ karmaṇi ca* (CV IV.1.141).

3 Cf. *ṣidgaurādibhyaś ca* (P IV.1.41), *ṣito ṅīṣ* (CV II.3.37).

4 Cf. *halas taddhitasya* (P VI.4.150), *halo yañādeḥ* (CV V.3.152).

5 *trayo lokās trailokī | cāturvarṇyāditvena ṣyañi striyāṃ ṣillakṣaṇo ṅīṣ sāmagrīvat |*

6 *nānāratnamarīcimālinī pronmīlan nijakāntisaṃpadā | pratyaṅgaṃ tava bhūṣaṇāvalī nītā śuddhavirāṭ parābhavam ||*

7 Cf. *vrīhyādibhyaś ca* (P V.2.116), *vrīhyādyata iniś ca* (CV IV.2.119).

8 Cf. *ṛnnebhyo ṅīp* (P IV.1.5), *ṛno ṅīp* (CV II.3.2).

9 *nānāratnānāṃ marīcimālā yasyā asti | vrīhyāditvād iniḥ |*

5. *cātuḥsamaṃ cūrṇam* (n. nom.) 'the powder made of four ingredients' (verse 40).[1] The word is an adjective qualifying *cūrṇam*. It is a secondary derivative from the compound stem *catuḥsama-* with the addition of the *taddhita* suffix *aṇ* in the sense of 'this is his.'[2] Śākyarakṣita explains the same as follows:

    Catuḥsamam 'four ingredients' are saffron and so on. *Cātuḥsama* is that which is related to it. The word *cūrṇam* 'powder' should be construed even with this (word *cātuḥsamam*).[3]

6. *adodhakam (ambakajātam)* (adj.) '(a legion of eyes) which imbibes this (form)' (verse 41).[4] This form is an *upapada-tatpuruṣa* compound of the pronominal form *adas* 'this' and the primary derivative *dhaḥ* which is derived from the root *dhāñ* 'to suck' by adding the suffix *ka* (= *a*). Thereafter the pleonastic suffix *kan* (= *ka*) is added to this compound in order to arrive at the form *adodhakam*.

    Śākyarakṣita explains the derivation in the following words:

    This (multitude of eyes) imbibes (lit.: drinks) this elixir vitae, which is (your) beautiful form. Hence, the suffix *ka* (= *a*) is added after the verbal root ending in the phoneme *ā, which* follows a word other than a prefix resulting in the form *adodha-*. When the suffix *kan* (= *ka*)is added pleonastically, it gives rise to the form *adodhaka-*.[5]

    In this explanation, we find an indirect reference to the Pāṇinian rule: *āto 'nupasarge kaḥ* (P III.2.3). The corresponding rule in the *Cāndra-vyākaraṇa* is *āto 'prādeḥ kaḥ* (CV I.2.2). In case of the second reference to the grammatical rule, nothing can be said decisively as the relevant rule in both grammars is *yāvādibhyaḥ kan* (P V.4.29, CV IV.4.12).

---

1 *sphārāmodā madhunidhir adhikaṃ cūrṇaṃ cātuḥsamam iva dadhatī | nīlābjaśrīr dala-sukhaśayanāsaṃparyāptabhramaravilasitā ||*

2 Cf. *tasyedam* (P IV.3.120), *tasya svaṃ rathād yat* (CV III.3.85).

3 *catuḥsamaṃ kuṅkumādi | tasyedaṃ cātuḥsamaṃ | cūrṇam ity atrāpi yojyam |*

4 *rūparasāyanabhāvanayā te vāsava eva paraṃ bahumānyaḥ | yena cirāya nirasta-nimeṣaṃ labdham adodhakam ambakajātam ||*

5 *ada idaṃ rūparasāyanaṃ dhayati pibatīty āto 'nupasargāt kaḥ | adodhaṃ | svārthe kani adodhakaṃ |*

7. *śyenī* (f. nom.) 'a feminine object of white colour' (verse 47).[1] The word is derived from the nominal stem *śyeta* denoting the white colour by adding the feminine suffix *ṅīp* and at the same time substituting the penultimate sound *ta* by *na*.[2] Śākyarakṣita describes the said derivation without quoting the relevant grammatical rule:

   Śyenī means 'of white colour.' The form is derived when the phoneme *ta* is replaced by *na* after the addition of (the feminine) suffix *ṅī* to the word *śyeta-*.[3]

8. *sragviṇī* (f. nom.) 'a woman (in this context, the goddess Sarasvatī) with a garland' (verse 54).[4] This feminine secondary derivative is formed by adding the possessive suffix *vini* to the word *sraj-*[5] with the further addition of the feminine suffix *ṅīp*.[6]

   sraj + *vini* (= *vin*) (P V.2.121)

   sraj + *vin* + *ṅīp* (P IV.1.5)

   srag + *vin* + *ī* (P VIII.2.30)

   srag + *viṇ* + *ī* (P VIII.4.2)

   sragviṇī

   Śākyarakṣita derives the said form as a part of the explanation of the compound *sadguṇasragviṇī*. He cuts the description of the derivation short and only mentions the *taddhita* suffix without quoting specific rule from any grammatical work:

---

1 *kīrtir artikartatas tava stavastomasadmano 'tisadmanohṛtaḥ* | *sāndracandracandrikārdracandanaśyeny alaṃkaroty alaṃ diśo daśa* ||

2 Cf. *varṇād anudāttāt topadhāt to naḥ* (P IV.1.39), *śyetaitaharitarohitāt to naḥ* | (CV II.3.34).

3 *śyenī śvetā* | *śyetaśabdād ṅīpratyaye takārasya natve rūpaṃ* | Please note that the Ms. reads *śveta°*. (Hahn 2013: 300). The reading is certainly faulty as the word *śyenī* is derived from *śyeta* and not from *śveta*. The feminine form of the latter is rather *śvetā*. Cf. *Kāśikā* on P IV.1.139: *anudāttād iti kim ? śvetā* |

4 *dīpyamānākhilālaṃkṛtiślāghinī puṇyabhājāṃ mukhāmbhojalabdhodayā* | *bhāratī bhāratīśa svabhāvojjvalā tvām upaiti svayaṃ sadguṇasragviṇī* ||

5 Cf. *asmāyāmedhāsrajo viniḥ* | (P V.2.121, CV IV.2.137).

6 Cf. *ṛnnebhyo ṅīp* (P IV.1.5), *ṛno ṅīp* (CV II.3.2).

> *Sraj* is a garland of those good qualities, which are peculiar to the lord; the woman, who possesses it as something worth mentioning, is *sragviṇī* 'having a garland.' (The form is derived) by adding the suffix *vini* having the (possessive) sense of the suffix *matup* to (the nominal stem) *sraj*.[1]

9. *ślāghinī* (f. nom.) 'a proud lady' (verse 54). The word is a feminine secondary derivative from the nominal stem *ślāghā*. It is derived by adding the possessive suffix *ini*[2] with the further addition of the feminine suffix *ṅīp*.[3] The word is a part of the larger compound *dīpyamānākhilālaṃkṛtiślāghinī*. Our author describes it as follows:

> One who has pride on account of all those glittering ornaments of poetic figures of speech is (*dīpyamānākhilālaṃkṛtiślāghinī*), the suffix *ini* is added to the nominal stem *ślāghā* as it belongs to the class of words beginning with *vrīhi* (to form the word *ślāghinī*).[4]

Here, too, there is no specific mention of any grammatical rule.

10. *kalikā* (f. nom.) 'holding, wielding' (verse 78).[5] This is a feminine primary derivative in the agentive sense. It is derived from the verbal root *kal-* 'to hold, to wield' of the tenth conjugation by adding the suffix *ṇvul* (= *aka*).[6]

kal + *ṇvul* (= *aka*) (P III.1.133)

kal + *aka* + *ā* (P IV.1.4)

kal + *ika* + *ā* (P VII.3.44)

---

1 *santo ye guṇā bhagavata eva teṣāṃ srag mālā* | *sā yasyā abhidheyatvenāsti* | *matvarthīyaḥ srajo viniḥ* | In the same context, Śākyarakṣita explains the intended pun on the word *guṇa-* in the word *sadguṇasragviṇī*: *san śobhano guṇaḥ sūtraṃ yasyāṃ tādṛśī srag asyā astīti sragviṇī* "one (i.e. Sarasvatī) who wears a garland with a beautiful thread."

2 Cf. *vrīhyādibhyaś ca* (P V.2.116), *vrīhyādyata iniś ca* (CV IV.2.119).

3 Cf. *ṛnnebhyo ṅīp* (P IV.1.5), *ṛno ṅīp* (CV II.3.2).

4 *dīpyamānā akhilā yā alaṃkṛtayaḥ kāvyālaṃkṛtayas tābhiḥ ślāghā yasyāḥ* | *vrīhyāditvād iniḥ* |

5 *pratibhayavapuṣām akaruṇacaritapraśamanavidhaye kva cid api kṛpayā* | *tava bhujaparighāvalir ativiṣamā vilasati vividhapraharaṇakalikā* ||

6 Cf. *ṇvultṛcau* (P III.1.133), *kartari ṇvultṛjacaḥ* | (CV I.1.139).

kalikā

It is a part of the larger compound *vividhapraharaṇakalikā* 'wielding different types of arms.'[1] Following his usual style, Śākyarakṣita explains the word referring simply to the main primary derivative suffix as follows:

> (It means:) it wields different types of arms. Hence, the suffix *ṇvul* is added (to the root *kal*). It, (i.e. the creeper like arm,) is such.[2]

11. *kuṭakam* (n. nom.) 'a receptacle' (verse 98).[3] This is a secondary derivative from the nominal stem *kuṭa* with the addition of the pleonastic *taddhita* suffix *ka* (*svārthe*).[4] It forms a part of the larger compound *ṛkkuṭakam*. Śākyarakṣita explains it in brief without quoting any specific rule:

> *Ṛkkuṭaka-* means a pot-like receptacle of the Vedic hymns, (i.e. the Ṛgveda, a collections of verses (*ṛc*)). The suffix *ka* is added pleonastically.[5]

12. *kṛtikokilakaḥ* (m. nom.) 'a cuckoo in the form of a bodhisattva who acts (for the welfare of others)' (verse 99).[6] The word is derived from the compound stem *kṛtikokila-* by adding the pleonastic *taddhita* suffix *kan* (= *ka*).[7] Here, too, Śākyarakṣita explains the derivation by mentioning merely the suffix along with its meaning. The explanation is as follows:

---

1 It may be noted that Dpaṅ lo tsā ba translates the word °*kalikā* into Tibetan as *sgrogs par byed rnams* 'producing sound.' It is, however, not clear what Jñānaśrīmitra actually intended to convey.

2 *vividhāni praharaṇāni kalayatīti ṇvul tādṛśī* |

3 *tava guṇavistarapraṇayapūtavacovibhavaṃ varada sa eka eva sumukho mukham āvahati* | *madhumayasāmadhāma yajuṣā sajuṣānugataṃ śravaṇasudhābhimānabhavanarkkuṭakaṃ ca vidhiḥ* ||

4 Cf. *yāvādibhyaḥ kan* (P V.4.29, CV IV.4.12).

5 *ṛcāṃ kuṭam iva kuṭaṃ* | *svārthe kaḥ* |

6 *tribhuvanasaṃmadapradajinavyavasāyamadhau sphuṭasahakāratāmahitam īhitam īśa tava* | *pravacanamañjarīsrutaśamāmṛtapānamudābhṛta yatiṣaṭpadaṃ kalakaṇatkṛtikokilakam* ||

7 Cf. *yāvādibhyaḥ kan* (P V.4.29, CV IV.4.12).

The Bodhisattvas[1] who act for the benefit of others are themselves cuckoos. The pleonastic suffix *kan* is added (to the word *kṛtijanakokila-*).[2]

13. *śrutirasabhid* (adj.) 'extinguishing (lit.: breaking) the desire of listening' (verse 101).[3] The said word is an initial part of the longer compound *śrutirasabhidākrandanādaikavṛttiḥ*. Here *bhid* is a primary derivative from the verbal root *bhid*. It is derived by adding the *kṛt* suffix *kvip* in the agentive sense.[4] Śākyarakṣita explains the form as follows:

    (*Śrutirasabhid* means) that which destroys the taste for listening, i.e. the desire of listening. Hence, there is an addition of the suffix *kvip*.[5]

14. *akhilavipadapavāham* (n. nom.) 'remover of all adversities' (verse 118).[6] Here the word under discussion is an *upapada* compound of *akhilā vipadaḥ* and the primary derivative *apavāha-*.[7] The word *apavāha-* is derived by adding the primary derivative suffix *aṇ* to the root *apa* + *vah-* with its object being an *upapada*.[8] In accordance with his usual practice, Śākyarakṣita explains the said derivation in a compact manner as follows:

    He removes, i.e. overpowers, all the adversities. With the addition of the suffix *aṇ*, (the form) *akhilavipadapavāham* (is derived.)[9]

---

1 Dpaṅ lo tsā ba in his Tibetan translation of the VMS translates the word *kṛti-* as *mkhas pa* 'a wise person.'

2 *kṛtijana eva kokilaḥ | svārthikaḥ kan |*

3 *durdāntānāṃ damanavidhaye kvāpi kāruṇyavegād dhatse mūrtiṃ caraṇaśikhayā khyātavikrānta yasyāḥ | trailokīyaṃ śrutirasabhidākrandanādaikavṛttir mandākrantā vrajati vilayaṃ nātha na svāsthyam āśu ||*

4 Cf. *kvip ca* (P III.2.76), *kvip-vij-manin-kvanip-vanipaḥ* (CV I.2.53).

5 *śrutirasaṃ śravaṇābhilāṣaṃ bhinattīti kvip |*

6 *tanvatsusphuṭam aviratam amitam amṛtarasakaṇam iva parito 'ṅgeṣu pratyālocana-samudayinavarasarasapadam asadṛśam atulaśrīkam | yat kṛcchrair api na sulabham aparavividhasukṛtavidhibhir abhiyuktātmā tvatsevātaruphalam iha samanubhavati tad akhilavipadapavāhākhyam ||*

7 Cf. *upapadam atiṅ* (P II.2.19), *kārakaṃ bahulam* (CV II.2.16).

8 Cf. *karmaṇy aṇ* (P III.2.1), *vyāpyād aṇ* (CV I.2.1).

9 *akhilā vipado 'pavahaty adhikrāmaty aṇi | akhilavipadapavāham ākhyā yasya tat |*

15. *upacitram* (*manaḥ*) (n. nom.) 'a mind filled with marvel' (verse 125).[1] This is a *prādi* compound in the *tatpuruṣa* category.[2] Śākyarakṣita explains the said form as follows:

    > (*Upacitram* means) that which has attained the state of marvel, i.e. amazement. The compound is formed as per the supplementary injunction (*vārttika*) *atyādayaḥ krāntādyarthe dvitīyayā.*[3]

    This injunction, common to both the Pāṇinian and the Cāndra traditions, can be considered as the second of the seven supplementary injunctions added by Kātyāyana to *kugatiprādayaḥ* (P II.2.18) or an injunction found in the CVṛ on *kuprādayo 'subvidhau nityam* (CV II.2.24). According to it, the prefixes *ati* and so on, conveying the sense of 'transcended and so on,' are compounded with a noun in the accusative case being the final member of the compound (to form a *prādisamāsa*). Since the injunction is identical in the traditions of Pāṇini and Candragomin, it is difficult to ascertain the exact source of Śākyarakṣita's explanation.

Thus, out of these fifteen derivations, eight are those of secondary derivatives, three of primary derivatives, two of compounds and one each of an *uṇādi*, and a feminine noun. Śākyarakṣita's description of these derivations is quite brief. In most of the cases, he simply refers to the main steps in the derivation and points out important suffixes with their nuances. Apart from these, at two places, we find explanations of peculiar morphophonemic changes. Elsewhere, such modifications are left to the knowledge of basic Sanskrit grammar on part of the readers. It may be argued that one who possesses the knowledge of basic Sanskrit grammar does not need this explanation as he knows the *sūtras* and the *vārttikas*. But one who does not know these would not be able to understand the explanation. Hence, this kind of grammatical explanation hardly serves the purpose.

Suffixes are usually taught without referring to a specific rule of grammar. Instead, we find a mention of *gaṇas* (word-classes) or other such condi-

---

1 *idam ardham abālaśaśiprabhaṃ bālaraviprabham ādadhad ardham | karuṇāvaśavarti bhavadvapuḥ kasya mano na karoty upacitram ||*

2 Cf. *kugatiprādayaḥ* (P II.2.18), *kuprādayo 'subvidhau nityam* (CV II.2.24).

3 *upagataṃ citraṃ āścaryam | atyādayaḥ krāntādyarthe dvitīyayeti samāsaḥ |*

tions responsible for the employment of a particular suffix. There is the only mention of an entry from the *Dhātupāṭha* – *uṣa dāhe*. It is attested in the *Cāndradhātupāṭha*. Out of the four references to the *gaṇas*, three are common to the Pāṇinian and the Cāndra tradition whereas the *nakhādi* class is found only in the *Cāndravyākaraṇa*. The only reference to the *Uṇādi* rule could not be attested decisively. In the above-mentioned fifteen derivations, the exclusive influence of the Cāndra grammar can be ascertained at two places and that of Pāṇini's *Aṣṭādhyāyī* at a single place. In all the remaining cases, no clear affiliation to any particular grammatical tradition, either that of Candragomin or Pāṇini, could be shown.

B. Morphophonemic Changes

At times, Śākyarakṣita's explanation of a particular form is limited to the description of morphophonemic changes like retroflexion. Five such cases are listed below:

1. *anuṣṭubhi* (f. locative) 'with regard to praise' or 'in the category *anuṣṭubh*' (verse 16).[1] This is a locative singular of the compound stem *anuṣṭubh, which* is derived from the prefix *anu* plus the verbal root *stubh*. Śākyarakṣita describes its derivation in the following manner:

   > The root *stubh* is in the sense of 'to stupefy.' Since verbal roots have a variety of meaning, in this case, it has the sense of praise,[2] therefore the word *anuṣṭubh-* means 'suitable (*anu*) praise (*stobhanam*).'[3] As per the rule *upasargāt sunoti* and so on (P VIII.3.65), the initial *s* (of the root *stubh-*) is replaced by *ṣ*.[4]

---

1 *yadguṇastutivistarād astasaṅgam anuṣṭubhi | dhīram ekam udīrayanty uttamaṃ padam udgatāḥ ||*

2 The primary meaning of the root *stubh-* in 1 PP is "to make joyful sound." Cf. MW (p. 1259). According to APTE (p. 1716), the root *stubh-* (1 *Parasmaipada*) means "to praise" and in the *Ātmanepada* "to stop." However, in the *Dhātupāṭhas* of the Pāṇinian and the Cāndra tradition, only the meaning 'to stupefy' is recorded.

3 According to MW (p. 40), the word *anuṣṭubh-* means "following in praise or invocation." APTE (p. 111) records the following meanings: "following in praise; speech."

4 *ṣṭubhu stambhe | anekārthatvād iha stutyarthaḥ | anurūpam stobhanam anuṣṭubh | upasargāt sunotītyādinā ṣatvam |*

Here the basis of Śākyarakṣita's explanation is Pāṇini's *Aṣṭādhyāyī*. The entry *ṣṭubhu stambhe* is found in the *dhātupāṭhas* of the Pāṇinian and the Cāndra tradition (PDh 1.421, CDh 1.416). However, the mention of the rule *upasargāt sunoti* and so on is a clear reference to Pāṇini's rule *upasargāt sunotisuvatisyatistautistobhatisthāsenayasedhasicasañjasvañjām* (P VIII.3.65). The corresponding rule in the Cāndra grammar is *prādīnāṃ susūsostustubhasthāsenisedhasicasañjasvañjām* (CV VI.4.50).

2. *triṣṭubhi* (f. locative) 'with regard to the praise of three things or in the category *triṣṭubh*' (verse 36).[1] This is the locative singular form of the compound stem *triṣṭubh*. Śākyarakṣita explains it as:

> The praise, i.e. admiration of one's own three (qualities), viz. appearance, virtues, and fame. (In this form, the phoneme *s* of *stubh* following the numeral *tri-*) is replaced by *ṣ* as the word belongs to the class of words beginning with *suṣāman-*.[2]

3. *atisadmanohṛt* (adj.) 'the one who exorbitantly captures the minds of good people' (verse 47).[3] While discussing this compound, Śākyarakṣita says:

> He, i.e. Mañjuśrī, exorbitantly captures the minds of good people. Hence the compound *atisadmanohṛtaḥ* 'of the one who exorbitantly captures the minds of good people.' (In case of this form,) there is an absence of the (nasal) substitute denoted by the siglum *ñam* as it is stated optionally.[4]

From the expression *ñamabhāvābhāvaḥ*, it appears that in this case Śākyarakṣita's explanation is based on a rule in the *Cāndravyākaraṇa*, which reads *yaro ñami ñam vā* (CV VI.4.140).[5] According to this rule, the

---

1 *rūpaṃ te guṇagaṇam atha kīrtiṃ saṃvīkṣyākhilam idam atiśāyi | bibhrāṇaṃ nijaviṣayavirāmaṃ mandaṃ triṣṭubhi jagad upajātam ||*

2 *tisṛṇāṃ rūpaguṇakīrtīnām ātmīyānāṃ stubh stutiḥ | suṣāmāditvāt ṣatvaṃ* | Cf. *suṣāmādiṣu ca* (P VIII.3.98), *suṣāmādayaḥ* (CV VI.4.89).

3 *kīrtir artikartatas tava stavastomasadmano 'tisadmanohṛtaḥ | sāndracandracandrikārdracandanaśyeny alaṃkaroty alaṃ diśo daśa ||*

4 *atyarthaṃ satāṃ mano haratīty atisadmanohṛtaḥ | vikalpitatvāt ñamabhāvābhāvaḥ |*

5 Cf. CVṛ on the same: *yaro ñami parato ñamādeśaḥ pratyāsanno bhavati vā* | "Before the consonants denoted by the siglum *ñam*, (i.e. all class-finals) (at the beginning of a *pada*) any consonant denoted by the *siglum yar*, (i.e. any con-

pada-final *d* of *atisad*- followed by *m* can be replaced by *n*. However, since the said rule is optionally applicable, there is no change in this case. It is noteworthy that the corresponding rule in Pāṇini's *Aṣṭādhyāyī* is *yaro 'nunāsike 'nunāsiko vā* (P VIII.4.45) where the word *anunāsika* is used instead of *ñam*.

4. *adhyā* (adj.) 'by the one without wisdom' (verse 126).[1] Occasionally Śākyarakṣita also discusses peculiar euphonic combinations. While discussing this form which is an instrumental singular of the form *adhī*- he comments:

> *Adhī*- means 'the one having no wisdom.' One should not become so. Since the prohibition is stated with respect to the word *sudhī*- by saying *asudhiyaḥ* 'except that of the word *sudhī*-' here, only the substitute denoted by the siglum *yaṇ* is applicable.[2]

This comment has a direct reference to the rule *kārakāsaṃkhyād oś ca supy asudhiyaḥ* (CV V.3.89). According to this rule, before nominal case terminations beginning with a vowel, which are denoted by the siglum *sup*, the final phoneme of nominal stems ending either in the phoneme *i* or *u* except that of the word *sudhī*- is replaced by a letter denoted by the siglum *yaṇ*, when these words follow either a *kāraka* or an indeclinable. The only condition being that these phonemes *i* and *u* do not follow a consonant cluster.[3] As far as the present form is concerned, the final phoneme *ī* of the word *dhī*- which follows the negative particle *na*, is replaced by *y*- before the instrumental singular suffix *ā*. Since the form under discussion is *adhī* and not *sudhī* as mentioned in the rule, the exceptional substitute *iya* taught by the rule *aci śnudhātubhruvāṃ yvor iyuvau* (CV V.3.83) does not apply in this case. Here, Śākyarakṣita's grammatical source is undoubtedly Candragomin's *Cāndravyākaraṇa* and not Pāṇini's *Aṣṭādhyāyī*, for the expression

---

sonant except *h*) (at the end of a *pada*) is optionally replaced by the most proximate consonant denoted by the siglum *ñam*."

1 *tattvasudhārasatṛptiviśeṣāt sakalasamīhitasiddhivaśād vā | tvaccaraṇānubhuvā bhavitavyaṃ bhavamathanaśruta na drutam adhyā ||*

2 *nāsti dhīr yasya tathā na bhavitavyam | asudhiya iti niṣedhād iha yaṇādeśa eva |*

3 Cf. CVṛ on the same: *kārakād asaṃkhyāc ca parasyāḥ prakṛter ivarṇāntāyā uvarṇāntāyāś ca sudhīvarjitāyāḥ supy ajādau parato yaṇ bhavati, na cet saṃyogāt parāv ivarṇovarṇau bhavataḥ |*

asudhiyaḥ occurring in our commentary does not figure in the corresponding Pāṇinian rule, which reads *na bhūsudhiyoḥ* (P VI.4.85).

5. *udabhārabandhura* (adj.) 'bending down on account of the load of water' (verse 146).[1] The next case of a morphophonemic change can be cited from the commentary on verse 146. It concerns the change of the word *udaka-* into *uda-* in a *tatpuruṣa* compound before the word *bhāra-*. Commenting on the compound word *udabhārabandhuraṃ*, Śākyarakṣita says:

> (The compound *udabhāraḥ* can be analysed as) *udakasya bhāraḥ* 'a load, i.e. a mass of water.' Before the word *bhāra-*, the word *udaka-* changes to *uda-*. (*Udabhārabandhura* means) bending down, i.e., bowing down on that account.[2]

As per the rules *udakasyodaḥ saṃjñāyām* (P VI.3.57) and *nāmny udakasyodaḥ* (CV V.2.65), the word *udaka-* is substituted by *uda-* before the final member of a compound when the compounded word is used as specific term (*saṁjñā*). Although Śākyarakṣita has not quoted a specific rule from any grammar, either that of Pāṇini or of Candragomin, his choice of words seems to be influenced by the explanation of the *Cāndravṛtti*. It is noteworthy that Śākyarakṣita uses the expression *udakasyodabhāvaḥ* which is also to be found in the *Cāndravṛtti*.[3] On the other hand, the author of the *Kāśikāvṛtti* chooses a different expression, viz. *udakaśabdasya saṃjñāyāṃ viṣaye uda ity ayam ādeśo bhavati.*

Out of the five cases discussed above, two concern with retroflexion, and one each with non-nasalization, substitution of a stem-final (*aṅgādeśa*) and substitution in place of a *pada* (*padādeśa*). References to a particular grammatical rule, an entry from a *dhātupāṭha* and a word-class (*gaṇa*) are found once each. It can be said with certainty that at least on three occasions Śākyarakṣita's comments rely on the *Cāndravyākaraṇa* whereas there is only one clear case of his adherence to the Pāṇinian grammar. In the remaining cases, no clear affiliation to any of the grammatical schools could be determined.

---

1 *taḍitojjvalaṃ jaladarāśim aniśam udabhārabandhuram | ghoraghanarasitam īśa tanuḥ kṛpayā kuto 'pi jayatīyam udgatā ||*

2 *udakasya bhāro rāśiḥ | bhāre udakasyodabhāvaḥ | tena bandhuraṃ namram |*

3 Cf. CVṛ on CV V.2.65: *udakasya saṁjñāyām uttarapade udabhāvo bhavati |*

III. Explanation of Unique Usages

As mentioned above, in the *Vṛttamālāstuti*, Jñānaśrīmitra combines the praise of different conducts of Mañjuśrī with the description of various metres belonging to different metrical genres. Since this is achieved by employing puns on particular words, two different interpretations of the same word become necessary to understand the intended meanings. At first, the word is interpreted to suit the praise of Mañjuśrī and secondly, the description of the metre. Sometimes, these interpretations involve discussions on grammatical issues without which their understanding is not possible. Four such cases are discussed in this section.

Apart from those, there are two cases: the first concerns a past participle of an intransitive verb used in the transitive sense and the second that of the reduplication of a verbal form. Śākyarakṣita discusses these peculiar usages from the point of view of grammar. Those are also discussed in the following section.

1. In the commentary on verse 13,[1] at first, Śākyarakṣita splits the expression *uṣṇihi* as *uṣṇi hi*. Here the particle *hi* has the sense of similarity and the word *uṣṇi* means 'in the hot season.'[2] The two together mean 'as in the hot season.'[3] Accordingly the translation of the verse would be as follows:

    Brightly shines the teaching of the Buddha
      after it has reached you—
    just as the splendour of the sun becomes extremely difficult to
      bear
    in the hot season.

    As for the second interpretation of the verse with regard to the metre, the word *uṣṇihi* is taken as a locative singular form of the word *uṣṇih-*, a metrical category to which the metre *sātireka* belongs.

2. Another such example can be cited from verse 17.[4] Here, the expression

---

1 *jājvalīti śāsanaṃ tvāṃ sametya saugatam | sūryadhāma duḥsahaṃ sātirekam uṣṇi hi ||*

2 For a detailed discussion of this form, refer to section II.A, no. 2.

3 *hiśabdaḥ sādṛśye | yathā uṣṇi uṣṇasamaye |*

4 *ghoramohatāmasāvaruddhabuddhilocanasya | ratnayaṣṭidīpikeva yā samāny abhūj janasya ||*

samāny abhūt is explained in the first place as a formation with the suffix *cvi* meaning 'what was uncommon before it became common.'[1] Thus, as a praise of Mañjuśrī, the verse can be translated as:

> For those beings, whose eye of wisdom
> was obstructed by the terrible darkness of delusion,
> that body of yours which was verily a lamp consisting
> of a stick beset with jewels, became commonly accessible.

When the verse refers to the metre, the same expression is interpreted as *samāny abhūt* where *samānī* is simply the name of a metre in the category *anuṣṭubh*.[2]

3. The next form to be discussed in this series is *avayavamatī* / *yavamatī* which occurs in verse 135. The metre described in this verse is named *yavamatī*. Jñānaśrīmitra very skilfully hints at this name during the course of describing Mañjuśrī's quality of compassion. He says:

> How is it possible to bring about the supreme wealth of welfare of others, if the compassion remains a mere mental state? (It is not.) Therefore, the very compassion in the appearance of this physical form (of Mañjuśrī) became one bearing the same designation, (namely, *avayavavatī* 'one endowed with physical limbs'), the feminine word with the suffix *matup* added after the word *avayava-*.[3]

Here the name of the metre *yavamatī* is hidden in the word *avayavamatī*, which in turn is mentioned in a very cryptic manner by referring to the grammatical components involved in its formation. This is well elaborated by Śākyarakṣita in his commentary as follows:

> Therefore, that very compassion in the appearance of the physical form of the Lord (Mañjuśrī), which has already been described, became *avayavavatī* ('endowed with physical limbs'), which is the form to be imitated. The word is equal to the form *avayava-mat-ī*, which is a mere imitation. (As for this form,) the (possessive) suffix *matup* is added after the sound, i.e. the word

---

1 *sādhāraṇībhavati smeti cvyantaḥ* |

2 *vṛttapakṣe 'nuṣṭubhi samānī nāma* ||

3 *caittamātrabhāvabhāji bhāvyate kva parā parārthasampad īdṛśī dayāyām* | *seyam etadākṛticchalād ato 'vayavadhvaner matup striyā samābhidhānā* ||

> *avayava-*. The very (combination) is feminine as it is a word ending in a feminine suffix. This is the meaning.[1]

After reading this complicated explanation one might ask why Jñānaśrīmitra chose this rather cryptic way of expression to describe Mañjuśrī. As an answer to this, Śākyarakṣita explains:

> On the metrical side, this is the metre *yavamatī* which bears the same name as the feminine word formed by adding the suffix *matup* after the word *yava-* that is to say, *yavamatī*. As per the rule *mād upadhāyāś ca mator vo 'yavādibhyaḥ* (P VIII.2.9), *ma* is not replaced by *va*. Since it is not possible to introduce the name (of the metre in its metrical structure) by adopting a regular word order, the earlier teachers themselves have used this elaborate expression.[2]

This explanation hints at a twofold problem: grammatical and metrical. The grammatical problem can be explained as follows: The feminine possessive form of the word *avayava-* is *avayavavatī*. Here, the phoneme *m* of the suffix *matup* is replaced by *v* as per the rule *mād upadhāyāś ca mator vo 'yavādibhyaḥ* (P VIII.2.9).[3] However, this regular form cannot serve the purpose as the name of the metre is *yavamatī*.

From the metrical point of view, the name of the metre *yavamatī*, which has a structure of three *laghu* and one *guru* syllable, does not fit in the metrical structure of this metre and hence could not be used in the metre as it is. In order to solve this twofold problem, Jñānaśrīmitra, like his predecessors, was forced to choose an expression, which could suit

---

1 *ataḥ seyaṃ dayaiṣoktalakṣaṇā yā bhagavadākṛtis tad eva cchalaṃ tataḥ | avayavadhvaner avayavaśabdān matup | sa eva strī | strīpratyayāntāvasthāparigrahāt | tayā anukaraṇamātrarūpayā samam abhidhānaṃ yasyā anukāryarūpāyāḥ | avayavavatīty arthaḥ* | What Śākyarakṣita wishes to convey is that here the intended word is *avayavavatī*, which, due to the metrical constraints, needs to be replicated (*anukārya*). *avayava* + the possessive suffix *mat(up)* + the feminine suffix *ī* = *avayava-mat-ī* is a replica of the intended form.

2 *vṛttapakṣe yavadhvaner matup striyā samābhidhānā yavamatī | mād upadhāyāś ca mator vo 'yavādibhya iti yavādipratiṣedhād vatvābhāvaḥ ṛjunā krameṇa saṃjñāpraveśo na nirvahatīti pūrveṣām evaiṣa vākyavinyāsaḥ* |

3 "The substitute phoneme *v* replaces the initial phoneme of the *taddhita* affix *matup* added after a nominal stem ending in or containing the phonemes *m* or *a* at the penultimate position excluding the class of words beginning with *yava-*."

both contexts. In this case, the chosen expression is a parallel grammatical description of the words *avayavavatī* and *yavamatī*.

From the commentarial explanation, it is quite evident that in this case, Śākyarakṣita's source of grammatical explanation is the Pāṇinian grammar and not the *Cāndravyākaraṇa*. The rule teaching the replacement of the phoneme *m* by *v* in the *Cāndravyākaraṇa* is *mād upāntāc ca mator vaḥ* (CV VI.3.35) where the prohibition *ayavādibhyaḥ* is excluded. In this grammar, the said prohibition is stated in a separate rule *na yavādibhyaḥ* (CV VI.3.38). Although the ms. of the VMSV reads *upadhāt* instead of *upadhāyāḥ* it seems to be a scribal error or an error that occurred in the course of transmission due to a possible confusion between *upāntāt* of the Cāndra system and *upadhāyāḥ* of the Pāṇinians.

4. Another instance worthy of note is to be found in verse 142.[1] This is a description of the metre *āpīḍa* in the category *padacaturūrdhva* in the section dealing with *viṣamavṛttas*. In this verse, once again Jñānaśrīmitra has skilfully incorporated the name of the metre by resorting to its grammatical analysis. It is noteworthy that in the metre *āpīḍa* the last two syllables of each foot are *guru* and the rest are *laghu*.[2] Considering this fact, the inclusion of the name *āpīḍa* containing two *guru* and one *laghu* syllables into the metrical scheme of this metre is impossible. In view of this difficulty, Jñānaśrīmitra once again adopted the device of referring to the intended name of the metre through the grammatical description of its components. The form *āpīḍaḥ* is a *prādi tatpuruṣa* compound of the prefix *āṅ* (= *ā*) meaning *abhividhi* ('complete, all-inclusive') and the word *pīḍaḥ* meaning 'the one endowed with compassion.' Hence, *āpīḍaḥ* means 'the one having all-inclusive compassion' (*samantād dayāvān*). Jñānaśrīmitra described the said components of the compound and their relation by using the grammatical parlance in such a way that when these are construed one arrives at the intended word describing Mañjuśrī as well as the name of a metre. He says:

   If you do not certainly become someone denoted by the word *pīḍaḥ* along with (the prefix *ā*) denoting complete inclusion (that

---

1 *iti nigaditajātau kṛtaviṣamacaraṇaracanāyām | laghuguruniyatibhṛti bhayam ayati ko na bhavasi na yadi niyatam abhividhivacanam anu pīḍaḥ ||*

2 *atrāntimadvayadvayaṃ guru śeṣaṃ laghu |*

is to say, *āpīḍaḥ* 'someone having all-inclusive compassion').[1]

It may be noted that the said explanation of the meaning of the prefix *ā* can be found in the *Aṣṭādhyāyī*'s rule *āṅ maryādābhividhyoḥ* (P II.1.13). Also cf. the *Kāśikāvṛtti* on *āṅ maryādāvacane*[2] (P I.4.89) and the *Cāndravṛtti* on *paryapābhyāṃ varjane* (CV II.1.82).[3] Śākyarakṣita explains it in his commentary in the following manner:

> The word denoting complete inclusion is the prefix *āṅ*. After that, i.e. together with it, *pīḍaḥ* becomes *āpīḍaḥ*. 'If you do not become fully compassionate' is the meaning.[4]

The same interpretation of the said expression also holds good for the metrical side of the verse. Śākyarakṣita comments:

> On the metrical side, the metre is called *āpīḍaḥ* where the word *pīḍaḥ* follows the word denoting 'complete inclusion' having the same meaning as explained before. It belongs to the category *padacaturūrdhva*, which has already been described; it consists of feet of uneven structure and moreover contains the fixed order of heavy and light syllables in the way as they are arranged in this *śloka*.[5]

Thus, by adopting such an ingenious method Jñānaśrīmitra could successfully include the name of the metre *āpīḍa* in a verse composed in the same metre that allows only two long syllables at the end of each foot.

5. Also of interest is an interpretation of the word *śānta-* found in the commentary on verse 55.[6] While commenting on *śānto dveṣāgniḥ* Śākya-

---

1 *bhavasi na yadi niyatam abhividhivacanam anu pīḍaḥ* |

2 *avadhiḥ - maryādā* | *vacanagrahaṇād abhividhir api gṛhyate* |

3 *ā Pāṭaliputrād vṛṣṭo deva iti maryādābhividhyor avadher eva pañcamī.*

4 *abhividhivacanam āṅ* | *tam anu tena saha pīḍa āpīḍaḥ* | *samantād dayāvān yadi na bhavasīty arthaḥ* |

5 *vṛttapakṣe nigaditāyāṃ padacaturūrdhvajātau kṛtaviṣamacaraṇaracanāyām etacchlokaprastārakrameṇa laghuguruniyamaṃ dadhatyāṃ satyāṃ* | *abhividhivacanam anu pīḍo vyākhyātārthaḥ* |

6 *bhaṅgaṃ nītās te pañcabāṇasya bāṇāḥ śānto dveṣāgnir mohajāḍyaṃ nirastam* | *nātha trailokyānugrahavyagramūrte saṃpat saṃprāptā vaiśvadevī tvayaiva* ||

rakṣita says:

> You pacified the fire of hatred. How is it (that the form *śānta* is interpreted in a transitive sense)? *Śānta* is a form where the sense of the causal suffix *ṇi* is included (in the meaning of the verbal root *śam*-).[1]

Thus, according to Śākyarakṣita, the form *śānta* is not a past participle of a mere intransitive root *śam*- meaning 'the one who is calmed down' as it appears to be. Rather in this particular case, it has a transitive sense that is to say, the word *śānta*- is used here in the sense of *śamita*-. In Sanskrit, there are certain roots, which are capable of conveying intransitive as well as transitive sense. Grammarians and commentators often explain the use of such intransitive roots in a transitive sense by stating that the meaning of the causal suffix *ṇi* is included in the root to turn it into a transitive root. Śākyarakṣita adopts the same technique to explain this peculiar usage.

6. In verse 119,[2] there is a reduplication of the verbal form *jayati jayati.* Śākyarakṣita explains this reduplication as follows:

> As for the expression *jayati jayati,* the reduplication (of the word) is either in the sense of 'agitation (*saṃbhrama*) or 'frequent repetition' (*ābhīkṣṇya*).[3]

The source of this explanation is the grammar of Candragomin and not Pāṇini's *Aṣṭādhyāyī*. Candragomin has prescribed the reduplication of a word in both the above-mentioned cases in rules *vīpsābhīkṣṇyayor dve* (CV VI.3.1) and *saṃbhrame yāvadbodham* (CV VI.3.14). As per rule VI.3.1, "the form is reduplicated when there is a sense of 'each and every' (*vīpsā*) or 'frequent repetition' (*ābhīkṣṇya*). ... (For example,) 'He gives water to each and every tree.' 'He cooks again and again.'"[4] According

---

[1] *tvayā śānto dveṣāgniḥ | kutaḥ | śānta ity antarbhūtaṇyarthe rūpaṃ |*

[2] *capalacaraṇapīḍitāgādhipopetapātālatālūcchaladvyālapālastutaṃ jayati jayati cāru kāruṇyakelisphuratpadmanarteśvarākāralīlāyitam | anibhṛtabhujadaṇḍaṣaṇḍapracaṇḍānilollāsitaḥ śrāntiśāntiṃ tanotīva te pralayasamayaśaṅkayā yatra lokatrayīdaṇḍakaś caṇḍavṛṣṭiprayāto 'mbudaḥ ||*

[3] *jayati jayatīti saṃbhrama ābhīkṣṇye vā dviruktiḥ |*

[4] Cf. CVṛ on CV VI.3.1: *vīpsāyām ābhīkṣṇye ca yad vartate tasya dve rūpe bhavataḥ | ... vṛkṣaṁ vṛkṣaṁ siñcati | ... ābhīkṣṇyaṁ paunaḥpunyam. pacati pacati |*

to rule VI.3.14, "when the speaker is agitated, then he should repeat the word as many times as is necessary for another person to understand the speaker's intention, for instance 'Snake! Snake! Snake!' or 'Wake up! Wake up! Wake up!'"[1]

From the above discussion, one may notice that some of these discussions involve grammatical discussions of general type, viz. the comment on the meaning of the particle *hi*, a mention of the suffix *cvi*, and the concept of *antarbhāvitaṇyartha*, that is the inclusion of the sense of the causal suffix *ṇi* into the primary meaning of a verbal root. Naturally, no mention of any particular grammatical rule can be found in such discussions. In two cases, viz. in the discussion on the form *jayati jayati* and *yavamatī* and *avayavamatī*, we find reference to specific grammatical rules. The first of the two is indirect and can be ascribed to the *Cāndravyākaraṇa*. The second is, however, direct, and is to be ascribed to Pāṇini's *Aṣṭādhyāyī*. In the last case, where the word *āpīḍa-* is hinted at in a cryptic manner, we find reference to the prefix *ā* by referring to its technical meaning that is popular in works of grammar.

IV. Explanation of Peculiar Compounds

The explanation of compounds is a special feature of Śākyarakṣita's commentary. He explains almost each compound occurring in a verse indicating its type merely by dissolution, and not by mentioning its designation. Occasionally, he suggests more than a single possible dissolution of a compound, thereby indicating different possible interpretations, for example, the compound *dalasukhaśayana°* (verse 40) is explained in two ways, first as a *karmadhāraya: dalaṃ pattraṃ | tad eva sukhaṃ śayanaṃ*[2] and secondly as a *tatpuruṣa: dale vā sukhena śayanaṃ.*[3]

Regarding the problematic cases of compounds, Śākyarakṣita indicates the underlying problem and its possible solution. Often in such discussions, he alludes to grammatical concepts, maxims, or rules. Four such instances are discussed below:

---

1 *prayoktuḥ saṁbhrame sati yāvadbhiḥ śabdaiḥ so 'rtho 'vagamyate tāvantaḥ śabdāḥ prayoktavyāḥ | ahir ahir ahiḥ ! budhyasva budhyasva budhyasva |*

2 '*Dalam* means 'leaf.' It is verily a comfortable bed.'

3 'Or, sleeping comfortably on the leaf.'

1. In verse 39,[1] there is a long compound *gīyamānasumanaḥsumanasvajjātikīrtivijayā*, which qualifies *nīlābjaśrī* 'the splendour of a blue water-lily' occurring in the next verse. The compound means 'that of which the victory over the fame of the class of flower best among the flowers is being sung.'[2] This is a *bahuvrīhi* compound having two main components, viz. *gīyamānaḥ* and *sumanaḥsumanasvajjātikīrtivijayaḥ*. Out of these two members, the first *gīyamānaḥ* is syntactically dependent on the compound word *dūratatasaurabhalobhasvāgatālipaṭalakvaṇitena* 'by the humming sound of the song of bees invited by the longing for a far-spread fragrance.' In a *bahuvrīhi*, both members of the compound are subordinate with respect to a qualificant noun. Now as a subordinate member dependent on another word, the word *gīyamāna*- cannot enter into a compound with the word *sumanaḥsumanasvajjātikīrtivijaya*-. As per the general rule of compounding, a word cannot form a compound with another word if it is syntactically dependent on a word, which is outside the domain of that particular compound.[3] However, there is an exception to the said rule when the compound, so formed, is capable of conveying the desired meaning. As regard to the compound *gīyamāna°*, Śākyarakṣita takes the same stand to justify it. He comments: 'Even though there is syntactic dependence, the compound does take place on account of being able to convey the intended meaning.'[4] Dr. DIMITROV notes other occurrences of this statement in his book *The Legacy of the Jewel Mind*. He says (2016: 656, note 157): "[t]he expression *sāpekṣatve 'pi gamakatvāt samāsaḥ* can be read, for example, in Prajñākaramati's *Bodhicaryāvatārapañjikā* on *Bodhicaryāvatāra* 2.17 (ed. DE LA VALLÉE POUSSIN 1901–14, p. 54; see also p. 310 [on 8.54] and p. 514 [on 9.92]), and in Ratna's *Ratnaśrīṭīkā* on *Kāvyādarśa* 3.1, 3.79 (ed. DIMITROV 2011, pp. 282, 350). It is often used in the commentarial literature."

---

1 *gīyamānasumanaḥsumanasvajjātikīrtivijayeva taveyam* | *bhāti dūratatasaurabhalobhasvāgatālipaṭalakvaṇitena* ||

2 *sumanasāṃ madhye suṣṭhu manasvatī manasvinī* | *parimalādiguṇenonnatā yā jātiḥ puṣpajātir jātipuṣpaṃ vā tasyāḥ kīrtis tasyā vijayaḥ parājayaḥ* | *sa gīyamāno yasyāḥ sā tathā* |

3 Cf. *Mahābhāṣya* (p. 318) on *samarthaḥ padavidhiḥ* (P II.1.1): *sāpekṣam asamartham bhavati* |

4 *sāpekṣatve 'pi gamakatvāt samāsaḥ* |

2. Another instance of *sāpekṣasamāsa* is *viśvabhāratī* (verse 131).[1] Here the word *viśvasya* is syntactically dependent on *prasabhākrānta°*, which is a part of another compound, *prasabhākrāntajagattrayīśikham*. In spite of this, it is compounded with *bhāratī* resulting into a *sāpekṣasamāsa*. As mentioned above, a noun, which is *sāpekṣa*, is not fit for compounding (*asamartha*) with another noun. Śākyarakṣita solves this problem by giving the same solution as before, viz. 'even though there is syntactic dependence, the compound still takes place because of its being able to convey the particular meaning.'[2]

3. An interesting case of a peculiar interpretation of a compound can be found in the commentary on verse 102.[3] Here Śākyarakṣita explains the compound *vyākhyānapreṅkhatkarakararuhodbhāsinī*, an adjective of *dorvallī* 'an arm creeper' as follows:

   > It is waving because of preaching and at the same time shining by the virtue of fingernails of the hand.[4]

   It is quite clear that Śākyarakṣita considers this compound as a *karmadhāraya* and hence, is faced with a problem of justifying the same. According to the primary rule of a *karmadhāraya* compound, a qualifier as an initial member of a compound is optionally compounded with a qualificant noun as a final member.[5] Thus, this type of compound presupposes a qualifier-qualificant (*viśeṣaṇa-viśeṣya*) relationship between its members. In our present case, both the members of the compound, viz. *vyākhyānapreṅkhantī* and *karakararuhodbhāsinī* are adjectives qualifying *dorvallī*. Since there is no *viśeṣaṇa-viśeṣya* relationship between the two, their compound is not possible. Anticipating this problem, Śākyarakṣita suggests a solution in the following words:

---

1 *padam ekam avekṣya te kṣaṇaṃ prasabhākrāntajagattrayīśikham | katham astu na viśvabhāratī nijadāsīva tava priyaṃvadā ||*

2 *sāpekṣatve 'pi gamakatvāt samāsaḥ |*

3 *śobhāsaṃpattiḥ śirasi guruṇaikena saivopajātā yā syāt kalpadroḥ śubhaphalanibhaṃ bibhrato bhadrakumbham | vyākhyānapreṅkhatkarakararuhodbhāsinī bhāti bhartur dorvallī ceyaṃ kusumitalatā vellitevānilena ||*

4 *vyākhyānena preṅkhantī cāsau karasaṃbandhinaḥ kararuhā nakhās tair udbhāsinī ca |*

5 Cf. *viśeṣaṇaṃ viśeṣyeṇa bahulam* (P II.1.57), *viśeṣaṇam ekārthena* (CV II.2.18).

In spite of both being qualifiers, their compound takes place when in expectation of a qualificant the qualifier-qualificant (*viśeṣaṇa-viśeṣya*) relationship is intended (between the two).[1]

Thus, according to Śākyarakṣita, it is possible to form a *karmadhāraya* compound even of two adjectives when a speaker intends a *viśeṣya-viśeṣaṇa* relationship between the two out of the expectation for a qualificant.

This might appear to be a clumsy way of explaining the compound. Although grammatical works allow compounds of adjectives under specific conditions,[2] the present case does not fit in any of these.

There is another possible way to explain this compound, which is as follows:

vyākhyāne preṅkhataḥ karasya ye kararuhāḥ, tair udbhāsinī |

Shining because of the fingernails of the hand, which is waving in discourse.

Śākyarakṣita, however, does not adopt this simpler way of explanation. Most probably, in his view, this is not the intended sense of the compound used by Jñānaśrīmitra. Here Śākyarakṣita seems to see a parallel structure in the compound *vyākhyānapreṅkhatkarakararuhodbhāsinīdorvallī* and the two expressions in the fourth *pāda*, viz. *kusumitalatā* and *vellitevānilena*. This is evident from his analysis of the compound into two adjectives, viz. *vyākhyānapreṅkhantī* that corresponds to *anilena vellitā* and *karakararuhodbhāsinī dorvallī*, which relates to *kusumitalatā*. Thus, Mañjuśrī's hand, which is waving because of giving a sermon, is like a creeper swaying due to wind and his hand, which is shining by the virtue of fingernails, is like a creeper full of flowers. This parallel structure not only explains why Śākyarakṣita interprets this compound as a *karmadhāraya* of two adjectives but also answers the query as to why he dissolves the compound *vyākhyānapreṅkhantī* as *vyākhyānena preṅkhantī* instead of *vyākhyāne preṅkhantī*.

---

1 *viśeṣaṇayor api viśeṣyam apekṣya viśeṣaṇaviśeṣyabhāvavivakṣāyāṃ samāsaḥ* |

2 Cf. *ktena nañviśiṣṭenānañ* (P II.1.60), *varṇo varṇena* (P II.1.69), *mayūravyaṃsakādayaś ca* (P II.1.72).

4. In the commentary on verse 124,[1] Śākyarakṣita discusses the form *udāranavanāṭyarasavat*, which is a part of a larger *bahuvrīhi* compound *udāranavanāṭyarasavallalitavṛttam*. The said form is derived by adding the suffix *matup* to the *karmadhāraya* compound *udāranavanāṭyarasāḥ*.[2] In the subsequent morphophonemic change, the *ma* of *matup* is replaced by *va*.[3] This explanation is followed by discussion about the propriety of this construction. It is based on Patañjali's *Mahābhāṣya* on the rule *varṇo varṇena* (P II.1.69). According to Patañjali, if compared, which mode of denoting a meaning is preferable, whether by using a *karmadhāraya* stem appended by a possessive suffix *matup*, or by a *bahuvrīhi* compound, then, the answer is: by using a *bahuvrīhi* compound as it is easy and brief from the point of understanding as well as expression.[4] The same point of discussion also figures later in Bhoja's *Śṛṅgāraprakāśa* (p. 482). Comparing the two modes, Bhoja says:

> It is brief when expressed by means of a *bahuvrīhi* containing a *karmadhāraya* as in the case of *yakṣaś cakre janakatanayāsnānapuṇyodakeṣu* ... and cumbersome when denoted by the way of a *karmadhāraya* appended by a possessive suffix *matup* as in the case of *ā kailāsād bisakisalayacchedapātheyavantaḥ* ... .[5]

Śākyarakṣita brings both the views in his discussion and defends Jñānaśrīmitra's usage of the form *udāranavanāṭyarasavat* from a grammatical point of view. He comments:

> (The expression) *udāranavanāṭyarasavat* can be analysed as something which possesses nine dramatic sentiments in abundance. Hence, there is an addition of the suffix *matup*. The

---

1 *prauḍhavaravajravanitāṅgaparirambhavilasatpulakajālakajagajjayatanutraṃ sāntrasavasāsramadhupānamadamuktavikaṭāṭṭahasitatrasadaśeṣasuradaityam | gāḍhavinigūḍhadayavismayamayāpratimaraudratanum advayamahārṇavanimagnaṃ śuddhaguṇadhāma karuṇābalam udāranavanāṭyarasaval lalitavṛttam abhivande ||*

2 Cf. *tad asyāsti asminn iti matup* (P V.2.94), *tad asyāsty atreti matup* (CV IV.2.98).

3 Cf. *mād upadhāyāś ca mator vo 'yavādibhyaḥ* (P VIII.2.9), *mād upāntāc ca mator vaḥ* (CV VI.3.35).

4 *karmadhārayaprakṛtibhir matvarthīyair abhidhānam astu bahuvrīhiṇeti | bahuvrīhiṇā bhaviṣyati laghutvāt* | Cf. Kaiyaṭa's *Pradīpa* on the same.

5 *karmadhārayabahuvrīhiṇā laghur yathā - yakṣaś cakre ... || karmadhārayamatvarthīyena gurur yathā - ākailāsād bisakisalayacchedapātheyavantaḥ ... ||*

> one having such type of charming behaviour is *udāranavanāṭya-rasavallalitavṛtta.* (This construction with a possessive suffix *matup* added to a *karmadhāraya* stem is justified) because the maxim 'the *bahuvrīhi* alone is to be favoured as compared to a *karmadhāraya* compound having a possessive sense denoted by the suffix *matup.*' is accepted only with regard to the view in favour of a compound. However, in the opinion of those who are exponents of non-compounding, a *karmadhāraya* compound having the possessive sense denoted by the suffix *matup* is also desirable as in the example *bisa*°.[1]

It is interesting to note that in the *Kavikāmadhenu* commentary on the *Amarakośa,* its author Subhūticandra, who was a senior contemporary of Śākyarakṣita, also discusses this issue. While commenting on the word *durgandha-* (AK I.6.5) he cites opinions of Kātyāyana, and Bhoja along with a quotation from the *Aśubhakathā* of Vibhākaravarman with regard to a *karmadhārayamatvarthīya* construction. Further in support of this construction, he adds that since the meanings 'excessive and so on' (*atiśayanādiḥ*) cannot be conveyed by a *bahuvrīhi* compound, a *karma-dhāraya* compound having a possessive sense denoted by the suffix *matup* is certainly desirable in order to express those meanings.[2] Although it looks quite certain that Śākyarakṣita's explanation is inspired by Bhoja's *Śṛṅgāraprakāśa,* we are unable to judge whether Subhūticandra's *Kavikāmadhenu* also played some role in shaping his argument. One thing is quite certain that this issue must have been discussed very keenly in the scholarly circles of Śākyarakṣita's time.

---

1 *udārā nava nāṭyarasā yasya santīti matup | tathābhūtaṃ lalitaṃ vṛttaṃ yasya | karmadhārayamatvarthīyād bahuvrīhir eveṣṭavyo lāghavārthaṃ ity asya samāsamata evābhimatatvāt | vyāsavādimate tu matvarthīyo 'pi | yathā bisakisalayaccheda-pātheyavanta iti |*

2 Cf. *Kavikāmadhenu* on AK I.6.5 (fol. 58a6–58b1): *viśeṣaṇasamāsāt matvarthīye cikīrṣite prakriyālāghavārtham anyapadārthasya eva nyāyyatvam iti duṣṭo gandho 'sya iti durgandhaḥ | tad uktaṃ kātyāyanena - karmadhārayamatvarthīyāt bahuvrīhir laghutvād iti | anye tu lāghavam anādriyamāṇā icchanty eva matvarthīyam | prayuktaṃ cāśubhakathāyāṃ vibhākaravarmaṇā - yad durgandhi yad āvilaṃ ... gṛdhrā iva || iti | śṛṅgāraprakāśe cābhihitam - dvividho vācyadharmo laghur guruś ca | ... bisakisalayacchedapātheyavantaḥ iti | kiṃ ca bahuvrīhiṇā atiśayanādir artho na gamyata iti avaśyaṃ tatpratipādanāya karmadhārayapūrvako matvarthīya eṣṭavyaḥ |*

V. References to Grammatical Concepts and Maxims

A number of references to different grammatical concepts and maxims evince Śākyarakṣita's thorough acquaintance with the grammatical literature. He has made use of these concepts and maxims to solve textual problems with regard to syntax and semantics, more precisely, the problems concerning issues like number, gender, and meaning of a word. These grammatical concepts and maxims are discussed in this section under four headings:

A. References to Grammatical Concepts

a. *Liṅgavipariṇāma*

1. In verse 81,[1] we come across a neuter word *atiśakvarībandhasāram* in the nominative singular case. The word signifies the category of metres and is continued in the following verses as a governing category (*adhikāra*). The following verse 82 describes Mañjuśrī in the Mālinī metre. In its explanation on the metrical side, Śākyarakṣita makes a reference to *liṅgavipariṇāma*, a traditional term denoting the gender transposition:

> On the metrical side, when here (in this verse) the word *atiśakvarībandham* is construed by effecting the gender transposition, (the verse means) this *mālinī* metre, which is excellent because of the atiśakvarī genre, is victorious.[2]

2. In the commentary on verse 97,[3] we find another reference to *liṅgavipariṇāma* 'gender transposition.' It runs as follows:

---

1 *svedapūravilasatpulakocchvasitais truṭatkañcukaṃ dadhati nirdhutam apy amarastriyaḥ | kāntikamram iva te samitāv atiśakvarībandhasāram urukampam anaṅgavijṛmbhitam ||*

2 *vṛttapakṣe 'tiśakvarībandhasāram iti liṅgavipariṇāmenātra saṃbandhāt | atiśakvarībandhasārā mālinīyaṃ jayati* | Note that the Ms. reads *vibhakti°*. This also appears to be a case of wrong transmission. Since both *atiśakvarībandhasāram* and *°sārā* are in the nominative case, the present case, where the former expression is in the neuter gender and the latter in the feminine, is rather an instance of *liṅgavipariṇāma* 'gender transposition' than *vibhaktivipariṇāma* 'case transposition.'

3 *kalpaśatopapāditamahāphalam iva vihitaṃ cañcalam etad āyur adhipa tvadavanatiparaiḥ | bhūṣaṇabhavyabhāvagamitaṃ śritagurukaruṇādigyativaṃśa pattrapatitaṃ kam iva jalaruhaḥ ||*

On the metrical side, when (the word *samudbhūtā*) is construed (with the expression *vaṃśapatrapatitam*) by effecting the gender transposition, (the verse means): The category *atyaṣṭi* attained its accomplishment in such a manner that the metre *vaṃśapatra-patita* is born.[1]

In verse 94,[2] we find the following expression: *atyaṣṭiḥ ... cchandaḥ ... pari-ṇatim avāpat ... tathā ... yathā ... samudbhūtā ... °śikhariṇī.* Here the word *samudbhūtā* occurs in the feminine gender. By the principle of ellipsis, it is continued in the following verses as a fixed formula describing metres in that section.[3] Though the feminine adjective *sambudbhūtā* is in agreement with the qualificant feminine noun *śikhariṇī,* it needs alteration as to its gender in the case of the neuter noun *vaṃśapatra-patitam.* Śākyarakṣita explains this alteration by means of *liṅgavipari-ṇāma.*

3. The next instance of *liṅgavipariṇāma* can be cited from the commentary on verse 106.[4] On the metrical side of the explanation of verse 105,[5] the word *atidhṛtimatā* is abstracted from the verse to match the qualificant feminine noun *meghavisphūrjitā.* The word *atidhṛtimatā* continues in the next verse denoting the category of the metre to which the metre *Śārdūlavikrīḍita* also belongs. Since *Śārdūlavikrīḍita,* as the name of a metre, is in the neuter gender, it is necessary to modify the qualifying word *atidhṛtimatā* into neuter as *°matam.* Explaining this process of gender transposition, Śākyarakṣita says:

---

1 *vṛttapakse 'tyaṣṭiś cchandas tathā pariṇatim avāpad yathā vaṃśapattrapatitaṃ samudbhūtam iti liṅgavipariṇāmena saṃbandhāt* |

2 *guṇānām atyaṣṭiḥ katham iha mamevāstu jagatām iti cchandaḥ svairaṃ pariṇatim avāpat tava tathā* | *yathā tvayy evāsmin paramarasabhedapraṇayanī samudbhūtā bhūtir nikhilasukhaśākhāśikhariṇī* ||

3 *atyaṣṭicchandas tathā pariṇatim avāpad yathā samudbhūteti mandākrāntāparyantam adhikṛtaṃ veditavyam* ||

4 *pāyād vo varabuddhavaṃśajaladher vṛddhau sudhādīdhitir mañjuśrīḥ paribhūta-manmathakathaḥ prajñāṅganāsaṃgame* | *bhīmabhrāntivibhāvarīparibhave bibhrad yatiṃ bhāsvato viśvakleśakuraṅgasaṅgaravidhau śārdūlavikrīḍitam* ||

5 *parārthe sthāsnūnām atidhṛtimatām īśa viśvānukampāmukhonmīlannānārasarasa-padākarṇayāvedayāmi* | *daśāṃ tām ādhehi kṣaṇam api guro pāvanīṃ pāvanānāṃ samantadhvāntāni praharasi yayā me 'ghavisphūrjitāni* ||

On the metrical side, when the word (*atidhṛtimatā*) is construed by means of gender transposition, (the verse means:) The metre *Śārdūlavikrīḍita* belonging to the *atidhṛti* genre.[1]

4. Another instance of *liṅgavipariṇāma* occurs in the commentary on verse 125.[2] Here while giving guidelines for construing the primarily neuter expression *idam ardham* and *ādadhad ardham*, with the concerned names of metres in different genders, Śākyarakṣita says:

 > The governing phrases (*adhikāra*) *idam ardham* and *ādadhad ardham* continue up to (the metre) *Viparītākhyānikā*. Wherever there is a difference in gender, these should be construed by following the method of *liṅgavipariṇāma*, i.e. gender transposition.[3]

 Hence, if the name of a metre is either in the masculine or feminine gender, then the governing phrase should be modified according to that particular gender.

b. *Ekaśeṣa*

Another important grammatical concept referred to by Śākyarakṣita is *ekaśeṣa*, the phenomenon of single remainder. In this word formation, out of the many identical word forms used in the same case, only one is retained, for example, *vṛkṣaś ca vṛkṣaś ca vṛkṣau, vṛkṣaś ca vṛkṣaś ca vṛkṣaś ca vṛkṣāḥ.*[4] This type of word formation is accepted only by Pāṇini. Candragomin, however, rejects it arguing that since words have multiple meanings accepting the single remainder is without purpose.[5]

A reference to the *ekaśeṣa* can be found at two places in the entire available commentary. As for the first, in the commentary on verse 88,[6] Śākyarakṣita

---

1 *vṛttapakṣe liṅgavipariṇāmena saṃbandhād atidhṛtimataṃ śārdūlavikrīḍitam* |

2 *idam ardham abālaśaśiprabhaṃ bālaraviprabham ādadhad ardham* | *karuṇāvaśavarti bhavadvapuḥ kasya mano na karoty upacitram* ||

3 *idam ardham ādadhad ardham ity adhikāro viparītākhyānikāṃ yāvat* | *yatra ca liṅgāntaraṃ tatra liṅgavipariṇāmena saṃbandhanīyaṃ* |

4 Cf. *Kāśikā* on *sarūpāṇām ekaśeṣa ekavibhaktau* (P I.2.64).

5 Cf. CVṛ on *lug aṇādiluky agoṇyādīnām* (CV II.2.87): *śabdasyānekārthatvād ekaśeṣānarthakyam* |

6 *atiratikarakatha katham iva samiyād aviratanavanavanava tava paramaiḥ* | *guṇagaṇaparimitim udadhiṣu yatibhiḥ suyatibhir agaṇitaguṇa maṇinikaraḥ* ||

remarks:

> One should understand that since there is a mention of the word *udadhiṣu* in the plural number, or as a single remainder, here (in this metre) the caesura is marked after every four letters.[1]

The second instance of an *ekaśeṣa* found in the commentary on verse 136 is discussed later in this paper in the section VI, no. 5.

B. References to Grammatical Maxims

a. *jātau ekavacanam*

1. In the commentary on verse 99,[2] while commenting on the singular number in two words, viz. *yatiṣaṭpadam* and *kṛtikokilakam*, Śākyarakṣita refers to the generally accepted grammatical maxim explaining the use of a singular number in the sense of a species (*jātāv ekavacanam*). He says: 'In both the cases, there is a singular number in the sense of a species.'[3] Thus, the words *yatiṣaṭpadam* and *kṛtikokilakam* should be understood as 'bees in the form of ascetics' and 'the cuckoos in the form of Bodhisattvas.'

   In this context, it is noteworthy that the said maxim occurs *verbatim* in the CVṛ on *lug aṇādiluky agoṇyādīnām* (CV II.2.87). The text reads: *saṃpanno yava iti jātāv ekavacanam* |[4] This is a clear testimony of the influence of the CVṛ on Śākyarakṣita's writing in this particular case. One may also refer to Pāṇini's rule I.2.58 for comparison: *jātyākhyāyām ekasmin bahuvacanam anyatarasyām* |[5]

---

1 *udadhiṣv iti bahuvacananirdeśād ekaśeṣād vā praticatuṣkaṃ yati .. .. .. lakṣito draṣṭavyaḥ* |

2 *tribhuvanasaṃmadapradajinavyavasāyamadhau sphuṭasahakāratāmahitam īhitam īśa tava* | *pravacanamañjarīsrutaśamāmṛtapānamudābhṛta yatiṣaṭpadaṃ kalakaṇat-kṛtikokilakam* ||

3 *ubhayatra jātāv ekavacanam* |

4 "As for the expression *saṃpanno yavaḥ* 'Fully grown barley' the singular number is in the sense of a species."

5 "The plural number is optionally used in the sense of a singular while designating a species."

2. A similar instance can be recorded from the commentary on verse 141.[1] Here commenting upon the singular number in the word *pādaḥ*, Śākya-rakṣita says: "The singular number is in the sense of a species. Thus it, (i.e. the word *pādaḥ*,) means 'feet.'"[2]

b. *saṃbandhibhedād bahuvacanam*

In the commentary on verse 148,[3] Śākyarakṣita refers to one more grammatical maxim, viz. *saṃbandhibhedād bahuvacanam* 'plural number on account of different relata.' Here the context is that of the use of plural number in the word *vikṛtāni* in the expression *bhṛkuṭīkaṭākṣadaśaneṣu kim api vikṛtāni bibhrataḥ.*[4] *Vikṛta* 'scary gesture' is a singular concept. However, in view of its association with three relata, viz. *bhrukuṭī, kaṭākṣa,* and *daśana,* it is mentioned in the plural number as per the previously mentioned maxim. The same has been elaborated by Śākyarakṣita in the following words:

> Scary gestures with respect to teeth along with frowning and side-glances. The plural number is because of the differentiation among the relata.[5]

Once more, the expression used by Śākyarakṣita can be traced back to CVṛ, this time on the rule *asaṃkhyaṃ vibhaktisamīpābhāvakhyātipaścādyathāyuga-patsaṃpatsākalyārthe* (CV II.2.2). Commenting on the word *abhāva-*, Dharma-dāsa, the author of the CVṛ, remarks: 'Absence is manifold on account of the differentiation among its relata.'[6] Though the context is different from the present one, the striking similarity in the expression cannot be easily ignored.

---

1 *aṣṭābhir akṣaraiḥ pādo 'soḍhas tadgāḍhamajjanād anuvṛddhaiḥ | guṇasāgara sāgarair apūritāṅgurīgarto viṣamaṃ daśāntare dayā padacaturūrdhvaṃ nayati bhāvam ||*

2 *jātāv ekavacanam | pādā ity arthaḥ |*

3 *bhṛkuṭīkaṭākṣadaśaneṣu kim api vikṛtāni bibhrataḥ | damayati tava bhuvanāni vapur lalitaṃ ca kiṃ tu vikaṭaṃ yad īdṛśam ||*

4 "Exhibiting in an inexplicable manner scary gestures of frowning, side glances, and teeth."

5 *bhṛkuṭīkaṭākṣeṇa yukteṣu daśaneṣu vikṛtāni | saṃbandhibhedād bahuvacanaṃ |*

6 *abhāvaḥ saṃbandhibhedād bahuvidhaḥ |*

As shown above, the concept of *ekaśeṣa* has its firm roots in the Pāṇinian tradition whereas the two maxims quoted in connection with the singular or plural number of the word are traceable to the Cāndra system of grammar.

VI. Semantic or Syntactic Interpretations

Śākyarakṣita's analysis of the VMS is not confined to the identification of word types, derivation of words, dissolution of compounds etc. Whenever he finds scope for a peculiar semantic analysis or different syntactic possibilities, he discusses them for the benefit of connoisseurs of the poem. He brings to their notice additional shades of meaning conveyed by a particular word or different possible nuances denoted by a particular case termination. On occasions, he displays how by splitting a word in different ways, by construing it differently, and by giving it a different interpretation, one can unfold the hidden beauty and poetic potentials of the poem. Five such cases are discussed below to corroborate the above statements:

1. 'An adjective with a conditional nuance.' Śākyarakṣita, while commenting on verses 12[1] and 20,[2] explains the respective expressions *tvadekaśaraṇam* and *ketanadaṇḍam* as 'an adjective with a conditional nuance' (*hetubhāvena viśeṣaṇam*). He thereby suggests an additional shade of meaning. Taking into consideration Śākyarakṣita's interpretation, the verses may be translated as follows:

   O Blessed One, be merciful,
   and turn your attention just a little bit
   to this stupid being
   since he has made you his sole refuge! || 12 ||

   When you bear the staff of your characteristic sign,
   then because of it, you display the grace of an excellent teacher,
   who is, as it were, instructing his disciples,
   the human beings, in rightful conduct. || 20 ||

---

1 *prasīda bhagavan vilokaya manāk | jaḍaṃ janam imaṃ tvadekaśaraṇam ||*

2 *ketanadaṇḍaṃ dadhato 'dhyāpayituṃ nītim iva | sadgurulīlā bhavato bhāti jaganmāṇavakam ||*

2. 'As an adverb or an adjective.' In the commentary on verse 16,[1] Śākyarakṣita proposes two explanations of the word *astasaṅgam* leading to two different interpretations of the verse. In the first instance, he interprets the word as an adverb to *vistarāt*:

> Because of the expansion, i.e. spreading (of the praise) in such a manner that the attachment would disappear, i.e. (the praise would be) free from attachment towards self-interest.[2]

As for this interpretation, the verse can be translated as follows:

> If one spreads, free of self-interest,
> the praise of the virtues of that (form of yours,) then (the Buddhas),
> who have (already) attained the highest position,
> will extol him as a unique wise person
> with regard to adequate praise.

As an alternative explanation, Śākyarakṣita accepts *astasaṅgam* as an adjective of *dhīram*: "Or alternatively, the word *astasaṅga-* is in the same case-relation with (the word) *dhīra-*."[3] This leads to an alternative meaning of the verse:

> If one spreads the praise of the virtues of that form of yours
> then (the Buddhas), who have (already) attained the highest position,
> will extol him as a unique wise person, free of self-interest,
> with regard to adequate praise.

It is difficult to judge at this point which interpretation out of the two is preferable to Śākyarakṣita.

3. 'An instrumental in the sense of a cause or means.' Sometimes Śākyarakṣita comments on the specific function of a particular case termination or a suffix. In verse 41,[4] while commenting on the use of an

---

1 *yadguṇastutivistarād astasaṅgam anuṣṭubhi | dhīram ekam udīrayanty uttamaṃ padam udgatāḥ ||*

2 *astasaṅgaṃ svārthāsaktirahitaṃ yathā bhavati tathā vistaraṇāt prathanāt |*

3 *athavā astasaṅgam iti dhīram ity asya padam ity asya vā samānādhikaraṇaṃ |*

4 *rūparasāyanabhāvanayā te vāsava eva paraṃ bahumānyaḥ | yena cirāya nirastanimeṣaṃ labdham adodhakam ambakajātam ||*

instrumental case in the word *rūparasāyanabhāvanayā*, he says: "Here, the instrumental is either in the sense of a cause or an instrument."[1] In the light of this explanation, the said word can be translated either as 'because of / by the constant practice of consuming the elixir vitae of your form.' Śākyarakṣita thus clarifies the specific syntactic role of the word in a verse.

4. 'Multiple interpretations.' The commentary on verse 57[2] presents a unique case of different possible explanations giving rise to as many as four different interpretations of the same verse. The expression *paramottamasaṃmatāḥ* in the first *pāda* is analysed in two different ways: As to the first, the expression can be split as *parama* and *uttama-saṃmatāḥ* where *parama* 'O the highest one!' is taken as a vocative referring to Mañjuśrī and *uttamasaṃmatāḥ* is explained as *uttamatvena saṃmatāḥ* 'those who are considered to be the best' referring to the great sages like Bṛhaspati and so on.[3] As for the second, the expression can be split as *paramottama* and *saṃmatāḥ,* where *paramottama* 'O the highest among the best ones!' is accepted as a vocative referring to Mañjuśrī[4] and *saṃmatāḥ* 'those respected ones' referring to Bṛhaspati and so on. Similarly, in the expression *drutavilambitam apy uditaṃ vacaḥ*, the compound word *drutavilambitam* is interpreted in two different ways: firstly as an adverb qualifying *uditam* and thus meaning 'even the quickly or slowly uttered speech' and secondly as an adjective of *vacaḥ* 'the speech' meaning 'the uttered speech even though quick or slow.'[5] Thus, ultimately, we can have four interpretations:

    a. 'O the highest one! Those who are considered to be the best, cherish even the quickly or slowly uttered speech in front of you.'

    b. 'O the highest among the best ones! Those who are respected, cherish even the quickly or slowly uttered speech in front of you.'

---

1 *hetau karaṇe vā tṛtīyā* |

2 *tava puraḥ paramottamasaṃmatāḥ pratibhayā vikalāḥ prativādinah* | *sulabhamūka-daśā bahu manvate drutavilambitam apy uditaṃ vacaḥ* ||

3 *he parama tava purata uttamatvena saṃmatā api prativādino bṛhaspatyādayaḥ* | "O the highest one! Before you even the opponents Bṛhaspati and so on even though they are respected to be the best ... ."

4 *paramottameti vā saṃbodhanam* |

5 *drutaṃ vā vilambitaṃ vā yad uccāritaṃ vacaḥ* | *kriyāyā viśeṣaṇam vacaso vā* |

c. 'O the highest one! Those who are considered to be the best, cherish even the quick or slow speech uttered in front of you.'

d. 'O the highest among the best ones! Those who are respected, cherish even the quick or slow speech uttered in front of you.'

These different interpretations not only disclose the different possible ways of understanding the poem, but also add to its poetic beauty.

5. 'Locative absolute or a single remainder.' In the commentary on verse 136,[1] Śākyarakṣita provides two alternative explanations of the word *ardhārdhe*. The word under discussion does not figure in the main text. It rather seems to be a part of a missing quotation defining the characteristics of the metre *atirucirā* in a manner different from that of Jñānaśrīmitra. The quotation seems to have been inadvertently omitted by the scribe. Śākyarakṣita's comment on the said word runs as follows:

> As for the word *ardhārdhe*, 'half' means a continuous text of thirty-one syllables. A half combined with another half is *ardhārdha*, when there are such halves. But if the form *ardhārdhe* is taken as ending in a nominative dual suffix, then it would be a case of single remainder (*ekaśeṣa*). In the opinion of others, this metre *atirucirā* should be known only by two halves without a prescribed division of feet. This is the meaning.[2]

Thus, according to Śākyarakṣita, the word *ardhārdhe* can be interpreted either as a locative absolute or as a nominative dual. With regard to the former, the word would mean 'when there are two halves.' In case of the latter, one has to accept the *ekaśeṣa* of the nominal stem *ardhārdha* as *ardhārdhaṃ ca ardhārdhaṃ ca ardhārdhe* according to the rule *sarūpāṇām ekaśeṣa ekavibhaktau* (P I.2.64). In this case, the word would mean 'the two halves having two halves each,' that is to say, having four feet. This latter interpretation as an *ekaśeṣa* goes contrary to the intended meaning of the quotation. According to the quotation, others intend to define this metre by the two continuous halves of thirty-one syllables each. However, as per the opinion of Jñānaśrīmitra, the metre *atirucirā*

---

1 *udayadaruṇakiraṇanikaraparikarakanakamayavimalahimakarajayanī | jayati nikhilajagadabhirucikṛtipaṭur atibhava tava tanur iyam atirucirā ||*

2 *ardhārdha iti ekatriṃśadakṣaram akhaṇḍam evārdham | ardhena yuktam ardham ardhārdhaṃ tasmin sati | dvivacanāntatve tu ekaśeṣaḥ syāt | avihitacaraṇavibhāgatveneyam atirucirā paramate 'rdhadvayenaiva veditavyety arthaḥ |*

contains four feet where the odd feet are of sixteen syllables and the even that of fifteen.[1] Thus, the alternative explanation of the word *ardhārdhe* as a nominative dual rather agrees with the opinion of Jñānaśrīmitra than the one expressed in the quotation.

In all these explanations, we do not find any trace of Śākyarakṣita's adherence to either Pāṇinian or the Cāndra school of grammars except for the last optional interpretation. In the case of the explanation of the word *ardhārdhe* as an instance of an *ekaśeṣa*, Śākyarakṣita clearly seems to rely on the Pāṇinian grammar as the *ekaśeṣa* is not accepted in the Cāndra system.

Conclusion

From the foregoing discussion, one can easily assess Śākyarakṣita's excellent knowledge of Sanskrit grammar and his command over the two grammatical systems, that of Pāṇini and Candragomin. The probable sources of his grammatical discussions are: a. *Aṣṭādhyāyī* of Pāṇini; b. *Vārttikas* of Kātyāyana; c. *Mahābhāṣya* of Patañjali; d. *Cāndravyākaraṇa* of Candragomin; e. *Cāndravṛtti* of Dharmadāsa; f. *Cāndravṛttipañjikā* of Ratnamati; g. *Kātantravyākaraṇa* of Śarvavarman; h. *Bodhicaryāvatārapañjikā* of Prajñākaramati; i. *Śṛṅgāraprakāśa* of Bhoja; j. *Kavikāmadhenu* of Subhūticandra; and k. *Dhātupāṭhas* of the Pāṇinian and the Cāndra system. His non-affiliation to any particular grammatical school indicates that the sectarian adherence did not mean much to the scholars of Śākyarakṣita's rank. They seem to look at these different treatises as different perspectives on language, which are sometimes contradictory and on occasions complementary.

From the depth of the grammatical discussions, and the technicalities involved in them, it is quite clear that they are meant for an educated reader of Sanskrit and not for a beginner. It is not possible for a common reader to understand Śākyarakṣita's condensed and subtle grammatical analysis without the basic knowledge of the Pāṇinian and the Cāndra system. This observation regarding grammatical discussions holds true even for Śākyarakṣita's discussions of lexicographical, metrical, and philosophical points. It would not be possible to understand his remarks on metrical matters or on entries from lexicons without the knowledge of

---

1 *etanmate tu prathamaḥ pādaḥ ṣoḍaśākṣaro dvitīyaḥ pañcadaśākṣara iti catuṣpadīyam atirucirā* |

these sciences. In the same manner, it is also mandatory to have a good understanding of Buddhist philosophy, especially that of Vajrayāna, to fully understand the *mūla* text and the commentary. A study of the relation of this work with the famous Buddhist work the *Mañjuśrīnāmasaṃgīti* "Chanting the names of Mañjuśrī" should be of immense interest. Another famous work, namely Abhayākaragupta's *Niṣpannayogāvalī*, describing all twenty-six *maṇḍalas* belonging to various Buddhist Tantric cycles, may be useful in order to understand the various manifestations of Mañjuśrī. The knowledge of *maṇḍalas* and the related ideas along with the Buddhist iconography is also necessary to unravel many knotty points in the text and the commentary.

Since Śākyarakṣita's comments on these topics are also brief and subtle like those on the grammatical points, it would be desirable to elaborate on them in separate research papers. Such an attempt would also prove helpful to understand lexicographical, metrical, and philosophical sources of these works. Only then, the scholarly community would be able to fully appreciate the beauty, and the value of the *Vṛttamālāstuti* and the *Vivṛti* and the depth of scholarship of their respective authors, Jñānaśrīmitra, and Śākyarakṣita.

Bibliography

Apte, V. S.

1957 The Practical Sanskrit-English Dictionary. Prasad Prakashan, Poona.

Bhoja: *Śṛṅgāraprakāśa*

1998 *Śṛṅgāraprakāśa of Bhoja*. Ed. by Venkatarama Raghavan, Part I. Harvard Oriental Series, 53. Cambridge.

Candragomin: *Cāndra-Vyākaraṇa*

1902 *Cāndra-Vyākaraṇa. Die Grammatik des Candragomin. Sūtra, Uṇādi, Dhātupāṭha.* Hrsg. von Bruno Liebich. Leipzig. (Abhandlungen für die Kunde des Morgenlandes, herausgegeben von der Deutschen Morgenländischen Gesellschaft unter der verantwortlichen Redaktion des Prof. Dr. E. V. Windisch. XI. Band. No. 4.)

1918 *Ca(!)ndra-vṛtti: Der Original kommentar Candragomin's zu seinem grammatischen Sūtra.* Hrsg. von Bruno Liebich. Leipzig. (Abhandlungen für die Kunde des Morgenlandes, 14.)

Deokar, Mahesh

2008 *Technical Terms and Technique of the Pali and the Sanskrit Grammars.* Miscellaneous Series, 23. Central Institute of Higher Tibetan Studies, Sarnath, Varanasi.

Dimitrov, Dragomir

2016 *The Legacy of The Jewel-Mind. On the Sanskrit, Pali, and Sinhalese Works by Ratnamati. A Philological Chronicle (Phullalocanavaṃsa).* UNIVERSITÀ DEGLI STUDI DI NAPOLI "L'ORIENTALE" DIPARTIMENTO ASIA AFRICA E MEDITERRANEO Series Minor LXXXII. Napoli.

Hahn, Michael

2013 "Śākyarakṣita's Vṛttamālāvivṛti on Jñānaśrīmitra's Vṛttamālāstuti (1)," in: South Asian Classical Studies, No. 8, pp. 265–330.

Jayāditya: *Kāśikāvṛtti*

1985 *Kāśika(!)vṛtti of Jayāditya-Vāmana (Along with Commentaries Vivaraṇapañcikā-Nyāsa of Jinendrabuddhi and Padamañjarī of Haradatta Miśra).* Ed. by Srīnārāyaṇa Misra. Ratnabharati Series - 5, 6, 7, 8, Varanasi.

Jñānaśrīmitra: *Vṛttamālāstuti*

1971 *Jñānaśrīmitras Vṛttamālāstuti. Ein Beispielsammlung zur altindischen Metrik.* Nach dem tibetischen Tanjur zusammen mit der mongolischen Version herausgegeben, übersetze und erläutert. Michael Hahn. Asiatische Forschungen, 33. Wiesbaden.

Monier-Williams, Monier

1979 *A Sanskrit-English Dictionary.* Etymologically and philologically arranged with special reference to Cognate Indo-European Languages. Oxford. [[1]1899]

Pāṇini: *Aṣṭādhyāyī*

1989 *Aṣṭādhyāyī of Pāṇini.* Roman Transliteration and English Translation by Sumitra M. Katre. Delhi. [Texas Linguistics Series [1]1987].

Patañjali: *Vyākaraṇamahābhāṣya*

1987 *The Vyākaraṇamahābhāṣya of Patañjali with The Commentary Bhāṣyapradīpa of Kaiyaṭa Upādhyāya and the Supercommentary Bhāṣyapradīpoddyota of Nāgeśa Bhaṭṭa*, Vol. I, Navāhnika (On the Aṣṭādhyāyī

Chapter 1, Quarter 1). Ed. with Notes and Variants by Bhargava Sastri Bhikaji Josi. Chaukhamba Sanskrit Pratishthan. Delhi [Repr].

Vāmana – See Jayāditya.

Subhūticandra: *Kavikāmadhenu*

Subhūticandra's Kavikāmadhenu Commentary on the Amarakośa (Part II). Edited by Lata Mahesh Deokar. Forthcoming.

*****